3

24.95
6CB

D1260911

The Civilization of the American Indian Series

THE
FOX
WARS

THE
FOX
WARS

The Mesquakie

Challenge

to New France

by R. David Edmunds
and Joseph L. Peyser

University of Oklahoma Press : Norman and London

Other Books by R. David Edmunds
The Otoe-Missouria People (Phoenix, 1976)
The Potawatomis, Keepers of the Fire (Norman, 1978)
(ed.) *American Indian Leaders: Studies in Diversity* (Lincoln, Nebr., 1980)
The Shawnee Prophet (Lincoln, Nebr., 1983)
Tecumseh and the Quest for Indian Leadership (Boston, 1984)
Kinsmen through Time: An Annotated Bibliography of Potawatomi History
    (Metuchen, N.J., 1987)

Other Books by Joseph L. Peyser
Letters from New France: The Upper Country, 1686–1783 (ed. and trans.)
    (Urbana and Chicago, 1992)
Fort St. Joseph Manuscripts: Chronological Inventory and Translations (Niles,
    Mich., 1978)

This book is published with the generous assistance of Edith Gaylord
    Harper.

Library of Congress Cataloging-in-Publication Data

Edmunds, R. David (Russell David), 1939–
        The Fox wars : the Mesquakie challenge to New France / by R. David
    Edmunds and Joseph L. Peyser. — 1st ed.
        p. cm. — (The Civilization of the American Indian series ; v. 211)
    Includes bibliographical references and index.
    ISBN 0-8061-2551-9 (alk. paper)
        1. Fox Indians—Wars.   2. Fox Indians—Government relations.
    3. Fox Indians—History—Sources.   4. Ethnohistory—New France.
    5. New France—History—Sources.   6. New France—Politics and gov-
    ernment.   I. Peyser, Joseph L., 1925–   . II. Title. III. Series.
    E99.F7E35   1993
    971.01'62—dc20   93-4098
                                                                                CIP

The paper in this book meets the guidelines for permanence and durabil-
ity of the Committee on Production Guidelines for Book Longevity of the
Council on Library Resources, Inc. ∞

Text design is by Cathy Carney Imboden. The text typeface is Meridien.

The Fox Wars: The Mesquakie Challenge to New France is Volume 211 in The
Civilization of the American Indian Series.

This book
is dedicated to
the Mesquakie People.

CONTENTS

Contents

x

ILLUSTRATIONS

MAPS

PREFACE

Any scholar familiar with the primary materials that relate to French-Indian relations in the Great Lakes region during the first four decades of the eighteenth century is aware that many of these documents contain extensive correspondence about the Fox Indians. Indeed, historians or anthropologists investigating a broad spectrum of activity by other Indian tribes often encounter considerable commentary regarding these peoples' relationships with the Foxes. Between 1710 and 1740 French officials in Quebec and Versailles spent an inordinate amount of time and effort developing policies designed to either integrate the Foxes into the French political-economic alliance or destroy them as a tribal entity. In conducting other research, both authors of this volume encountered much of this correspondence and were struck by the rich ethnohistorical content of the documents.

Other historians and anthropologists had examined facets of the Fox, or Mesquakie, experience, but with the exception of Louise Phelps Kellogg, none had attempted to examine, survey, and analyze the entire scope of the Fox-

French relationship. Early in the twentieth century anthropologists such as William Jones and Truman Michelson investigated many components of contemporary Mesquakie culture, and at midcentury several anthropologists from the University of Chicago conducted considerable field research among the Mesquakie people near Tama, Iowa. During the early 1970s Fred McTaggart examined and provided very valuable insights into contemporary Mesquakie oral traditions and culture. Yet all of these scholars focused primarily upon the evolution of Fox, or Mesquakie, culture in the late nineteenth or the twentieth century.

In contrast, William T. Hagan, in *The Sac and Fox Indians* (Norman, 1958, 1980), discussed the Sac and Fox experience during the nineteenth century, though he concentrated primarily on the Sacs and their activities in the Black Hawk War. Joseph Herring also discussed the Sac and Foxes' experience after their removal to Kansas, and Michael Green wrote a master's thesis and several articles on those Mesquakies who either refused to remove to Kansas or returned to Iowa in the decade preceeding the Civil War.

Until recently, with the exception of Kellogg's two chapters in *The French Regime in Wisconsin and the Old Northwest* and her extended essay in the *Proceedings of the State Historical Society of Wisconsin,* historians have written relatively little focused specifically on the Fox-French encounter. Raymond Hauser's M.A. thesis examined these events, and he has written on the Fox conflict with the Illinois Confederacy. Richard Lortie's master's thesis studied the economic factors associated with the warfare between the Foxes and the French. David Edmunds has investigated Potawatomi-Fox relations, but from the Potawatomi perspective. Joseph Peyser has closely examined the great battle that the Foxes fought against the French and their allies on the prairies of Illinois in 1730, and has traced the fate of many of the Fox prisoners captured by the French and other Indians. While Kellogg attempted to survey the broad scope of Fox-French relations and place them within a general discussion of French colonial policies, she did not have access to more recently discovered documents that provide additional information about this relationship. In *The Middle Ground*, Richard White has analyzed French-Indian relations, but he devotes only twenty-five pages to the Fox-French conflict.

Plans for this volume originally were formulated in 1984 when the two authors first met in South Bend, Indiana. At that time Edmunds had completed *The Potawatomis: Keepers of the Fire* (Norman, 1978), which includes a chapter on that tribe's participation in the Fox wars. Peyser recently had translated and edited *Fort St. Joseph Manuscripts* (Niles, Mich., 1978), a series of documents on the French occupation of the St. Joseph Valley in the late seventeenth and early eighteenth centuries. Each of us admitted that he had been fascinated by the documentary evidence that the Foxes periodically disrupted the French fur trade during this period, and we lamented that no detailed, scholarly history of the events had been published. After an extended initial conversation, we agreed to collaborate on this project and to coauthor such a volume. *The Fox Wars: The Mesquakie Challenge to New France* is the result.

This is designed as an ethnohistory of the Foxes' epic struggle to maintain their identity and existence in the face of overwhelming adversity. We have attempted to trace Fox history from the late precontact period through the middle of the eighteenth century and to describe and analyze the events surrounding the tribe's conflict with New France. Although, like other historians, we have been forced to rely on French documents, we have tried to incorporate Fox, or Mesquakie, oral traditions and to present these events as much as possible from the Fox perspective. This task has been demanding but also pleasurable. It is impossible to study the history of the Mesquakie people without developing a sense of admiration for their courage and perseverence. Indeed, many of the people and events portrayed in this volume approach heroic stature, and as most historians familiar with this period are aware, the Foxes' endeavor to maintain their identity and independence is a struggle of epic proportions. We have attempted to place the struggle within a valid historical context and to analyze the motives and actions of all sides.

Any historian, anthropologist, or other author who writes about the history of the Mesquakies, "the People of the Red Earth," is immediately faced with problems of nomenclature and synonymity. They referred to themselves as Mesquakies, as do the modern Mesquakie people near Tama, Iowa. In the late seventeenth and early eighteenth centuries, however, other Algonquian tribes of the western Great Lakes region and the upper Mississippi Valley frequently called them Outagami, using a Chippewa word meaning "People of the Opposite Shore." In contrast, the French almost always referred to the Mesquakies as Renards, or "Foxes." About 90 percent of the anthropological and historical references to the tribe also use the term Fox. As we were writing the book, we at first attempted to use the term Mesquakie when the tribe would have been referring to itself or when the Mesquakie people initiated any sort of action. In contrast, when the French were taking action against the tribe, or when the French officials were communicating about the tribe, we utilized the term Fox. Such a distinction, although well-meaning, created considerable confusion within the text, and since most anthropologists and historians use the term Fox, as do most library reference systems, we finally decided generally to use Fox when discussing our subject. We have, however, used Mesquakie in particular instances where it seemed most appropriate.

We are indebted to many institutions and individuals for their assistance with this project. Financial support was provided by the Eli Lilly Endowment; the Faculty Research and Development Committee at Indiana University South Bend; the D'Arcy McNickle Center for the History of the American Indian, at the Newberry Library; the Texas Christian University Research Foundation; and the National Endowment for the Humanities Summer Stipend Program. In conducting our research, we have received invaluable assistance from many people who supervise special collections, archives, and manuscript collections. We particularly would like to express our appreciation for the efforts of André Desrosiers, Michel Wyczynski, and Victorin Chabot, at the National Archives of Canada; John Aubrey and the late Michael Kaplan, at The Newberry Library; and James Keller and Christopher Peebles, at the Glenn A. Black Laboratory of Archaeology, Indiana University. Ray DeMallie, of the American Indian Research Institute, Indiana University, graciously agreed to assist in the compilations of documents; while Lucien Campeau, S.J., at the Maison des Pères Jésuites, Saint-Jérôme, Québec; Helen Tanner and Francis Jennings, at The Newberry Library; Olive P. Dickason, at the University of Alberta; and Lenville Stelle, of Parkland College, shared their cartographic, historical, ethographic, and archaeological knowledge with us. Appreciation also is extended to William C. Sturtevant of the Museum of Natural History, Smithsonian Institution, for his assistance in obtaining illustrations; and to George Aubin, at Assumption College, and particularly Paul Voorhis, at Brandon University, for their assistance with Fox nomenclature. Those names that have been translated correctly are attributable to them. The mistranslations, when they have occurred, are our own. Appreciation also is extended to Don Wanatee of the Mesquakie tribe for his insights into modern Mesquakie culture; and to Spencer Tucker, of Texas Christian University, for his assistance with our word-processing problems.

R. DAVID EDMUNDS
JOSEPH L. PEYSER

THE
FOX
WARS

CHAPTER ONE

THE WEST
IN CHAOS

On August 4, 1701, Louis-Hector de Callières, governor general of New France, arose shortly after dawn, recited his prayers, and thanked God for his assistance in achieving what the governor anticipated would be the diplomatic coup of his administration. After half a century of warfare the Iroquois Confederacy and the tribes from the western Great Lakes finally had been persuaded to assemble at Montreal to establish a permanent peace. If their efforts were successful, Callières and other French officials believed that the internecine bloodshed that had plagued the Great Lakes–St. Lawrence valley would be ended and both the fur trade and New France would prosper.

The formal ceremonies held at Montreal in August 1701 were the culmination of considerable French enterprise. Following the Peace of Ryswick (1697) Louis XIV had ordered Callières's predecessor, Louis de Buade, comte de Frontenac, to initiate the intertribal peace negotiations, but the aged Frontenac had died in November 1698 and the burden of responsibility fell on Callières's shoulders.

Throughout 1699 and 1700 he met with delegations from both the Five Nations and the western tribes, first cajoling one side, then persuading the other, until in September 1700 representatives of the Ottawas, the Hurons, the Abenakis, and the Iroquois Confederacy met in Montreal and signed a peace agreement. Yet Callières was concerned that only three French-allied tribes had put their marks on the document, and moreover, both sides still held large numbers of captives. Consequently, he instructed the Indians to reassemble at Montreal during the following summer when delegates from all the western tribes could be in attendance. Presents would be distributed, prisoners would be repatriated, and the peace treaty would be celebrated with pomp and ceremony.[1]

During the following months Callières took steps to ensure that the formalities of 1701 would be a success. In October 1700 he dispatched Father Jean Enjalran and Augustin Le Gardeur de Courtemanche to Michilimackinac to inform the western Indians of the recent peace agreement and to escort them to Montreal for the formal ceremonies. Enjalran and Courtemanche also were instructed to intercept any war parties that the western tribesmen had sent against the Iroquois, and to be certain that these French-allied Indians brought their Iroquois prisoners to Montreal for repatriation. Meanwhile, Callières mediated a dispute between the Ottawas and the Iroquois and met again with Teganissorens, an Onondaga chief, and other Iroquois leaders to foil a British attempt to keep the Five Nations from attending the upcoming conference."[2]

Enjalran and Courtemanche arrived at Michilimackinac in December, but found that most of the Ottawa and Huron residents of the straits had abandoned their summer villages and were scattered through the forests in small hunting camps. Enjalran remained at Michilimackinac while Courtemanche proceeded down the eastern shore of Lake Michigan to the St. Joseph River, where he was welcomed by villages of Potawatomis and Miamis, and scattered lodges of several other tribes. Alarmed to learn that the Potawatomis recently had sent a war party toward the Senecas, Courtemanche informed them of the recent peace agreement and persuaded other warriors to intercept the war party and escort it back to the St. Joseph. After receiving promises that the assembled Indians would attend the peace ceremonies at Montreal, Courtemanche traveled on to the Illinois Confederacy, then returned to the Chicago region, where he convinced the Ouiatanon band of the Miamis also to participate in the proceedings. In the spring he journeyed north along the western shore of Lake Michigan, enlisting the support of the Sacs, the Foxes, the Winnebagos, the Kickapoos, the Mascoutens, and the Menominees. Near Green Bay he met with several tribes and persuaded them not to retaliate against the eastern Sioux, who recently had attacked the Indians in what is now Wisconsin. By early summer Courtemanche had returned to Michilimackinac, where he assembled representatives from all those tribes, and in July he embarked for Montreal with a flotilla of over one hundred canoes filled with western warriors.[3]

On July 22, 1701, French soldiers at Montreal saluted Courtemanche's entourage with artillery salvos, as over seven hundred Indians beached their canoes near the juncture of the Ottawa and St. Lawrence rivers. During the following twelve days Callières met both privately and in public with representatives of the western Indians and the Iroquois, quietly assuring all the tribes of both sides' good intentions. In addition he interceded in a series of minor quarrels regarding the exchange of prisoners, and attempted to ameliorate several disputes in which the Foxes, the Sacs, the Kickapoos, and the Mascoutens were embroiled with both the Chippewas and the Sioux in Wisconsin. Speaking for the Foxes, Noro (The Porcupine) accused the Chippewas of murdering one of his kinsmen. He complained about recent French attempts to prevent coureurs de bois from visiting the western tribes, and lamented that his people had become "beggars." He also asked for French traders and priests to visit his village, for according to Noro, if the Foxes "had a black robe, a blacksmith, and several Frenchmen among us, the Chippewas would not be bold enough to attack us."[4]

Callières eventually persuaded the Fox and Chippewa delegates to smoke the calumet together, but he was less successful in resolving the Fox-Sioux difficulties. When the Foxes and their allies demanded that Pierre Le Sueur and other French traders barter no more arms or ammunition to the Sioux, Callières was evasive in his reply. Aware that the Wisconsin tribes still planned to retaliate against their enemy, Callières asked the Foxes to postpone any action until he could contact "the Great Onontio" (Louis XIV) for advice on the matter.[5]

Although Callières was willing to discuss other problems, some unnamed epidemic had erupted among the Indians at Michilimackinac, and the arrival of warriors from that region transmitted the disease to Montreal. Afraid that the assembled Indians might blame the French for the malady, the governor hurried to conclude the proceedings. In an open field outside the city French workmen constructed a large enclosure with covered galleries to both shelter French dignitaries and serve as a focus for the final ceremonies. On August 3 a great fire pit was dug, and three oxen were slaughtered, then placed in huge kettles and boiled over the coals. Large quantities of other food and drink were prepared, and on the morning of August 4, 1701, almost thirteen hundred Indians assembled within the enclosure to share in Onontio's bounty. In addition, the galleries were lined with uniformed French troops, French dignitaries, and a considerable assemblage of "ladies and all the fashion of the town" who had come to share in the spectacle.[6]

They were not disappointed. Inspired by Callières's preparations, the Indians attired themselves in tribal splendor. Although the Iroquois were dressed in their finery, their increased use of European clothing diminished their impact on the assembled French population, who were fascinated by the rich ceremonial costumes of the western tribes. After preliminary speeches by Callières and other officials, representatives from the different tribes stepped forward to present short replies and to make their mark upon the document. Onanguisse (Shimmering Light) of the Potawatomis, who pledged that he was willing to obey Onontio "even unto the death," was dressed in a buffalo robe with his head covered by the skin and horns of the animal. Ouabangué, a Chippewa leader from the Sault Ste. Marie region, wore a long fur robe and a halo of feathers. He too pledged his loyalty to New France.[7]

Most striking however was Miskousouath, who spoke for the Foxes. Cloaked in a bearskin, Miskousouath had covered his face and head with red paint, and although he wore a scalp lock, he had adorned his head with a French wig, which was also red in color. Like the other tribal leaders, Miskousouath stepped forward to sign the document, but unlike the others, he was more guarded in his professions of fealty. The Foxes, he declared, had no Iroquois prisoners to exchange. The few Iroquois whom they had captured had either escaped or had long since been repatriated. "Moreover," he concluded, "though I am much involved with the Sioux, I have never had any great quarrel with the Iroquois."[8]

After that speech, the Fox chief doffed his wig, which brought a "great outburst of laughter" from many of the French spectators in the galleries. Callières did not share in their amusement. Miskousouath's lukewarm professions of loyalty, his denunciation of the Sioux, and his thinly veiled overtures to the Iroquois were not lost on the governor. Like other knowledgeable French officials, Callières

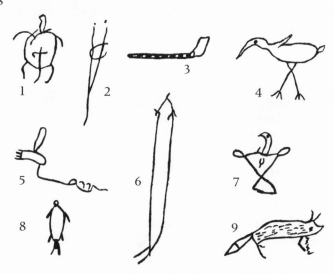

Some of the thirty-nine tribal marks on the great 1701 peace treaty of Montreal between the Iroquois and the French and French-allied tribes. The manuscript identifies the marks as follows: *(1)* Toarenguenion, a Seneca; *(2)* Souc8on, for the Oneidas; *(3)* Garonhiaren, a Cayuga; *(4)* Chippewa chief 8abanqué (Ouabangué); *(5)* Chichicatalo, chief of the Miami village at the St. Joseph River; *(6)* Le Rat (Kondiaronk), chief of the Hurons; *(7)* Winnebago village chief 8aban; *(8)* the Sacs; *(9)* the Outagamis (Foxes). Copied from the National Archives of Canada, MG18, C12.

was aware that the Foxes often had vexed his government, and Miskousouath's speech seemed to underscore their recalcitrance. The Fox-French relationship had never been harmonious, but it soon would worsen.[9]

Frenchmen first officially encountered the Foxes when Father Claude Allouez had established a Jesuit mission among several large villages of Ottawas and Petuns who were encamped at Chequamegon Bay, on the southern shores of Lake Superior. In 1666 or 1667 a trading party of

120 Fox men, women, and children, accompanied by Indians from several other tribes, arrived at the mission to barter their furs for French trade goods. Attempting to spread the gospel, Allouez met with the Indians. He later described the Foxes as a populous tribe, "given to hunting and warfare," who inhabited a country that lay "southward toward the Lake of the Ilimouek" (Lake Michigan). He indicated that they grew large quantities of corn, but were not proficient canoeists, preferring to make "their journeys by land, bearing their packages and their game on their shoulders." Allouez also hinted that the Foxes had some previous contacts with French coureurs de bois, for he added, "It is said of them and of the Osuaki (Sacs), that when they find a man alone and at a disadvantage, they kill him, especially if he is a Frenchman."[10]

Allouez may have encountered the Foxes in Wisconsin, but tribal traditions trace their origins farther east. The Foxes believed that they once had lived on the shores of the Atlantic, but had migrated up the St. Lawrence Valley eventually to occupy eastern Michigan and northwestern Ohio.[11] Some historians and anthropologists argue that the Foxes abandoned lower Michigan, fleeing the Iroquois and the Neutrals during the Great Dispersal of the 1640s and 1650s, but there is strong evidence to suggest that they migrated to Wisconsin before that time. Both the Foxes and the Chippewas agree that the Chippewas, not the Iroquois or the Neutrals, drove the Foxes from Michigan's lower peninsula. If such traditions are historically valid, then the Foxes would have vacated the lower peninsula before the Iroquois expansion. In addition, when the French reached Michilimackinac, both the Chippewa and the Ottawa residents of the region referred to the Foxes as the Outagami, or "the People of the Opposite Shore," a name suggesting that they had occupied the eastern shores of Wisconsin for some time.[12] Moreover, if they had once lived in the Saginaw and Detroit areas, and had shared in the traditional Woodland culture of the region, their way of life had changed markedly by the last quarter of the seventeenth century. When French travelers first entered their villages in Wisconsin, they found that Fox subsistence patterns more closely resembled the prairie-dwelling tribes of Illinois or Iowa than the Woodland peoples of Michigan or northern Wisconsin.[13]

In 1669, when the Jesuits began to proselytize among the Foxes, they found them living in eastern Wisconsin. During October, Allouez encountered Fox tribespeople intermixed with Sacs, Potawatomis, and Winnebagos residing in three intertribal villages along the western shores of Green Bay. Other Foxes were scattered in winter camps as far distant as Chicago, but most of the tribe evidently lived at Ouestatimong, a fortified village of over two thousand men, women, and children, located on the Wolf River near modern Leeman, Wisconsin.[14]

In April 1670 Allouez journeyed to Ouestatimong, which he described as being "in an excellent country—the soil, which is black there, yielding them Indian corn in abundance." The Foxes welcomed him to their village and listened politely to his attempts to spread the gospel, but they informed Allouez that one of their hunting camps in northern Illinois recently had been mistakenly attacked by the Iroquois, and they "were too dispirited to speak, being all occupied in mourning their dead." According to the Foxes, the Iroquois had been seeking revenge against the Potawatomis, but instead had fallen upon the small village of Foxes, killing almost seventy women and children, and capturing thirty others while the men from the camp were absent hunting. The Foxes thanked Allouez "for having come to visit and console us" and asked the priest to dwell in their midst and "teach us to speak to the great Manitou." A Fox spokesman also pleaded with Allouez to intercede with the Iroquois and "tell them that they have taken me for some one else. I do not make war on them, I have not eaten their people."[15]

Allouez assured the Foxes that he would carry their requests to French officials in Canada, and he admonished the Indians to "fortify themselves in their resolution to obey the true God." Before leaving their village, he announced that he was founding a new mission, St. Marc, in their midst. No priest was yet available for permanent residency, but Allouez assured the Indians that a black robe would regularly visit their village. He later informed his superiors that although neighboring tribes still held the Foxes "in very low estimation," the tribe would provide a "glorious and rich harvest for a zealous and patient Missionary."[16]

The "harvest" was much leaner than Allouez anticipated. Throughout the 1670s the Foxes welcomed Allouez and other priests to their villages, but their acceptance of the gospel was markedly affected by secular concerns such as economics and politics. At first the Foxes seemed eager for the black robes' message. Allouez returned to Ouestatimong during February 1671, and although many tribesmen complained that they recently had been cheated by French traders, they listened politely to his teachings. Prominent warriors tolerated his denunciation of their polygynous marriages, and several parents allowed the priest to baptize their children. Moreover, two adults, an aged man and a woman, also embraced Christianity, and Allouez reported that the Foxes, from whose "haughty natures" he had expected nothing "but jests, repulses and mockery," were "being changed from wolves into lambs."[17]

Throughout 1671 and 1672 interest in the black robes' manitou seemed to increase. From the Foxes' perspective, the new faith cost little, and although most tribespeople evidently made little attempt to embrace the totality of the priest's teachings, Roman Catholicism seemed to offer a new set of symbols whose medicine was potentially very powerful. Long-embroiled in a series of conflicts with both the Sioux and the Chippewas, and facing new aggression from the Iroquois, the Foxes were willing to incorporate

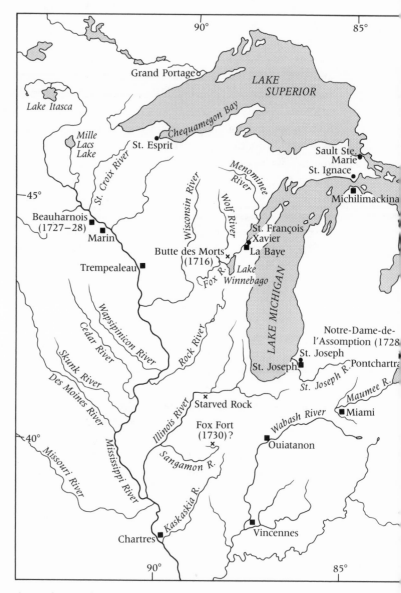

The Northwest, 1645–1740

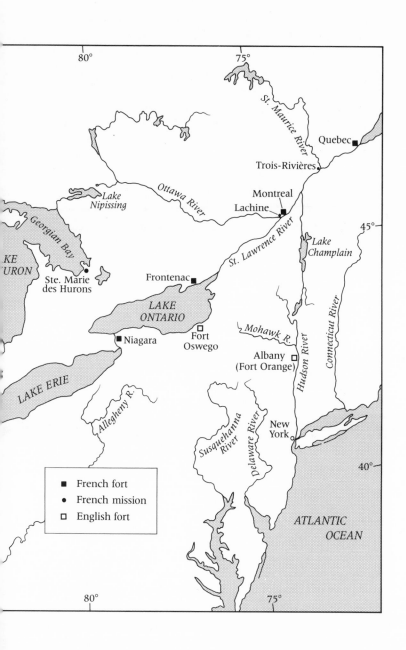

80°   75°

St. Maurice River

Quebec ■

Trois-Rivières ●

Ottawa River

Lake
Nipissing

Montreal
Lachine ■

45°—

Georgian Bay

St. Lawrence River

Lake
Champlain

KE
URON

Ste. Marie
des Hurons ●

Frontenac ■

Connecticut River

LAKE
ONTARIO

■ Niagara

Fort
Oswego □

Mohawk R.

Albany □
(Fort Orange)

Hudson River

LAKE ERIE

Allegheny R.

Susquehanna
River

Delaware River

New
York ●

40°—

■ French fort
● French mission
□ English fort

ATLANTIC
OCEAN

80°   75°

new manitous into their cosmology if such spirits offered them medicine. Before he had departed from Ouestatimong, Allouez had erected a large cross, and in the months that followed many of the Foxes incorporated the symbol on their lodges and possessions. Moreover, they had been fascinated by the ritual of the mass, and when Allouez returned to their village in November 1672, he found many of the tribespeople making the sign of the cross on numerous, if sometimes inappropriate, occasions. During Allouez's brief visit in their village about fifty Foxes accepted Christianity, and late in November, when the priest left Ouestatimong, much of the tribe seemed to be under the Jesuit's influence.[18]

Conditions changed in the months that followed. During November 1672, convinced that the symbol of the cross would enhance their endeavor, a small party of Fox warriors painted crosses on their weapons and clothing before leaving to attack the Sioux in what is now eastern Minnesota. They surprised a small camp of their enemies and, on returning to Ouestatimong, praised the new medicine, "proclaiming everywhere that they were solely indebted to it for such good success." But other Foxes who later followed their example were ambushed by the Sioux and suffered over thirty casualties. When Allouez again visited their village in the spring of 1673, the Foxes were much less hospitable. They refused to share their lodges with the priest, and he was forced to "seek shelter in an old Cabin that was open on all Sides." Some tribespeople remained interested in his teachings, but others declared that "prayer had caused them to die" in their warfare against the Sioux. Tribal leaders confronted Allouez, asking, "How can we pray to God? He does not love us; he loves only our enemies, for he always Delivers us into Their hands, and hardly ever Delivers any of them into ours." Allouez attempted to answer their questions, but when a woman whom he had recently baptized suddenly sickened and died, his influence among the Foxes diminished.[19]

Fox attempts at reconciliation with the Iroquois also threatened the Jesuits' efforts. Still convinced that the Iroquois attack on their hunting camp had been a mistake, the Foxes sent emissaries to the Senecas during the fall of 1672. Pleading that they had never attacked the Iroquois, the Foxes admitted that they held a few Iroquois prisoners in their villages, but said these captives had been given to them by neighboring tribes. The Foxes assured the Iroquois that the prisoners had been adopted and "they are living . . . as [our] children." In response, the Senecas promised friendship, but they warned the Foxes against both the French and the Jesuits. When the emissaries returned to Ouestatimong, Allouez attempted to negate the impact of the Iroquois message, but the offers of an Iroquois alliance had been extended and the Foxes would not forget them.[20]

Other circumstances further weakened the Foxes' ties to the Jesuits. Although Allouez and other priests shrewdly incorporated certain Fox beliefs with Catholic teachings (for example, Fox traditions of fasting were redirected toward Lent), they were less tolerant of other tribal ceremonies. The priests particularly disliked the Fox reliance on dreams and visions, which the priests considered to be at best superstitious and at worst a form of devil worship. At first the Foxes tolerated the priests' denunciation of such practices, but when Allouez and others attempted to prevent young men from experiencing a vision quest, they encountered the wrath of many tribal elders. In response, the priests refused to baptize all who adhered to such traditions, but their decision then limited most of their converts to young children, the infirm, and the elderly.[21]

The Foxes also were dismayed at the priests' reaction to several natural disasters. In the summer of 1675 the Foxes' corn crop was severely damaged by a late freeze, and during the following autumn much of the sparse harvest was afflicted by a fungus that destroyed the ears in the storage pits. Weakened by food shortages during the winter of

1675–76, many of the Foxes fell prey to an epidemic that swept through their villages. Although Allouez assured them that "God visits them with his scourges to make them more amenable to our Instructions," the Foxes took little consolation in such suffering and wondered if the old manitous were angry because the tribe had forgotten them.[22]

They also wondered why the black robes and their French "children" continued to befriend their enemies. While St. Marc struggled, Catholic missions among the Illinois Confederacy prospered, and many of the Illinois tribesmen were readily converted to Christianity. Although Allouez urged the Foxes to live in peace with neighboring tribes, in the mid-1670s they were attacked by Illinois war parties, many of whom included warriors who were ostensibly Christians.[23] Other French-allied tribes treated the Foxes with contempt, reporting to the French that they considered the Foxes to be "avaricious," "thieving," and "quarrelsome." Potawatomis living near Green Bay attempted to prevent French traders from entering the Fox villages, keeping the tribespeople at Ouestatimong so "destitute" of trade goods "that they aroused the compassion" of the few traders who visited them.[24]

The Foxes also were plagued with other intertribal squabbles. During the 1670s and 1680s they quarreled intermittently with the Ottawas, and warriors from Ouestatimong or outlying camps were embroiled in kinship vendettas with neighboring villages of Miamis and Mascoutens.[25] Eager to maintain peace in the west, Nicolas Perrot and other French officials mediated many of these disputes, but they were less successful in controlling hostilities between the Foxes and the Chippewas. Warriors from Ouestatimong still were embittered over their fathers' forced exodus from Michigan, and their resentment of the Chippewas was fanned by competition between the two tribes over hunting and trapping grounds in northern Wisconsin.[26]

The Chippewas also warred against the Sioux, but in the early 1680s both tribes combined to attack the Foxes. In 1680 or 1681 a huge Sioux-Chippewa war party (approximately eight hundred men) attacked Fox settlements in east-central Wisconsin. The Foxes rallied and repulsed their attackers, but they suffered over fifty casualties, including one prominent village chief whose death caused considerable consternation. The Chippewas also captured several Fox children. In retaliation, during 1682 the Foxes struck back at a Chippewa village near Michilimackinac, where they killed and decapitated several Chippewa warriors, seized twelve Chippewa women and children, and also captured two Ottawa women who had been visiting in the Chippewa camp. Enraged, the Ottawas threatened to join with the Chippewas in a new series of raids against the Foxes, and French officials at Michilimackinac were hard pressed to prevent intertribal warfare from engulfing the fur trade in Wisconsin.[27]

The Jesuits attempted to mediate the dispute, but the Foxes refused their reconciliation. Accusing the French of favoring their enemies, the Foxes drove several traders from Ouestatimong. The Potawatomis and the Winnebagos near Green Bay also tried to arrange an exchange of prisoners, but the Foxes feared that if they relinquished their Chippewa and Ottawa captives, they would have no hostages to prevent additional attacks by those tribes. They clung to their prisoners even though they grieved for their women and children still held by the Chippewas.[28]

Nicolas Perrot finally ended the stalemate. Returning from Montreal, he arrived at Michilimackinac in the spring of 1683, and learning of the conflict, he immediately embarked for Green Bay and the Fox villages. Well-versed in Indian politics, Perrot met with the Foxes and warned them that among their captives were the relatives of several prominent Chippewa leaders. According to Perrot, the Chippewas were losing their patience, and unless the Foxes allowed him to return with the prisoners, the Chippewas would assume that the Foxes already had burned them. They would then kill their Fox captives and join with the Sioux and the Ottawas to attack the Fox villages. But if the prisoners were relinquished, Perrot promised that the Foxes' kinsmen also would be returned.[29]

The Foxes were divided in their response. Okimaouassen, a leader of the Fox clan and the brother of the recently slain chief, at first declined to give up his prisoners. Embittered, he repeatedly refused to smoke the calumet with Perrot, and at first he resisted efforts by members of other clans who also argued in Perrot's favor. During the evening, however, the region was subjected to a series of extremely violent thunderstorms, which the Foxes interpreted as a sign that the manitous were displeased with Okimaouassen's recalcitrance. Frightened, Okimaouassen changed his mind, and after Perrot assured the tribe that he would temporarily reside in their villages as a guarantee against further Sioux and Chippewa raids, Okimaouassen relinquished his captives.[30]

Perrot's efforts brought a temporary respite to the Fox-Chippewa hostilities, but the dispute still simmered. Four years later, in 1687, a war party of young Fox warriors encountered a hunting camp of Chippewas in western Wisconsin while en route to attack the Sioux. Envisioning the Chippewas as easy prey, they surprised the camp, and although they did not kill any of its occupants, they captured three young women and one adolescent boy. They carried the captives home to their village, where the Fox elders were contacted by representatives of neighboring tribes who demanded that they surrender the prisoners to the French for repatriation to the Chippewas. Alarmed by the incident, Fox chiefs sent a messenger to trader Daniel Greysolon Duluth, who was passing through Green Bay, and asked him to come to their village. When he arrived, they apologized for the attack and relinquished the prisoners. Duluth carried the captives back to Green Bay and informed the Chippewas, who sent a small party of warriors to escort the former prisoners back to their villages. Ironically, however, as the party passed through northern Wisconsin, they were again attacked by another Fox war party, who mistook the Chippewas for a hunting camp of Sioux. The Chippewa warriors immediately fled, and when the Foxes realized that they had recaptured the hapless women, they pursued the Chippewas, attempting to return the captives. Unable to overtake their quarry, the Foxes were afraid to release the women since they might become lost and starve in the forest. Consequently, they escorted the captives back to the Fox villages near Lake Winnebago, where the women again were surrendered to the French. The prisoners eventually returned to their homes, but their odyssey did not endear the Foxes to the Chippewas.[31]

Fox antipathy toward the Chippewas paled in comparison to their hatred of the Sioux, and like their feud with the Chippewas, the Fox-Sioux quarrel had simmered for decades. During the middle years of the seventeenth century the Foxes had occupied the fertile valleys surrounding the Fox-Wisconsin portage in south-central Wisconsin, but pressure by the Sioux had forced their evacuation of the region, and by the 1670s the Foxes had withdrawn toward Green Bay where Allouez first visited their villages along the Wolf River. Yet even there they feared Sioux attacks, for Allouez indicated that Ouestatimong and other Fox villages were heavily fortified, surrounded by oak palisades reinforced by earth embankments.[32]

From those villages the Foxes joined with Miamis, Mascoutens, and other neighboring tribes to launch a series of campaigns against the Sioux in Minnesota. Warfare between the two tribes flared intermittently throughout the 1670s, with neither side able to achieve any military dominance. Sioux warriors usually outnumbered the Foxes and their allies, but the latter were better armed since they had greater access to French trade goods.[33]

Unfortunately, as the decade ended, the balance of power shifted precariously against the Foxes. In 1679 Sioux delegates, eager for French firearms, met with Chippewa tribesmen from the southern shores of Lake Superior and agreed to make peace in exchange for access to French trade goods. Encouraged by what seemed to be an unlimited economic opportunity, French traders led by Duluth attended the conference, and after the peace negotiations Duluth returned with the Sioux to their villages, where he bartered his trade goods for beaver pelts. He also promised that other Frenchmen would soon arrive to meet the Sioux demands for arms and ammunition. In 1680 Duluth returned to Michilimackinac via the Wisconsin and Fox rivers portage. Although the Foxes recently had established several new villages on the Fox River, they did not welcome the trader into their lodges. They had defended themselves against the Sioux in the past, but new Sioux war parties armed with French muskets constituted a more serious threat, Commercial ties between the French and Sioux did not bode well for the Algonquian tribes of central Wisconsin.[34]

During the 1680s scores of French traders entered the Sioux villages and the Foxes' apprehension mounted. In late 1680 or early 1681 a Sioux war party surprised a Fox hunting camp in western Wisconsin, killing several Fox warriors and carrying others up the Mississippi to the Falls of St. Anthony, where they first tortured, then burned them. Other skirmishes occurred, and in 1686 when Nicolas Perrot established Fort St. Antoine just above the mouth of the Chippewa River, the Foxes and their allies were incensed. During the fall of 1686 the Foxes and Mascoutens sent scouts to Perrot's post, ostensibly to trade for gunpowder, but in reality to ascertain the strength of the garrison and the quantity of supplies cached in the fort's storehouse. They learned that the fort was poorly defended, and in November a large war party of Foxes, Kickapoos, and Mascoutens approached the post, intending to kill Perrot and his employees, loot the storehouse, and then continue on into modern Minnesota, where they planned to attack neighboring Sioux villages. Friendly Miamis warned Perrot of the war party's approach, and before the main body of Indians arrived, he sent a messenger, asking that several prominent chiefs meet with him privately inside the palisade. There, through a ruse, he convinced the chiefs that the number of French traders present in the fort was far larger than they had anticipated. Perrot gave them presents, but he also upbraided them for planning the attack, and placed them under arrest as hostages against the good behavior of their followers. Convinced that their plot had failed, the Foxes and their allies complained bitterly about French trade with the Sioux, but they eventually returned to their villages.[35]

The Sioux retaliated. Well armed by a growing coterie of traders, the Sioux grew bolder and again swept through Wisconsin. In response the Foxes blamed the French and waylaid traders along the Fox-Wisconsin waterway in a futile attempt to prevent guns and ammunition from reaching their enemies. In 1689 they also enlisted the Mascoutens in an unsuccessful plot to attack Perrot again, but when this conspiracy failed, they redirected their hostility back toward the Sioux.[36]

The bloodshed continued. In 1690 Fox warriors overwhelmed a small village of Sioux employed to hunt and trap for French traders in west-central Wisconsin. Although the Foxes "slew many, and took several captives," the Sioux reciprocated; and in revenge the Foxes again enlisted the Mascoutens and Miamis. Intending to surprise their enemy with a winter campaign, the Foxes waited until December 1690 before advancing into western Wisconsin, where they planned to join with large numbers of their allies and attack Sioux villages along the upper

Mississippi. Unfortunately, the Sioux learned of their advance, and although the deep snow prevented them from mustering all of their warriors, the Sioux sent a war party of over four hundred men to intercept the Foxes. Informed of the impending raid, Perrot and other traders used their influence to prevent the Miamis and Mascoutens from joining the Foxes, and by mid-January the latter found themselves isolated in western Wisconsin. Aware of their vulnerability, the Foxes fortified their camp, but when their shamans dreamed visions of disaster, they sent messengers to Perrot, begging him to intercede in their behalf. Eager to forestall any further disruption of the fur trade, the trader persuaded the Sioux to return to their villages. The Foxes retreated back to the Fox River, but the tribesmen who survived the ill-fated campaign were so shaken that they considered withdrawing from Wisconsin and moving to the Wabash Valley.[37]

The warfare continued. During the middle 1690s Fox and Mascouten warriors overran a Sioux village on Lake Pepin, losing fifteen warriors but killing all the Sioux who resisted. Although the Foxes carried many Sioux captives back to their villages, the Mascoutens sought revenge for their warriors who had fallen in the attack, and in the aftermath of the battle they tortured and burned over two hundred prisoners, many of whom were women and children. Perrot intervened to ransom other captives, but the Sioux still demanded revenge, and the Mascoutens prepared to seek shelter among the Iroquois. Afraid that the brunt of the Sioux retaliation would fall on their villages, the Foxes made plans to follow the Mascoutens, but French traders persuaded the Sioux to remain in their villages, and in 1696 the grateful Foxes agreed to a temporary armistice. Their hostility toward the Sioux did not diminish, but the temporary respite from armed conflict enabled them to consolidate their forces and to renew their ties to the Iroquois.[38]

Although the Foxes had been devastated when the Senecas mistakenly had attacked their camp in 1670, they had not retaliated.[39] Indeed, in the aftermath of the incident, when the Miamis turned several Iroquois captives over to the Foxes "to be eaten, in reprisal for the Iroquois [attack]," the Foxes protected the hapless prisoners. Seeking closer ties with the Iroquois, the Foxes sent a messenger to the Senecas, offering to exchange their captives and to make a permanent peace. The Senecas responded favorably, bestowing presents on the Fox emissary and promising that they would focus future raids upon the Shawnees or the Illinois Confederacy. Arrangements were made to exchange the prisoners through French officials in Montreal, and when the Fox warrior returned to Wisconsin he was accompanied by a small delegation of Iroquois warriors, who offered the Foxes and neighboring tribes trading opportunities with British merchants at Albany. To the Jesuits' dismay, the Foxes and their neighbors were so favorably impressed that they provided the Iroquois visitors with two canoe loads of pelts and other presents, before escorting the Iroquois back to Niagara.[40]

Fox ties with the Iroquois posed an immediate danger to the French fur trade, and officials at Montreal attempted to disrupt the growing friendship. Daniel de Rémy, sieur de Courcelle, the governor of New France, instructed French agents in Wisconsin to remind the Foxes and their neighbors "that they ought to remember all the treacheries of the Iroquois" who had caused "the destruction of a great many of their finest young men." Indeed, according to the French, the Iroquois only wished to lure the Foxes into their country to dominate them, and once the Foxes were "surrounded by their enemies, they would find no way to extricate themselves." Meanwhile, Jesuit missionaries among the Iroquois were ordered to inform the Senecas that the Foxes still harbored great bitterness toward them and that Fox warriors planned to journey to the Seneca

homeland "less in search of merchandise than to learn the
location of Iroquois villages." According to the Jesuits, the
Foxes' primary intention was to attack the Iroquois, and
"teach them that they must always look upon them [the
Foxes] as enemies."[41]

The French efforts initially were successful, and economic ties between the Foxes and the Iroquois at first failed
to develop. But the Foxes continued to regard the Iroquois
as potential allies, and they were reluctant to join the
French in military campaigns against the Five Nations. In
1684, when Perrot attempted to rally the western tribes in
support of Governor Joseph-Antoine Le Febvre de La
Barre's ill-fated campaign against the Senecas, the Foxes
begrudgingly agreed to send a contingent of warriors to
join with French forces at Niagara. Yet some wandering
pro-British Mohicans advised them against the venture,
and they were easily dissuaded.[42]

The failure of La Barre's expedition and his subsequent
willingness to abandon some of his western allies (the Illinois Confederacy) to Iroquois retaliation did little to enhance French prestige within the Fox villages. Consequently,
in 1687, when La Barre's replacement, Jacques-René de
Brisay de Denonville asked the western tribes to participate
in his campaign against the Five Nations, the Foxes (much
embroiled with the Sioux) refused. They eventually sent a
war party as far east as Detroit, but there they again were
turned back by pro-British Indians and returned to Wisconsin. Denonville's army burned several Seneca villages,
but in 1689 the Iroquois retaliated with a vengeance, surprising French settlements at Lachine and killing over one
hundred colonists. When news of the onslaught reached
Wisconsin, the Foxes ransomed several Iroquois prisoners
from the Illinois Confederacy and sent the captives back to
the Senecas, carrying Fox offers of a renewed alliance.[43]

The Fox overtures were received favorably by the
Iroquois. During the 1680s Seneca war parties had deci-

mated the Illinois Confederacy and had struck at the Mascoutens and Miamis, but they remembered the Foxes' previous offers of friendship and had not attacked their villages. Indeed, during the 1680s Iroquois envoys attempted to lure the Foxes and Ottawas into the growing British trade network, chiding the Foxes that the French had abandoned them in favor of more lucrative markets among their Sioux enemies.[44]

The Foxes responded by renewing their plunder of French traders traveling to the Sioux, and by mistreating the Jesuits' blacksmith at Green Bay, whom they forced to repair their weapons, then beat so severely that he "had to take to his bed" to recover from the pummeling. Perrot eventually persuaded them of their folly, and they reluctantly allowed French traders to pass through their villages; but they remained aloof from French influence and continued to court the Iroquois. In 1694 part of the tribe conspired with the Mascoutens and Kickapoos to "join with the Iroquois and English" at a new village on the Wabash, and although these plans failed, officials in Canada warned that such a realignment of Indian loyalties "would have very pernicious consequences" for French control of the west.[45]

Yet other events emerged that temporarily bridged the growing chasm between the Foxes and Onontio. During the previous two decades a few Fox warriors had visited the French settlements, but their sojourns had been unpleasant and they had returned to Wisconsin complaining that French officials had been less than cordial and that they had been cheated by merchants at Montreal and other posts.[46] By the 1690s, however, the Foxes and other western tribes relied on the fur trade for many of the necessities of life and they wanted access to French merchandise. Although they still resented French commerce with the Sioux, more-perceptive tribal leaders realized that they could not eliminate all ties with New France, or their people would starve in their villages. Consequently, in 1695, when Nicolas Perrot escorted a small flotilla of western tribesmen to Montreal for an audience with Count Frontenac, a handful of Fox warriors led by Makkathemangoua (Black Bear), the son of Okimaouassen, the chief from the Fox River, accompanied the party.[47]

The decision by Okimaouassen to send his son to Montreal reflected a change of heart, for a decade earlier he had been reluctant to smoke the calumet with Perrot and had opposed French efforts to solve the Fox-Chippewa quarrel. His decision also reflected a growing division within the Fox tribe over their policy toward New France. Although a majority of the tribe's warriors, including Noro, remained suspicious of French policy, a significant minority led by Okimaouassen (mostly members of the Fox clan) argued that the tribe could not sever its ties with the French without risking economic and political isolation. In retrospect, Okimaouassen's faction sought no binding alliance with New France but were pragmatic enough to realize that neither the British nor the Iroquois could sustain the Foxes if the latter were completely alienated from New France and her allies in Wisconsin.[48]

Perrot's party arrived in Montreal on August 14, 1695, and two days later Frontenac met with the western Indians. After delegations of Potawatomis, Sacs, Menominees, and Miamis assured Frontenac of their loyalty, the youthful Makkathemangoua, speaking through a Potawatomi interpreter, spoke for the Foxes. He admitted that many of his kinsmen were embroiled in warfare with the Sioux, but he pointed out that Okimaouassen and his followers had attempted to keep the peace and were obedient to Onontio. Moreover, unlike many members of his tribe, Makkathemangoua did "not approve of my Nation wishing to make an alliance and peace with the Iroquois."[49]

Following the speeches, the Potawatomis warned Frontenac that Makkathemangoua and the other Foxes could not be trusted, but in the two weeks during which Frontenac formulated his reply, the Foxes joined with the other western Indians in Perrot's party to assist the French against an Iroquois war party on Lake St. Francis. On September 3, 1695, they reassembled in Montreal, where Frontenac praised the tribesmen who had supported New France and chastised those whose loyalty was suspect. Speaking to the Foxes, the governor thanked both Makkathemangoua and his father (Okimaouassen) for their fidelity, but he warned Makkathemangoua that "your Nation has quite turned away from my wishes; it has pillaged some of my young men [and] . . . grossly insulted me, and defeated the Sioux whom I now consider my Son." If the Foxes would change their ways, the governor promised to place the tribe "under my protection, though it does not deserve it"; otherwise the Foxes would face French retaliation. Frontenac also cautioned that Noro and other Fox chiefs must stop their intrigues with the Iroquois, who could never be trusted and who only wished to "deceive and devour" the Foxes. Finally, the governor urged the Foxes and other tribes of east-central Wisconsin to establish new villages at Green Bay "to execute with more facility and readiness the orders I should send to them."[50]

Although the Foxes and other Wisconsin tribes refused to relocate their villages in the Green Bay region, Makkathemangoua's trip to Montreal temporarily ameliorated Fox-French relations. After returning from the St. Lawrence, the young Fox warrior worked diligently in the French behalf, persuading many of his fellow tribesmen to join with his father's faction. Noro and his followers still opposed such policies, but by late 1696 Fox elders informed Perrot that they would relinquish their Sioux prisoners and make peace with their enemies if the French would guarantee that the Sioux would reciprocate. One year later, when a delegation of Fox warriors returned to Montreal, Frontenac again scolded them for the misdeeds of some of their young men, but he lavished presents on them and complimented them for their increased friendship. Moreover, to the Foxes' delight, he added, "No more powder and iron will be conveyed to the Sioux, and if my young men carry any thither, I will chastise them severely."[51]

Frontenac's promises of "no more powder and iron" to the Sioux was only part of a general trade policy instituted in 1696 that forbade French citizens to carry trade goods to the western tribes. Motivated by a glutted fur market, and inspired by Jesuit concern over the debauchery of French coureurs de bois among the western Indians, the policy provided that the tribespeople could still bring their pelts to Montreal but no traders would be allowed to visit the Indians' villages. In retrospect, the policy failed miserably. By the 1690s the western tribes had become enmeshed in the fur trade and they much preferred to purchase commodities from visiting merchants rather than make the arduous voyage to Montreal. Accordingly, the Indians in the west were faced with a growing shortage of trade goods, and by 1697 even the Potawatomis complained that they lacked "powder, iron, and every other necessary which you [the French] were formerly in the habit of sending to us." In addition, the scarcities rekindled intertribal conflicts in Wisconsin and inspired the Iroquois to reopen their trade offensive to the western tribes.[52]

Surprisingly, the Foxes remained aloof from most of those activities. Their habitual antipathy toward French traders had precluded an adequate supply of trade goods in their villages, and the diminished quantity of merchandise had less impact among them than among many other tribes. Indeed, during 1697–98 they supported Perrot's efforts to maintain peace between the Sioux and the Wisconsin tribes, and in 1698 when the Sioux surprised and killed a large encampment of Miamis, the Foxes advised the Miamis against any retaliation. In response, Miami spokesmen met with the more-militant anti-French faction led by Noro, who still wished "to irritate his tribe against the Frenchmen," but his efforts were neutralized by Okimaouassen and Makkathemangoua. Okimaouassen's followers also protected Perrot and several other French from the Miamis and the Mascoutens, escorting the Frenchmen back to Green Bay and providing them with food and other supplies. The Foxes still refused Perrot's endeavors to solicit their assistance against the Iroquois, but unlike the Ottawas, the Hurons, and some Chippewas, they remained temporarily aloof from the Iroquois trade offensive. In response, Perrot described the Foxes' conduct as "altogether discreet [sic]," but he was far too optimistic. The Foxes had protected Perrot and other French traders, but they still despised the Sioux, and even Okimaouassen and his followers refused to allow any trade goods to pass through their villages en route to Sioux villages in Minnesota. Moreover, by 1700 they had become embroiled in another quarrel with the Chippewas, and although few lives were lost on either side, one of the Foxes slain in the resulting skirmish was a prominent warrior and a close kinsman of Noro, a leading member of the anti-French faction.[53]

Therefore, when Courtemanche visited the Fox villages during the spring of 1701, tribal leaders agreed reluctantly to accompany him to Callières's grand council. Noro, Miskousouath, and other Fox warriors attended the proceedings, and they listened politely to the French promises of abundant trade goods and peace with the Iroquois. Unquestionably, the pledges of increased trade appealed to these tribesmen, but the treaty with the Iroquois held little promise. As Miskousouath reminded Callières, "Though I am much involved with the Sioux, I have never had any great quarrel with the Iroquois." After the conference, the Fox delegation returned west. In Montreal they had eaten Onontio's oxen and had tasted his brandy; they had also heard his promises, but considerable skepticism still reigned in the villages along the Fox and Wolf rivers. Callières had offered no assistance against the Sioux, and those old enemies still threatened their villages. Fox ties to the French remained tenuous. Onontio might rule in Montreal, but his power was limited in Wisconsin.[54]

CHAPTER TWO

PEOPLE
OF THE
RED EARTH

Centuries ago, when the world was inhabited only by manitous and animals, Gisha Manitou, the chief of the manitous, took a wife and sired four sons. The two eldest, Wisaka and Kiyapatha, were especially blessed, and even in their youth it was apparent that they would develop powers greater than those of the other manitous. Jealous of their gifts, the others conspired against them and killed Kiyapatha, but Wisaka, aided by his grandmother, Mother of the Earth, gained hegemony over the other manitous. Some he killed. Others he drove under the earth or into the sky, where their campfires can be seen scattered along the Great White River (the Milky Way). Some were transformed into Thunderers, beings who ride upon the south wind and are guardians of the people. Then Wisaka met with the animals, and assisted by the turtle, buzzard, muskrat, wolf, and other beasts, he shaped all the mountains and valleys found on the earth.[1]

To inhabit his world, Wisaka scooped up blood-red clay and created his people. And he made their eyes and hair as black as the forest at midnight. Then Wisaka taught his people how to hunt, and grow corn, and perform the dances and ceremonies that would bring them good medicine. And he provided them with all the knowledge they needed to live peacefully with one another. Finally, Wisaka left his people and journeyed far to the north, where he built a lodge among the ice and snow, but he promised to return one day and take them to a new home beyond the western sunset where they would be reunited with their loved ones who had gone before them. After his people were safe in the west, Wisaka again would return, and he would destroy their old homeland. And since his people's skin was the color of the clay from which he had formed them, Wisaka called his children Mesquakie, or "the people of the red earth."[2]

The French called Wisaka's people the Renards, or the "Foxes." Although the French had first learned of them from the Hurons and the Chippewas, and early French documents often refer to the Foxes by their Chippewa name, Outagami ("People of the Opposite Shore"), officials in Canada eventually perpetuated the misnomer supplied by French traders. Fox traditions indicate that when their ancestors first encountered the traders, the Frenchmen inquired about their identity. Since clan or family ties have always been important to the Fox people, and since these particular Mesquakies were members of the Wahgohagi, or Fox clan, the Indians answered that they were Foxes. Misinterpreting their reply, the French reported back to their superiors that a tribe of Indians named "the Foxes" lived in Wisconsin.[3]

The Foxes shared linguistic and cultural ties with some of their neighbors. They spoke a dialect in the Algonquian language group very similar to those spoken by the Sacs and the Kickapoos, and members of all three tribes could easily communicate with each other. There is strong evidence to suggest that the Mascoutens, a tribe absorbed into the Kickapoos early in the nineteenth century, also spoke a similar dialect. Of the other Algonquian languages, Shawnee is probably the closest to that of the Fox group, but significant differences in vocabulary and grammar separate the two. Within the Fox group, the Fox and Sac dialects were so similar that Indian agents meeting with the combined Sac and Fox tribes during the early nineteenth century did not differentiate between the two and reported that both tribes spoke the same language. Of course, such linguistic evidence suggests that the ancestors of all of these tribes had been closely associated and that the split between the Foxes and Sacs had occurred relatively late.[4]

When the Foxes first welcomed Allouez and other Jesuit missionaries into their villages, they were living along the Wolf River, but by 1700 they had scattered from Green Bay up the Fox River to the portage at the Wisconsin. Several of their major settlements were heavily fortified. Surrounded by log palisades, these summer villages consisted of rectangular frame houses constructed of poles and covered with elm bark. Some were sixty feet long and provided shelter for several families. Fox villagers entered the structures at either end and rested or slept upon wide pole benches, covered with rush mats, that stretched along opposite walls of the building. Personal possessions or clan objects were stored beneath the benches or hung from the ceiling. During excessively warm weather Fox women removed part of the elm-bark sheeting to provide better ventilation. On cool nights small campfires might be kindled within these structures, but during the warm months most of the cooking took place outdoors or in brush shelters adjoining the buildings.[5]

For the Foxes and their neighbors, summer was a time of plenty. In the spring Fox women planted extensive fields of corn in the fertile bottomlands and small prairies that adjoined the Fox-Wisconsin waterway, and after the corn reached sufficient height to prevent it from becoming entangled, crops of beans, squash, and pumpkins were

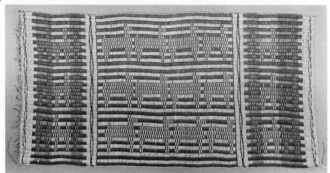

The Mesquakies used reed mats like this for both floor coverings and the outer shell of their wigwams. The mats were woven from bulrushes that grew along the banks of rivers and lakes in northern Illinois and Wisconsin. Those used as floor covers often incorporated dyed rushes woven into geometric or other patterns as in this example from about 1830. Field Museum of Natural History, Chicago (neg. 11105, cat. 34990)

cultivated amidst the corn rows. In midsummer, when the ears were well formed but still tender, part of the corn was harvested and the Foxes gorged themselves on green corn, often boiled in large kettles with venison, ducks, or wild turkeys. The remainder of the corn, in addition to the beans, squash, and pumpkins, was allowed to ripen to maturity and was harvested during the late summer or autumn.[6]

Although corn remained the staple of Fox existence, they supplemented that crop with a multitude of other vegetable foods gathered from the forests and prairies. They were especially fond of maple sugar, which they manufactured from the sap each spring and stored and used as a condiment. They also dug and harvested many tubers, including wild potatoes and groundnuts, from the forest. In season, Fox women and children picked wild strawberries, blackberries, grapes, and plums. Hickory nuts, walnuts, and hazelnuts were harvested in the fall, but unlike the Chippewas and the Menominees, the Foxes made relatively little use of the wild rice that grew in the lakes on the northern borders of their homeland.[7]

This wigwam, constructed of reed mats by Winnebagos in the 1920s, was almost identical to those used by the Mesquakies in the late seventeenth and early eighteenth centuries. Nebraska State Historical Society (D517:54–45)

Fox hunters provided the meat that flavored the rich stews that simmered over their campfires. Most tribe members preferred venison or bear, but the men and older boys also hunted elk, raccoon, rabbits, squirrels, and other small animals. Large numbers of waterfowl were taken on a seasonal basis, and during the summer Fox hunting parties left their villages to travel to the prairies of Illinois or Iowa where they killed buffalo. After an initial feast, the Fox women would dry the remainder and carry it back to their villages. Although fish and turtles were sometimes taken, they were not a food of choice and were eaten only when other forms of animal protein were unavailable.[8]

Summer also was a festive period when the population concentrated in the large villages enjoyed a series of social events and religious ceremonies. During the summer members of clans that extended throughout the tribe assembled together to participate in the rituals that reaffirmed their kinship. Sometimes the sacred clan bundles were opened by the elders who served as their guardians, and the members of the clan shared in their medicine. At other times social dances such as the Swan Dance were performed, or the entire village participated in the Buffalo Feast, which invoked the manitous' assistance for a successful hunt. On other occasions lacrosse was played with a ferocity that amazed those Jesuits who were fortunate enough to witness the matches. And yet, all these events, regardless of their religious, economic, or kinship significance, were surrounded with sufficient festivity to make the summer months a joyous time for the Fox people.[9]

In contrast, the winter months were a time of quiet reflection. During the Moon of Rutting Elk (late September–early October) most of the Foxes left the major summer villages and scattered in smaller hunting camps through the forest. Occupied by extended families or similar kinship groups, these temporary settlements consisted of small round "wigwam" structures built of poles covered by woven reed mats. Although less spacious than the summer houses (their diameter rarely exceeded fifteen feet), the winter dwellings were more tightly constructed. Bearskins and buffalo robes served as door and floor coverings, and heated by a central fire pit, the winter houses provided a warm, if smoky, environment.[10]

Although some hunting continued during the winter, in the cold months the Foxes were much more sedentary, and family members of all ages spent considerable time huddled around their campfires. Food harvested and prepared during the past summer was parceled out from skin bags or metal containers, while adults fashioned or mended clothes, weapons, and other utensils. During this season all members of the family would sit quietly by the fire listening to the elders recite the stories of how Wisaka, the other manitous, and the animals created the world and taught humankind its secrets. For the Foxes these stories had a profound significance. Not only did they provide a rational explanation for the universe, they also reinforced traditional tribal values such as courtesy, generosity, and loyalty to the kinship group.[11]

The personal life cycle of the Fox people reflected such traditions. Unlike Europeans, who lived within a sociopolitical structure characterized by a hierarchy of power, Fox society was more egalitarian. Political, kinship, and economic ties reflected relationships between equals rather than the vertical framework of social and economic classes common in European societies. Consequently, while most European parents instructed their children always to submit to the proper authority (that is, that they should "mind"), Fox parents urged their children to be more independent. Indeed, according to early French observers, the Foxes' discipline over their children was very lax, though children sometimes were scolded or doused with cold water and occasionally were forced to blacken their face and fast, a punishment that caused them considerable public humiliation.[12]

But the Foxes cherished their children, and many members of the extended family shared in their upbringing. Children were nurtured and cared for by their parents, but aunts, uncles, and grandparents also played important roles. Relationships between children and grandparents were particularly close. Since age sometimes prevented the grandparents from participating in the strenuous economic activities that had filled their younger years, they had more time to devote to their grandchildren than they earlier had spent with their children. Consequently, they shared their accumulated knowledge with their grandchildren and if the parents disciplined their child, the grandparents often interceded in the child's behalf. Ties between such alternate generations were strong, and for the Foxes, terms such as "grandfather" or "grandmother" incorporated qualities of affection and respect that transcended the strictly generational features of such kinships.[13]

Surrounded by relatives, Fox children were reared in preparation for their later roles in life. Children of both sexes were strapped in cradleboards until they were old enough to walk. Then they were supervised by female relatives until age six or seven. When boys were old enough to be trusted with weapons, their father, uncles, or brothers taught them to use a bow and arrow, to hunt, and fish, and to accept the responsibilities of a Fox warrior. During the preadolescent years boys also were encouraged to spend time with their peers in the forest, perfecting the activities in which they would engage as adults. In contrast, mothers and other female relatives taught Fox girls those skills they would need as women. At the age of seven a girl began to sew clothes for her dolls, and when she reached ten, she assisted her mother and aunts in preparing meals and in cultivating corn and other crops. Meanwhile, the women of her kinship group instructed her regarding the proper behavior expected of a Fox woman.[14]

At puberty Fox children formally entered adult life. With the onset of her first menstrual period a Fox girl was isolated in a special lodge and instructed that during her period she should have no contact with any male member of the tribe. Because the Foxes believed that menstrual blood held the potential for catastrophe, her mother and aunts informed the girl that she was forbidden to even touch a man or his belongings during her period. She was forced to cook for herself or was supplied with food by her grandmother, and when her period ended, her female relatives bathed her in a stream, then scratched her legs and back with a sharp object until her blood flowed so that she would be assured of a normal menstrual cycle. Finally, all her old clothing was burned, she was dressed in new finery and returned to her family as a young woman.[15]

Fox boys entered manhood less formally, but after learning the skills necessary for adult life, an adolescent was encouraged to sequester himself in the forest and to fast in anticipation of receiving a vision from a protective spirit that would provide him with his personal medicine. The spirit or manitou might also inform him of certain items that should be incorporated into his medicine bundle and would provide him with medicine for the rest of his life. After receiving his vision, the young man continued to hunt for his family, but he also looked forward to becoming a warrior. Under ordinary circumstances young men did not join war parties until their sixteenth birthday, and novices often were assigned such duties as guarding the camp until their older kinsmen believed that they had acquired enough experience to protect themselves. After proving himself in battle, however, a young man was privileged to paint his face with vermilion and change his name, casting off the appellation of his childhood and assuming a new title more befitting a warrior.[16]

Most Fox men married during their late teens or early twenties, while Fox women usually married three to four years earlier. After a brief courtship, the young man or a member of his family might approach the girl's family and offer goods or his services for her hand. If the woman's family accepted, the marriage was consummated. The man was obligated to hunt only for his wife's family for a period of two to three years, or until the birth of their first child. The couple might then establish their own residence or move in with the husband's family. Polygynous marriages took place, but almost always these were sororal, with the man marrying sisters or perhaps a cousin of his first wife.[17]

After the birth of their first child a Fox couple settled into the routine of adult life. Women planted, cultivated, and harvested the crops while men hunted, trapped, or participated in warfare. Seasons passed, children were raised, and the all-important kinship groups continued. Fox men and women, once young themselves, passed through middle age and became the family's elders. Like their grandparents and parents before them, they relished their interactions with their grandchildren, and when the winter winds howled down from Wisaka's lodge place, they too entertained their family by passing on the rich tribal traditions around the winter campfires.[18]

And when death came, like their fathers before them, they accepted it as part of the natural order of things. Kinsmen of the deceased appointed a nonrelative to supervise the funeral. The body was dressed in the dead person's finest clothing, sprinkled with tobacco, and surrounded by the utensils that he or she would need for the journey into the afterlife. Usually seated in a shallow grave, the deceased faced west, and after a formal farewell or eulogy was recited, the body was buried and the grave covered with either rocks or a small grave house. Dogs were strangled to serve as guides to the lands beyond the sunset, and the property of the dead person was then distributed to those who had assisted with the burial. After a funeral feast, close relatives of the deceased entered a formal mourning period that might last for as long as four years. During this time the spouse of the deceased was expected to remain solemn, dress in a disheveled manner, and refrain from contact with members of the opposite sex. Finally, if the deceased had been killed or had died at a relatively young age, the surviving members of his or her kinship group held a formal adoption ceremony and inducted another person of the same sex and approximate age into the family.[19]

After death, the spirits of deceased Foxes journeyed beyond the sunset where Wisaka's younger brother, Kiyapatha, who had been killed by the manitous, had prepared several villages for them. All Foxes traveled toward Kiyapatha's dwelling place, but Wisaka promised that only

those tribespeople who had honored their kinship obligations and had lived in a virtuous manner would proceed beyond the first village. They would pass across a bridge over a swift river and would then achieve true happiness, but if the spirits of evil men and women attempted to cross the bridge, they would fall into the water and be swept away to the domain of Machi Manitou (the evil spirit).[20]

The interplay of good and evil formed an intricate part of Fox cosmology. Some of the early Jesuits reported that the Foxes believed that only one supreme being ruled the universe, but such an assertion reflects the priests' simplistic perspective on Fox religion. Although the Fox people were convinced that Gisha Manitou ruled over the other manitous, his power was not complete, nor did he often interfere in the affairs of the tribe.[21]

More pertinent to the Foxes were a series of other manitous whose particular interests or activities impacted on their daily

A captive Fox chief and woman from Alexandre de Batz's 1735 watercolor of Indians from several nations. The chief's hand is resting on the head of a domesticated whooping crane. Peabody Museum of Archaeology and Ethnology, Harvard University (photograph by Hillel Burger, no. N28063)

life. Of course, Wisaka had made the world and provided for his people, but his friend Cawan lived in the south and his lodge was the home of the Thunderers, the manitous who rode the wind and watched over the Fox people. The Thunderers constantly moved across the horizon striking at evil with their lightning bolts, and the Foxes considered them to be especially protective of the tribe's interests. Also beneficial was the Sun. The Foxes called him their "Grandfather" because he provided them with warmth and light, but he sometimes was harsh and did not let them gaze intently on his face. In contrast, the moon, their "Grandmother," was gentler. She allowed her grandchildren to look directly at her, and she furnished them with many of the good things that they used in their daily life.[22]

In addition to the celestial manitous, other spirits occupied the earth and shaped the lives of the Fox people. Of special importance were the spirits who lived in the earth, for they provided both men and the Thunderers with fire. Other manitous were personified by animals who bestowed particular gifts on Wisaka's children. Toads and crows possessed special knowledge that helped shamans heal the sick, while deer and hummingbirds endowed their favorites with speed and agility. Snakes were renowned for their wisdom, while raccoons blessed their favorites with adaptability and craftiness. Other manitous lived in streams, trees, boulders, and other natural environments, and all could on occasion have a profound impact on Fox life.[23]

So could witches. Like other Algonquian-speaking people, the Foxes believed that witches flourished in their midst. Servants of Machi Manitou, the witches used their power to cause sickness or to sow disharmony within Fox society. Witches were especially active at night, assuming the form of animals (especially bears) or passing through the forest as a ball of blue-green light. For example, the Foxes believed that witches could cause the corn crop to fail and were responsible for stealing the souls from corpses. To counteract their evil power, the Foxes relied on the medicine of their shamans. These medicine people (both men and women) could cure illnesses by sucking out foreign objects that witches had secretly injected into their victims' bodies, or they could provide herbal remedies, charms, and information to help individual Foxes counteract the malevolent spells cast on them. Yet many Foxes were convinced that even friendly shamans periodically dabbled in the evil arts, and these medicine people were both feared and respected.[24]

Although the friendly manitous had once supplied the Fox people with everything they needed, by the beginning of the eighteenth century conditions were changing. At the time when French traders first entered their villages, the Foxes were a self-sufficient people. They procured their food from the fields, streams, and forests, and they fashioned the utensils and implements that they needed from wood, stone, or animal products. Men wore deerskin breechcloths, leggings, and shirts, while women wore leggings and loose-fitting deerskin dresses. Both sexes wore moccasins. In the winter they wrapped themselves in buffalo robes or, preferably, bearskins, and they adorned themselves with ornaments made of bone, porcupine quills, and native copper. Adult males shaved their head except for a scalp lock, while the women wore their hair long and often braided. Both sexes periodically painted their face and bodies with black and vermilion.[25]

The Foxes long had participated in the intertribal trade network that stretched across the Great Lakes and Mississippi Valley, but before the development of the European-sponsored fur trade they had bargained their surplus commodities only for luxury items (moose hides and skins from more-northern animals, copper, shell beads, tobacco, and so on) or for food products that supplemented their basic diet. In exchange they traded agricultural produce, such as surplus corn or beans, or the tightly woven rush mats fashioned by Fox women that were used as floor coverings and in the construction of winter houses. In the precontact period much of the intertribal trade was closely tied to ceremonial reciprocity that existed between neighboring tribes. Goods were exchanged within a framework of mutual gift giving, and both sides honored both themselves and each other by demonstrations of generosity. Such interchanges were attended with much formal ceremony, and the exchange of goods, while economically important, was ostensibly secondary to the social or political significance of the interaction. Therefore, hard bargaining had no place within the exchange of commodities, for a tribe would only dishonor themselves and insult their neighbors by insisting that they receive a larger quantity of trade items than their neighbors had proffered.[26]

The European-sponsored fur trade irrevocably altered the old system. The introduction of French manufactured trade goods, particularly metal utensils and firearms, did not immediately transform Fox life, but these items were so markedly superior to traditional tools fashioned from wood, bone, or stone that the demand for such commodities was instantaneous. Trade muskets, while sometimes inaccurate and undependable, were superior weapons to bows and arrows. And what Fox man or woman could resist the temptation of brass pots and kettles; steel needles, knives, and awls; iron hatchets; brightly colored sashes; silver jewelry; glass beads; and oil-based paints in black or vivid blues, greens, and vermilion? Of course, Fox hunters still scoured the forests killing game for their families, but they also turned their attention to securing those pelts (beaver, ermine, and otter) that the French and the British so seemed to covet. Within a generation the wondrous European luxury goods became necessities. Fox women still tilled their fields, but they discovered that metal hoe blades were much more serviceable than bone or stone,

This wooden spoon with a beaver-shaped handle illustrates the wooden implements made and utilized by the Mesquakies. Field Museum of Natural History, Chicago (neg. 110953)

and they badgered their husbands to obtain them. Trade muskets needed lead and powder, and even durable iron or tin kettles eventually cracked and needed to be replaced. Moreover, as Fox warriors traveled to Montreal or other French settlements, they developed a thirst for "Onontio's milk" (French brandy), and when French coureurs de bois carried kegs filled with the fiery liquid into the west, they demanded many beaver pelts before the kegs were opened.[27]

Such tariffs markedly changed the nature of the trade system. Before the French trade the exchange of commodities had been within the framework of a ceremonial

reciprocity, but by 1700 the generosity that had characterized earlier transactions had been replaced by the demands
of the marketplace. French and British traders occasionally
plied their Indian customers with gifts, but such merchandise was designed to lure trading partners. In contrast, Fox
warriors found that French merchants, both at Montreal
and in Wisconsin, demanded payment for trade goods that
once had been luxuries but now were becoming necessities. And since the supply, and as a result the price, of such
goods fluctuated, due to exigencies over which neither the
traders nor the Indians had much control (economic policies established in France, maritime transportation, warfare), the Foxes and their neighbors often were angered
over the scarcity and considerable expense of trade merchandise. Quid-pro-quo demands for payments in exchange
for gunpowder, lead, and other necessities violated such
traditional Fox values as generosity and the communal dis-
tribution of available resources, and French traders who
followed such policies were seen as greedy and lacking in
any pretense of courtesy or etiquette.[28]

Moreover, both history and the Foxes' geographic location within the French trade network placed them at a
disadvantage. Since they had been driven into Wisconsin
by the Chippewas, and had arrived earlier than those
tribes who had fled the Iroquois, the Foxes' ties with the
French were considerably more tenuous than those of later
arrivals such as the Potawatomis and Miamis. Their early
exodus from Michigan precluded any major participation
in the French-Huron trading empire, and after the Iroquois
destruction of Huronia, French trade with the Chippewas,
traditional Fox enemies, also discouraged initial contacts
between the Foxes and the coureurs de bois. In addition,
their location in central Wisconsin placed them at the
western terminus of the initial French trade network, so
that goods transported from Montreal were often in short
supply and necessarily highly priced. Indeed, during the

1660s and 1670s the Foxes were so isolated that they were perennially short of French trade goods, and other Indians described them as "destitute" and as "barbarians." Hoping to profit from the Foxes' economic deprivation, the Potawatomis at Green Bay endeavored to monopolize trade with the tribe and prevent French merchants from visiting the Fox villages.[29]

The Potawatomi efforts were unsuccessful, but the small number of French traders who journeyed to the Fox villages could not meet the tribe's growing demands. Moreover, aware that the Foxes desperately needed their merchandise, many of the coureurs de bois charged exorbitant prices, which only added to the Foxes' frustration. In response, younger warriors sometimes seized the traders' goods, leaving in payment the pelts which they had intended to exchange, but which were considerably less than what the French merchants expected. Of course, such commerce did not endear the Foxes to the traders, who in turn became more reluctant to travel to the Fox villages. Therefore, as the Foxes grew more dependent on European technology, their access to such merchandise seemed to diminish.[30]

French attempts to extend the fur trade to the Sioux markedly increased the Foxes' frustration. Although the Sioux were more numerous than the Foxes, and the two tribes had warred for decades, the Foxes had been able, with some difficulty, to defend their homeland in east-central Wisconsin. They had been assisted in this struggle by their limited acquisition of French arms, but if the Sioux also gained access to such technology, the Foxes feared that their position would become untenable. In contrast, French traders were eager to extend their commercial network onto the plains, and the populous bands of the eastern Dakotas invited such penetration. Compared to the Sioux, the Foxes offered a limited market. French traders did not necessarily choose between the two tribes, but they refused to allow Fox objections to preclude their westward expansion. Therefore, the Foxes watched in dismay as Perrot and other French merchants paddled their heavily laden canoes up the Fox River to the Wisconsin portage. Embittered, the Foxes could not even participate in this trade, for the merchandise that was in such short supply in their villages was destined for their enemies. Not surprisingly, angry Fox warriors pillaged the canoes of traders who were en route to the Sioux villages, or they attempted to exact tribute from the coureurs de bois who passed down the Fox-Wisconsin waterway returning from the Mississippi.[31]

The Foxes' ambivalent relationship with the French and their fur trade also created stress within the tribe's social and political systems. Kinship groups permeated Fox society and delineated much of the tribe's formal political organization. Although the exact number of clans among the Foxes during the first quarter of the eighteenth century remains unknown, evidence suggests that at least eight exogamous patrilineal kinship groups functioned within the tribe. The separate clans differed in size, influence, and the role they played in tribal politics, but each group assumed certain responsibilities that prominent clan members had fulfilled for generations. For example, the village or peace chiefs almost always were members of the large and influential Mucqua, or Bear, clan, and those positions may have been hereditary within certain subdivisions of that group. In contrast, the Wahgohagi, or Fox clan, usually supplied the tribe's war chiefs, and was responsible for greeting strangers or visitors new to the villages. Like the Bear clan, the Fox clan also was a populous kinship group with considerable prominence. Another large clan, the Neneemekee, or Thunder people, could supply both village and war chiefs, but members usually played a secondary role in assuming such leadership positions. The Mowhay, or wolf clan, also was numerous, but its members were a "lower grade of people" who could be councilmen but could not be chiefs. Several smaller clans such as the Pukkee (Partridge), Ahawuck (Swan), Meshaway (Elk), and Ashegunuck (Bass), also were relegated to subordinate positions.[32]

In addition to political roles, the clans served other functions. Each clan maintained sole possession of a series of names that could only be given to members of its lineage. These names could be bestowed at birth or at puberty, or to new members of the tribe (usually prisoners) adopted to replace kinsmen who had been killed or had died of natural causes. Indeed, the Foxes' willingness to replace fallen relatives with captives similar in age and sex to the deceased was a key to the tribe's resiliency. Although the Foxes suffered catastrophic casualties in their warfare with the French and other tribes, they continually replenished their ranks with prisoners who were adopted and who evidently were willing to espouse the Fox cause. Of course, the tribes of the Iroquois Confederacy followed a similar practice, but the Foxes' adoption policies were more inclusive than those of most other Algonquian-speaking tribes in the Great Lakes region.[33]

Clan activities were augmented by a loose loyalty to two divisions resembling moieties that enrolled all members of the tribe. Largely social and ceremonial in function, the divisions, named Kiskoha and Tohkana, were symbolized by the colors white (Kiskoha) and black (Tohkana), and they organized their members for games, dances, and other occasions. Tribe members were assigned to each division at birth. The first child born to Fox parents was assigned to the division of his or her mother, the second to the father's division, and so on, alternatively. Led by informal chiefs, these divisions fostered a friendly competition at dances and lacrosse games and helped diffuse intratribal tensions.[34]

Disputes between families or individuals also were mediated by the village councils. Composed of the leading spokesmen for the families or clans present in the village, these informal bodies met intermittently to discuss problems and issues that confronted the village's inhabitants. They dealt with such matters as the maintenance of the village's palisades, the dispersion of villagers for the winter hunt, or general policies regarding war or peace. Deliberative in nature, they attempted to achieve a consensus before reaching any final decision. Although the political unit was the village when most of the Fox tribe lived in a large fortified village such as Ouestatimong, the council representing such a population center actually functioned as a tribal council.[35]

Under ordinary circumstances the village councils possessed only limited coercive powers and relied on tribal tradition and peer pressure to enforce their decisions. Obviously, within the framework of a relatively small tribal society, common backgrounds, experiences, and interests fostered a perspective that was shared by most members of the tribe. Significant deviations from the common world view were immediately suspect, and since most Foxes achieved their identity primarily as members of a family and kinship group, any belief or activity that engendered criticism from one's relatives was particularly undesirable. Indeed, a Fox's primary allegiance was to his or her bloodline, and if a member of another family killed or injured a kinsmen, the family of the perpetrator was expected to cover the death or injury with presents. If such compensation was not forthcoming, the victim's kinsmen initiated a vendetta.[36]

It was hoped, however, that mediation by the village chief precluded such violence. Usually a prominent middle-aged or older male member of the Bear clan, the village chief served as counselor, mediator, and conciliator. Although the position was hereditary within that clan, the village chief achieved and maintained his position through his followers' faith in his wisdom and sound judgment. Like the council, he could only advise and provide guidance, and if his followers became displeased with his leadership, they could refuse his counsel and withdraw from the village. Although the authority of the village chief was limited among most of the Algonquian-speaking Great Lakes tribes, it probably was least persuasive among the Foxes, whom Indian agent Thomas Forsyth described as paying "no respect to their chiefs at any time, except necessity compels them."[37]

In contrast, by 1700 the power of the war chiefs had increased. Traditionally members of the Fox clan, war chiefs were experienced warriors whose success on the warpath inspired other men and attracted a following. In happier times village chiefs and their councils had dominated tribal affairs, since war chiefs played major roles only during those infrequent periods when the tribe was threatened. Unfortunately, however, by 1700 the Foxes had experienced over a quarter century of intermittent warfare that had thrust the war chiefs into positions of continued prominence. In a constant state of alarm, the Foxes repeatedly were forced to rely on the leadership of the war chiefs, whose influence increased while that of the village chiefs diminished. In addition, since warfare emerged as a factor that dominated the Foxes' existence, the warrior also was aggrandized as a role model in Fox life. By 1700 adolescent Fox males fasting on a vision quest no longer sought to be primarily a hunter, a trapper, or a trader. Warfare was now a necessary, not a secondary, facet of Fox life. Young Fox warriors seeking the respect or admiration of their kinsmen still condescended to seek deer or beaver in the forests, but they saw the warpath as the primary road to success.[38]

The status of Fox warriors also was enhanced by the growing importance of the Kiyagamohag, or warriors society. Composed of younger Fox warriors, usually aged eighteen to thirty-five, the Kiyagamohag were considered to be the defenders of the Fox homeland, and when the Sioux, Chippewas, or other enemies threatened the Fox villages, the Kiyagamohag were "the first to go, others follow afterwards." The Foxes believed that members of the warrior society possessed special "manitou power, and the manitous look upon them with favor." They carried powerful medicine bundles to protect themselves from enemies, and if, on returning from the warpath, they danced and feasted in honor of fallen comrades, Kiyapatha would readily welcome the dead into the spirit world.[39]

Although membership in the Kiyagamohag was open to all the clans, traditionally only members of the Wahgohagi, or Fox clan, could serve as war chiefs. Yet, by 1700 the role of warfare in Fox society had achieved a position of such prominence that many members of the Kiyagamohag who were not part of the Wahgohagi lineage also aspired to such leadership. Breaking with the past, warriors from other clans also began to recruit followers. They too fasted, blackened their faces, and prepared a small lodge apart from the village. In the midst of the lodge they kindled a fire, and near the smoke hole they hung a belt of red wampum or a piece of red cloth. If other Fox warriors wished to join them on the warpath, they entered the lodge, passed their hands over the wampum or cloth, and shared some tobacco. When enough warriors had been recruited, the war party left the village, singing the Shegodem, or war song. If they were successful, they returned to their homes in triumph. Before entering the village, the war chief sent a younger member of the party to announce their arrival. In response, the villagers assembled to congratulate them on their good fortune. Dances were held and plunder and prisoners were distributed. If the war party had been defeated, however, they entered the village separately, each individual returning quietly to his lodge.[40]

The Fox villagers who welcomed their kinsmen back from Onontio's great conference at Montreal in 1701 probably were aware of many of the changes that were transforming their society. Most realized that they had become dependent on the fur trade for many of the necessities of their existence, and although they were hard pressed to supply sufficient pelts to obtain such commodities, they were determined to have them. Firearms, metal utensils, beads, and brandy had all become a part of Fox life, and just as the People of the Red Earth were eager to acquire the products of European technology, they were determined to keep these goods from their Sioux enemies.

Sitting beside their campfires, perceptive Fox men and women must have reflected on the changing nature of tribal politics. For some the age-old order of things seemed to be deteriorating. No longer were their lives governed by the traditional wisdom of the village chiefs and the council of elders. More and more, they seemed to be subject to a chaos of warfare, which was encouraged, if not precipitated, by young men seeking the admiration of their peers. Eager for recognition, these warriors disregarded the traditional clan-dominated political system and often ignored the advice of their older kinsmen. For younger men seeking honors on the warpath, these were heady times, but for their older, more-conservative kinsmen the seasons were fraught with danger. Wisaka and the Thunderers had withdrawn to their lodges, and their people now faced Machi Manitou.

The Foxes' relationship with other indigenous peoples only added to the confusion. Because of Onontio's bidding they maintained a tenuous peace with the Sioux and Chippewas, but their enmity, especially toward the Sioux, threatened to boil over into warfare. French officials continually warned them against the Iroquois, and in 1670 a war party from the Five Nations had mistakenly struck at Fox hunting camps, but such forays paled in comparison to threats by the Sioux or the Chippewas. Moreover, Iroquois traders now offered promises of plentiful and less-expensive British trade goods if the Foxes would leave Onontio and embrace the League of the Hodenosaunee.[41] Nevertheless, some Foxes remained wary of the Machi Nadoway and still sought an accommodation with Onontio.[42] Perhaps they could gain access to French trade goods without bending to Onontio's will. Perhaps the Kickapoos, the Mascoutens, or other tribes might be enlisted in an alliance. Perhaps they could dissuade the French from trading with their Sioux enemies. For the Foxes, the opening years of the eighteenth century were a time of transition. Not surprisingly, transition also brought chaos.

CHAPTER THREE

REAPING
THE
WHIRLWIND

No one ever accused Antoine de la Mothe Cadillac of underestimating his own abilities. Born in Gascony in 1661, Cadillac arrived in North America in 1683 and first settled at Port Royal in Nova Scotia. Serving as an officer in the colonial Troupes de la Marine, he established close ties with Frontenac, and in 1694, through the governor's influence, he was appointed commander of the French post at Michilimackinac. Although Cadillac became enamored with the west of New France, he disliked Michilimackinac, which he described as "the most terrible place imaginable . . . neither bread nor meat is eaten there, and no other food to be had but a little fish and Indian corn". In contrast, although he had never personally visited the region, he proposed that a new French post be established at Detroit, which he claimed was blessed with "a milder climate, more fertile farmlands, and an abundance of both fish and game."[1]

A French post at Detroit also offered Cadillac the potential for considerable financial success. If given command of the post and allowed to invest in the fur trade at that location, Cadillac promised French officials that he would administer the post to the Crown's advantage. He would, of course, reap certain personal profits, but he assured Callières that he would first limit the quantity of fur brought down from the west until the current surpluses in Canada had been depleted. In addition, he planned to relocate the Ottawas, the Hurons, the Miamis, and other tribes to the Detroit region. Such a nucleus of staunchly pro-French Indians, supported by a strong military post, would both preclude British influence and serve as a base for future campaigns against the Iroquois. His proposal failed to mention, however, that the resettlement of these tribes at Detroit also would make the post the most lucrative center for the French fur trade in the west.[2]

Cadillac's proposals ran afoul of the Jesuits, who also sought to dominate Indian affairs in the west. Cadillac had quarreled continually with the missionaries while serving as commandant at Michilimackinac, and he complained to Callières that he had found only three ways of pleasing them: "The first is to let them do as they like; the second, to do everything they wish; the third, to say nothing about what they do." Yet the earlier bickering at Michilimackinac paled in comparison to the crescendo of Jesuit protest over the establishment of a new post at Detroit. The "black robes" already were well ensconced in missions among the Ottawas and the Hurons at Michilimackinac, and if the tribes moved to Detroit, the Jesuit missions would be stripped of their converts. Moreover, they were aware of Cadillac's animosity, and were particularly alarmed about his plans to welcome Franciscan Récollet missionaries to his post. Meeting with Ottawa and Hurons chiefs in Montreal, Jesuit priests warned them that Cadillac would lure them to southern Michigan only to abandon them, and that they "would be eaten by the Iroquois."[3]

Although the Jesuit protests continued, Cadillac was successful. In 1701, having secured the support of officials in France, Cadillac led an expedition of about two hundred French and Indians from Montreal to Detroit. A Jesuit priest accompanying about fifty soldiers in Cadillac's party encouraged the soldiers to return to the St. Lawrence, but Cadillac learned of the plot and forestalled the sedition. They reached Detroit in July, and within six weeks a palisade, church, and several houses had been constructed. In the following months Cadillac met repeatedly with Ottawa and Huron leaders, and by the end of the year about four thousand members of the two tribes had established villages in the region. During 1702, following an invitation by the Hurons, Miamis relocated near the post from the St. Joseph River in western Michigan, while additional Hurons and several lodges of Chippewas from Michilimackinac and Sault Ste. Marie also added to the burgeoning Indian population.[4]

By 1705 Detroit was flourishing. Cadillac facilitated a further exchange of prisoners between the Iroquois and several of the western tribes, and although the French trade goods were more expensive than those of the British, growing numbers of Senecas brought their pelts to Detroit for exchange.[5] Meanwhile, both the French population and their influence at the post expanded. In 1702 Cadillac's wife and children joined him in Michigan, as did the wife and family of his second-in-command, Alphonse de Tonty. Additional houses were constructed, and fields were cleared along the Detroit River. St. Anne's Church was established, and its records indicate that several of the French soldiers and settlers married Indian women. By 1706 the French or Canadian population had increased to two hundred and seventy, and Cadillac wrote to the governor-general, Philippe de Rigaud de Vaudreuil, requesting that a school be organized "for teaching the children of the savages with those of the French in piety, and for teaching them our language by the same means." He also sought permission to uniform, arm, and train (at the colony's expense) one hundred Huron warriors who would serve as soldiers.[6]

But the tranquility did not last. The newly resettled Indians quarrelled among themselves, and the bickering led to bloodshed. The Jesuits may have been involved. Embittered over the withdrawal of the Hurons and some of the Ottawas to Detroit, the Jesuits continued to criticize the post, and priests among the Weas, the Illinois Confederacy, and those Ottawas remaining at Michilimackinac used their influence to undermine Cadillac's efforts. They were assisted by traders at Michilimackinac and merchants among the Illinois who also envisioned the growing fur trade at the new post to be a threat to their fortunes.[7]

In 1706, while Cadillac was absent in Quebec, an unnamed Christian Potawatomi, who had been living among the Miamis on the St Joseph River, informed the Ottawas at Detroit that the Miamis were plotting to attack them. According to the Potawatomi, the Miamis planned to wait until the Ottawa warriors had left Detroit to go on the warpath against the Sioux; then they intended to fall upon the Ottawas' village and kill their women and children. Although the rumor was at best questionable, some of the Ottawas believed the Potawatomi and, led by an old chief known as Le Pesant (The Heavy Man), they made a preemptive strike against the Miamis. In the aftermath of the attack, the Miamis sought assistance from the French and the Hurons. Étienne de Véniard de Bourgmont (Bourgmond), who was commanding Fort Pontchartrain in Cadillac's absence, provided sanctuary to the Miamis and ordered his men to fire upon the Ottawas. The Hurons also sided with the Miamis, and before the firing ended, a handful of Miamis, about thirty Ottawas, and several Hurons were killed. One French soldier also was slain, and the Récollet priest was murdered by the Ottawas. The Jesuits disavowed any responsibility for these events, blamed Cadillac, and used the affair to lure part of the Ottawas back to Michilimackinac.[8]

In response, Cadillac placed the blame on the Jesuits and the Ottawas, and demanded that the latter surrender Le Pesant, whom he promised to turn over to the Miamis. The Ottawas reluctantly complied, but their chiefs pleaded both with Cadillac and with French officials at Montreal, and although Cadillac at first placed the incorrigible old Ottawa in chains, he later released him.[9]

The affair did not bode well for either Cadillac or the French. Although Cadillac still referred to his post as the "Paris of America," much of its lustre had tarnished. His enemies at Montreal and Quebec used the uprising to refocus the French fur trade through Michilimackinac, and Vaudreuil ignored Cadillac's requests for additional assistance. Moreover, both Cadillac and Vaudreuil had hoped that the Indians would interpret Le Pesant's release as indicative of French magnanimity, but the Miamis were embittered, while the other tribes accused the French of vacillation. Indeed, most of the Indians from the western Great Lakes were dumbfounded over Cadillac's response. Had not the Ottawas broken the peace? Were Le Pesant and his young men not responsible for the deaths of two Frenchmen? Had not the Ottawas defied Bourgmont and fired upon his garrison? Onontio might cajole and threaten in Montreal, but in the west his power still was limited.[10]

At first the Foxes remained aloof from Cadillac's problems. In 1701 they had returned from the great conference at Montreal ostensibly at peace with the French and their allies, but the intertribal cauldron still simmered in Wisconsin. During 1703 the Foxes sided with the Sacs against their old enemies, the Chippewas, and although Jesuit priests from Michilimackinac defused the quarrel, the Foxes' distrust of their northern neighbors continued unabated. Three years later they listened to Ottawa envoys who urged them to attack Miami villages along the St. Joseph River, but they wisely refused. Since the Miamis were warring with the Sioux, the Foxes still considered them to be friends, and for the Foxes, events at Detroit were overshadowed by concern over conditions in Wisconsin.[11]

Much of that concern focused upon the continued trade between French merchants and the Sioux in Minnesota. Although the trade was illegal, Green Bay swarmed with coureurs de bois who continually attempted to tap the rich Sioux markets. Alarmed by such commerce, the Foxes systematically plundered French traders passing along the Fox-Wisconsin waterway, or they exacted such an extensive tribute from these merchants that the Sioux trade was scarcely profitable. Ironically, they were encouraged in these activities by Cadillac, who envisioned the Wisconsin trade as a threat to Detroit. Defending the Foxes to Vaudreuil, Cadillac wrote, "I do not think they [the Foxes] are far wrong," since the coureurs de bois "were carrying aid to their enemies."[12]

While the Foxes remained wary of the Sioux, they increased their contacts with the Iroquois. The great conference in 1701 had made a tenuous peace between the Five Nations and the western tribes, and delegates from the Iroquois Confederacy used the new tranquility to visit Detroit, Michilimackinac, and other posts. Ostensibly, these Iroquois visitors spent their days trading with the western Indians, but they also carried offers of British friendship. Although some of the tribes reported the overtures to French officials, the Foxes met quietly with the Iroquois, carefully considering the advantages of the British alliance. Okimaouassen again cautioned his people to remain within Onontio's family, but other, younger leaders were more sympathetic to the Iroquois proposal. Makkathemangoua broke with his father and spoke in favor of the alliance, while leaders such as Oninetonam and the

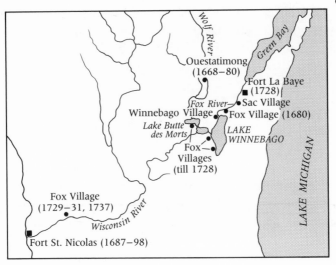

The Fox-Wisconsin waterway

great chiefs Lalima and Pemoussa (Man Who Walks) also were receptive to the offer. From the Fox perspective, Onontio's goods were costly. The British king offered a cornucopia at half the price. Still, many Foxes remained uncertain. Although they held little loyalty to Onontio, they were skeptical of the "Sauganash."[13]

Cadillac provided them with an answer. Although the dispute between the Ottawas and the Miamis should have forewarned the commander about the perils of concentrating several different tribes at one post, Cadillac continued in his efforts to lure Indians to the Detroit region. Eager for personal profit, in 1710 he sent messages to the Sacs, the Foxes, the Kickapoos, the Mascoutens, and other tribes clustered along the Green Bay–Fox–Wisconsin waterway, inviting them to relocate in eastern Michigan. Cadillac assured his superiors that the resettlement would terminate the incessant Sioux-Algonquian warfare in Wisconsin and also would curtail the influence of the illegal coureurs de bois. He did not mention that the successful resettlement of these tribes at Detroit would revitalize the post and make it again the focus of the western fur trade.[14]

Some of the Foxes, Kickapoos, and Mascoutens accepted the offer. Led by Makkathemangoua, Oninetonam, Lalima, and Pemoussa, two villages of Foxes left Wisconsin during 1710 and moved to Michigan. Accompanied by some Kickapoos and Mascoutens, they first settled along the headwaters of the St. Joseph and Grand rivers. Then one village of Foxes followed Makkathemangoua and Oninetonam (The Wea) on to Detroit, where they encamped during the winter of 1710–11. For the Foxes, the resettlement offered several advantages. They now resided farther from the Sioux threat but closer to the British. In addition, since they had removed to Detroit at Cadillac's request, they assumed that Onontio would grant them special favors.[15]

Things did not go as the Foxes expected. First, Cadillac, who had invited them to Detroit, was relieved of his command and assigned to a new post in Louisiana. His temporary successor, Jacques-Charles Renaud Dubuisson, did not favor the relocation and considered the Foxes and their allies to be troublemakers. The Foxes did much to confirm Dubuisson's suspicions. Envisioning themselves as the new "masters at that place," the Foxes pilfered French livestock at Detroit and created a general nuisance. They treated the Miamis and Hurons with contempt, and openly boasted of their plans to trade with the British. Meanwhile their kinsmen and allies on the Grand and St. Joseph rivers became embroiled in a series of quarrels with the Piankashaws, the Weas, and the Illinois Confederacy. Several lives were lost on both sides, and Dubuisson complained bitterly to officials in Montreal that the Foxes had "brought nothing but disorder."[16]

In response, Vaudreuil requested that the Fox, Kickapoo, and Mascouten leaders from Michigan journey to Montreal, where he met with them early in March 1711. As-

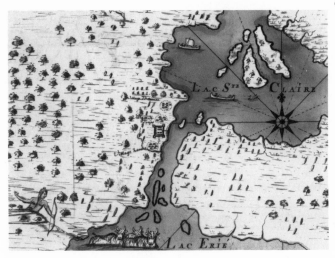

Detail from a map of early Detroit, drawn about 1703. In 1712 the Fox village was located probably on the site of the short-lived Mohican (Loup) village shown here immediately north of Fort Pontchartrain. The Ottawa village is farther north, and the Huron village is south of the French fort. Reproduced from a photograph (Ph. 902 [ca. 1703]) in the National Archives of Canada, with the permission of the Service historique de la Marine, which holds the original (Carte du lac Ste. Claire, Recueil 67, no. 74).

suming the Foxes to be the dominant party in the alliance, the governor informed them that he "wished the country of Detroit to be peaceful, that I encourage all my children there to take all possible care to that end. . . . It will only depend upon you, Outagamis, whether there shall be rest and peace in those parts." He condemned their warfare with the Miamis, Weas, and Piankashaws, and demanded that they cease their raids against the Illinois. He also warned them that they would be forced to make reparations for the deaths of the other tribesmen, and finally, in a dramatic reversal of Cadillac's policies, Vaudreuil suggested that the Foxes should "go back to your old village [in Wisconsin], where the bones of your fathers are, and a great part of your people also, rather than settle in a

Philippe de Rigaud de Vaudreuil, governor-general of New France from 1703 to 1725. Reproduced from a painting by Henri Beau (1863–1949) in the National Archives of Canada (C-10614).

strange place where you may be insulted by all the tribes. Reflect once more, Outagamis, on what I have just said to you, for it is for your preservation.[17]

The governor's pleas had little impact on the Foxes. They returned to their villages, but their truculence continued. On the upper Grand River, Pemoussa and Lalima's people taunted the great Ottawa chief Saguima, while the Mascoutens, led by Kuit and Onabimaniton, continued to quarrel with both the Ottawas and the Potawatomis. During the fall of 1711 the Kickapoos, who had established a village on the Maumee River, launched an unsuccessful raid against the Miamis, while at Detroit the followers of Makkathemangoua and Oninetonam boasted that they had received British belts and that the Iroquois had asked them to "cut the throats" of the French garrison. Not surprisingly, such claims did not endear the Foxes to the other

Indians at Detroit, and early in 1712 Makkathemangoua and Oninetonam abandoned their village and, with part of their people, fled to the Senecas.[18]

Saguima, the war chief of the Ottawas, did not take the Fox taunts charitably. Although he spent his summers in the Ottawa village at Detroit, during the winter of 1711–12 he had encamped with kinsmen on the Grand River, and when he heard that the neighboring Foxes and Mascoutens had both threatened his life and referred to him as a coward, he was sorely offended. Conspiring with Makisabi (The Eagle), a chief of the Potawatomis, Saguima first made peace with the Illinois Confederacy, then enlisted their support against the Foxes. Makisabi also secured the assistance of the Miamis (no mean feat, since the Ottawas and the Miamis had fought at Detroit just five years previously), and rallying his new allies on the Grand River, Saguima planned to fall upon Pemoussa and Lalima's village. Yet, to his initial dismay, in April 1712 he learned that those Fox chiefs had left their winter camps and had moved to Detroit, intending to eventually follow their kinsmen to the Senecas.[19]

Not to be undone, Saguima, Makisabi, and their allied tribesmen fell upon the Mascoutens. Unlike the Foxes, the Mascoutens had remained in their hunting camps on the headwaters of the St. Joseph River, and the sudden onslaught caught them by surprise. The attack took place at daybreak, and in the ensuing melee the Mascoutens lost sixty warriors and over one hundred and fifty women and children. The Ottawas and the Potawatomis suffered thirteen killed and about fifty wounded. Fleeing the slaughter, the Mascouten survivors retreated toward Detroit, where they sought refuge in the new Fox village.[20]

At Detroit, Pemoussa and Lalima's people already had assumed the scurrilous role recently vacated by their kinsmen who had gone east. "Speaking always with much insolence, and calling themselves the owners of all the country," they had arrived at the post in early April. Ignoring Dubuisson's protests, the Foxes established a fortified camp "at about fifty paces" from Fort Pontchartrain and promptly began to kill and eat "the fowls, pigeons, and other animals" belonging to the French settlers. They also insulted the resident Ottawas and Hurons, and when these tribesmen, in conjunction with French traders at the post, protested against their arrogance, the Foxes threatened to murder them.[21]

The arrival of the Mascouten refugees both alarmed and infuriated the Foxes. After listening to accounts of the massacre, Fox warriors set fire to part of the Ottawa village and seized several Ottawa women as hostages. Among the captives was Saguima's wife, who had been visiting with kinspeople in the village. Suspecting the French of complicity in the attack, the Foxes and the Mascoutens surrounded Fort Pontchartrain, limiting access to the post, while their leaders met in council deciding what retribution should be taken. Unknown to Pemoussa and Lalima, however, they harbored a traitor in their midst, for a Christian convert named Joseph, a Fox warrior married to a Potawatomi woman, relayed their plans to Dubuisson.[22]

The French were considerably more frightened than the Foxes. Although Dubuisson disliked the Foxes, he was ignorant of Saguima and Makisabi's conspiracy, and the attack upon the Mascoutens surprised him. Moreover, he was ill prepared to defend Fort Pontchartrain. Most of his food stores were cached outside the palisade, and his garrison consisted of only thirty French soldiers. Dubuisson immediately sent messengers to the Ottawas and the Hurons who still were in their winter camps, pleading with them to send assistance. Meanwhile he brought in as much corn and other food as he could obtain and strengthened the palisade. Dubuisson also ordered a detail of soldiers to level St. Anne's Church and all other buildings that were near enough to provide cover for Fox marksmen. He explained his actions by informing the Foxes that he feared an attack by the Miamis, but Pemoussa was not deceived, and after the French settlers sought shelter inside the fort, the Foxes began to fire at anyone who ventured outside the palisade.[23]

While Dubuisson was strengthening Fort Pontchartrain, the Foxes fortified their camp, constructing a low wall of felled trees around their village. The Hurons, whose camp was located nearby, also enclosed their village, and although most of their warriors were hunting with the Ottawas, they were able to prevent the Foxes from burning their wigwams. Meanwhile the Fox siege continued. At night Dubuisson was able to send messengers to the Huron camp, but the errand was dangerous. Relying on stealth, the messengers risked being discovered by Fox sentinels. If they were apprehended, they were killed.[24]

But help was forthcoming. On May 13 Jean-Baptiste Bissot, sieur de Vincennes, arrived from the Miami country, accompanied by seven French traders. Surprising the Foxes, he was able to dash through their lines and reach the safety of Fort Pontchartrain without suffering any casualties. Shortly thereafter the Hurons sent word that Makisabi had arrived in their camp and that he would soon be followed by Saguima and almost six hundred friendly Indians. Risking attack, Vincennes sortied to the Huron village, where he confirmed the report. He also reported back to Dubuisson that the Ottawas, the Potawatomis, the Hurons, and their allies would accept no quarter and were determined to exterminate the Foxes.[25]

Although Pemoussa and his warriors learned of Makisabi's arrival, they were not intimidated. They had quarreled with those tribes before, but the French had always interceded and bloodshed had been kept to a minimum. Moreover, they had returned to Michigan at Cadillac's request. Therefore, when Saguima and his host of warriors emerged from the forest, the Foxes taunted them, sending

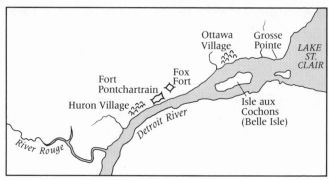

Detroit, 1711–1712

out a small war party who shouted their defiance. As the French-allied Indians advanced, however, the Fox warriors retreated back to their camp. Meanwhile Saguima, Makisabi, and the Huron and Illinois leaders entered the French fort to confer with Dubuisson, while the remainder of the newly arrived tribesmen surrounded the Fox village.[26]

Both Dubuisson and Vincennes welcomed their allies, but they were intimidated at "having so many nations around us of whose good intentions we were not certain." The Frenchmen would have preferred that Saguima and Makisabi simply force the Foxes to return to Wisconsin, but the Hurons were particularly determined to destroy the Foxes, and they falsely reported to Saguima that Pemoussa had burned Saguima's wife and the other Ottawa hostages. Incensed, the Ottawas and Potawatomis now vowed to "forever put out the fire" of their enemies. Concluding that "nothing else could be done, but to be silent, and to put the best face upon the affair," Dubuisson acquiesced in his allies' decision. He distributed powder and lead, and promised the assembled Indians he would lead them against "our common enemies."[27]

The mood in the Fox camp was much less sanguine. Surprised at the large number of warriors who surrounded his village, Pemoussa took store of the Foxes' supplies of food and ammunition. Since his warriors had seized part of the garrison's provisions, Pemoussa believed that his people could withstand a limited siege, but they were particularly short of water. In the past it had been a simple matter for them to fill their water jugs from the Detroit River, and they had dug no wells in their village. Now they were surrounded and access to the river was impossible. Moreover, unlike the Foxes, whose haphazard siege of Fort Pontchartrain had allowed French and Huron couriers to slip in and out of the palisade, Saguima and Makisabi's followers seemed determined to contain Pemoussa's people in their village. Yet all was not lost. Pemoussa knew that his Indian opponents had no stomach for a prolonged siege, and the Fox village was so well defended that his enemies would not risk a frontal assault. In addition, Fox messengers had been dispatched to the Kickapoo villages on the Maumee River, and Pemoussa hoped that they in turn would seek assistance from Makkathemangoua's and Oninetonam's people among the Senecas. The Foxes had withstood adversity in the past. Perhaps Wisaka would again smile upon his people.[28]

The siege of the Fox villages began on May 13, and at first the Foxes remained defiant. After the initial volleys, Pemoussa joined his warriors at the wall opposite the French fort and chided Dubuisson for his treachery. Shouting above the din of battle, Pemoussa reminded the Frenchman that Cadillac had asked the Foxes to resettle at Detroit, "and yet thou declarest war against us. What cause have we given for it?" As the combatants stopped firing to listen to the Fox chief, he pointed out that among the western tribes "there are no nations . . . whom thou callest thy children who have not wet their hands with the blood of Frenchmen." Why then, according to Pemoussa, were the French "joining our enemies to eat us?" Therefore, if the Foxes "shed the blood of Frenchmen" in defending their village, "my Father cannot reproach me." And finally, in a statement of defiance, Pemoussa warned his enemies that the Foxes were "immortal." No matter how great the odds, his people ultimately would prevail. They could never be defeated.[29]

Pemoussa's words angered Dubuisson's allies, and before the Fox chief could finish his speech, they resumed their firing. In response, the Foxes placed several red blankets over the walls of their village and shouted that they soon would similarly cover the earth with the blood of their enemies. In addition, they raised other red blankets on long poles, which they said represented British flags, and they boasted that they now had "no father but the English."[30]

But Pemoussa underestimated his enemies. Since the walls surrounding the Fox camp were relatively low, Dubuisson constructed two large fortified scaffolds, approximately twenty feet in height, which enabled the French and their allies to fire down into the Fox village. In response, Pemoussa and his followers dug trenches in which they sought shelter, but French marksmen still made open movement in the village hazardous, and the Foxes continued to suffer casualties. To counter the threat, a sortie by Fox warriors captured an abandoned French house that was outside the Fox fort yet sufficiently close to Fort Pontchartrain that Fox warriors could fire from its rooftop at the French scaffolds. Protected by bags of earth that they carried to the roof, they effectively cleared the scaffolds of French marksmen. But Dubuisson fired canisters of grapeshot at their position, and the warriors were forced to abandon the house and retreat back into their village. Meanwhile, the long-awaited assistance from the Kickapoos failed to materialize. Although the Kickapoos and some scattered villages of Mascoutens sent warriors to Pemoussa's aid, they were intercepted by the Ottawas. Carried by their captors to Detroit, the hapless Kickapoo and Mascouten prisoners were systematically tortured and killed within sight of the Fox village.[31]

Aware that his position was deteriorating, Pemoussa proposed a duel. Twenty Fox warriors would meet eighty of their enemies in an open field adjoining the two forts. If the Foxes won, the French and their allies would let them return to Wisconsin. If the French were victorious, the remainder of the Foxes and Mascoutens would capitulate. Yet the French refused and the firing continued. Pemoussa then asked for a truce. He informed Dubuisson that the Foxes still held the three Ottawa women, including Saguima's wife, and that they wished to negotiate terms for their surrender.[32]

Surprised that the women still were alive, Dubuisson immediately agreed to the proposition. Accompanied by two Fox warriors, Pemoussa entered Fort Pontchartrain, where in the midst of his enemies he offered to give up his life to save his people. He asked Dubuisson to continue the cease-fire for two days while the Foxes and the Mascoutens conferred, "to find a means of turning away your wrath." He also spoke to the assembled Indians, requesting them to "soften the heart of our father, whom we so often have offended," and reminding them that many members of their tribes had intermarried with the Foxes. According to Pemoussa, "You are our kindred. If you shed our blood . . . , you shed your own." But Dubuisson countered by demanding that the Foxes first relinquish the women. Only then would the French consider any mercy. And the assembled warriors reiterated Dubuisson's position. If Pemoussa and his people "wished to live," they must "surrender their captives."[33]

But the Foxes were betrayed. Two hours later Pemoussa sent three envoys with the women back to Fort Pontchartrain, where the prisoners were surrendered. Believing that they had met the French terms, the Fox and Mascouten spokesmen asked Dubuisson to "cause all the nations, who are with you to retire." They admitted their guilt in first firing upon Fort Pontchartrain, but asked for permission to leave Detroit so that they might "seek provisions for our women and our children," then return to Wisconsin. But as Dubuisson later confessed to his superiors, "as I had now the three women, whom I sought, *I did not care to keep fair with them.*" Instead of dispersing his allies, the commander did nothing, and Makouandeby, the chief of the Illinois, informed the envoys that their people's fate was sealed. Denouncing the Foxes as "dogs," Makouandeby accused the envoys of being British agents and ordered them to leave Fort Pontchartrain, for "as soon as you shall re-enter your fort, we shall fire upon you."[34]

Incensed by the betrayal, the Foxes fought back with a vengeance. Although the French continued to fire at their village, the Foxes launched hundreds of fire arrows at Fort Pontchartrain, setting fire to the thatched roofs of the barracks and to the storehouses containing foodstuffs. Using mops and buckets, French civilians eventually extinguished the flames, but the fires destroyed a large quantity of provisions. Some of the French lost heart. Several of the traders inside the fort asked Dubuisson for permission to flee to Michilimackinac, while many of the Indians complained that Dubuisson no longer had sufficient food to feed his allies. In addition, dispirited Miami and Illinois warriors lamented that Pemoussa's followers "were braver than any other people," and despite their losses, they could never be defeated. Dubuisson successfully diffused the dissension, but after two weeks of fighting, French morale was deteriorating.[35]

In the Fox village conditions had become desperate. Critically short of water, the Foxes made repeated sorties toward the Detroit River, but each was beaten back with considerable loss of life. By the last week in May they had depleted their food supplies, and since French marksmen continued to fire into their village, they were unable to bury their dead. The decomposing bodies spread a pestilence, and weakened by malnutrition, almost seventy women and children perished. Yet, the Foxes fought on, conserving their gunpowder but still returning sufficient fire to keep their enemies from storming their village.[36]

Late in May Pemoussa sought another armistice. Accompanied by Lalima and the two Mascouten chiefs Kuit and Onabimaniton, he entered the French fort under a flag of truce to once again plead for his people. The chiefs carried gourd rattles and chanted supplications to the manitous, and they were accompanied by seven young women whom they offered to the French as hostages. Most impressive was Pemoussa. Bedecked in green paint and adorned with wampum, he again pleaded for his women and children and offered many belts of wampum to symbolize the Fox atonement. Dubuisson remarked that he now was "touched with compassion at their misfortunes," but the French-allied Indians would have none of it. During the past two weeks the Foxes had killed many of their attackers, and their kinsmen and comrades sought revenge. Although Dubuisson intervened, he was hard pressed to keep the other Indians from murdering the envoys. Convinced that any peaceful solution was impossible, Pemoussa and his comrades retreated back to their village.[37]

Now devoid of hope, the Foxes and Mascouten refugees met in hurried council. Desperately short of food, water, and ammunition, if they remained in their village they faced annihilation. Of course any attempt at flight would make them vulnerable to their pursuers, but better to endeavor to escape, in the hope that some of their people might survive, than face certain death or captivity in their village. And yet, if they were to be successful, they would need Wisaka's blessing. The Thunderers had always protected their people. Perhaps they would again appear and deliver the Foxes from their enemies.[38]

On the evening of May 30, 1712, Wisaka seemed to provide an answer. A long line of late spring thunderstorms

swept westward across southern Michigan, and as night
fell, the Detroit region was inundated. Fleeing the rain, the
Foxes' besiegers took refuge in the French fort or the
Huron village. Aware that their enemies had sought shelter, the Foxes and Mascoutens hastily packed their scanty
stores of food and ammunition, and at midnight they
abandoned their village and silently made their way
through the sodden forest. They traveled northeast, following the Detroit River, desperately hoping to secure canoes
to cross over into modern Ontario, then retreat toward
Niagara. Moreover, the Grosse Pointe region near the outlet of Lake St. Clair held an abundance of wild potatoes
and groundnuts, food which could be quickly dug or harvested. Although they were aware that the river posed a
formidable obstacle, they believed that their enemies would
assume that they had fled south to the Kickapoos along the
Maumee River; or perhaps the French would look for their
trail west of Detroit, supposing that they were en route
back to Wisconsin.[39]

But again the Foxes miscalculated. The French and their
allies did not discover the Fox flight until morning, but
they easily discerned their direction. Following in their
wake, a large force of French and Indians led by Vincennes
tracked the hapless refugees to the Grosse Pointe region.
Fox scouts reported the pursuit, and with their backs
against Lake St. Clair, Pemoussa and his warriors made
their final stand. Firing from ambush, they killed forty of
their enemies before Vincennes brought in reinforcements
and all chance of escape was lost. After an additional four
days of fighting, Pemoussa again proposed to surrender
himself and his warriors if the French would spare their
families. To his surprise, Vincennes replied that if they immediately laid down their weapons he would "grant their
lives and safety."[40]

Once again, the French reneged on their promises.
Pemoussa and his warriors had no sooner abandoned their

weapons and stepped forward before the French and their allies fell upon them with a vengeance. Disarmed, the Fox and Mascouten warriors were "cut in pieces" while their women and children were bound and stripped of their meager possessions. When the slaughter ended, the French-allied Indians temporarily spared about one hundred Fox warriors, including Pemoussa, whom they intended to torture in their villages. Fortunately, however, en route back to the fort, these Fox warriors secured a knife, cut their bindings, and most escaped into the forest.[41]

Their wives and children were not so lucky. They were distributed among the French and their allies either as slaves or as captives. Particularly vindictive, the Hurons amused themselves by torturing or shooting "four or five of them every day" until they had killed all their prisoners. In retrospect, French officials at Detroit and Michilimackinac estimated that the Foxes and their Mascouten allies lost almost one thousand men, women, and children.[42]

In his official report of the siege and subsequent French victory, Dubuisson boasted that "these two wicked nations [the Foxes and Mascoutens], who so badly afflicted and troubled all the country," had been destroyed. Other French officials were not so sanguine. At Michilimackinac, Jesuit priests warned that large numbers of Foxes still lived in Wisconsin, where they maintained close ties with the Sacs and Winnebagos. Tribesmen loyal to New France cautioned that refugee Foxes among the Senecas were using all their influence to bring the Iroquois Confederacy into the conflict, while the Kickapoos and the remnants of the Mascoutens still vowed to avenge their fallen kinsmen. The Ottawas suggested a preemptory military strike against Fox villages in Wisconsin, but at Montreal Governor Vaudreuil wavered, unsure over which policy to follow.[43]

Much of Vaudreuil's indecision was motivated by his concern over the Fox refugees among the Iroquois. Oninetonam and Makkathemangoua's people had fled to the Senecas during the winter of 1711–1712, and many of the Fox warriors who escaped their captors after the battle near Lake St. Clair also sought sanctuary among the Five Nations. Eager to avenge their fallen kinsmen, during the autumn of 1712 a small party of refugee Foxes led by a war chief named The Thunderer hovered near the Niagara portage, intending to ambush any French or allied tribesmen en route from Montreal to the west. Although the Senecas did not join the war party and eventually informed the French that the Foxes lay in ambush, they refused Vaudreuil's request that they either surrender the refugee Foxes or send them home to Wisconsin. Instead they assured the governor that the refugees had promised to relinquish their troublesome "Fox spirit, in order to take the Seneca spirit which works toward good ends and always listens to its father Onontio." Unconvinced, Vaudreuil admonished the Senecas to remain at peace and advised them to distribute the Foxes throughout their villages so that "no longer being one body they will not be able to instill in you what is evil in them and involve you in spite of yourselves in a war which can only harm your true interests."[44]

By the spring of 1713 such a war already was raging in the west. Pemoussa and some of the refugees from Detroit returned to Wisconsin, where their account of the French betrayal incensed their kinsmen. Seeking revenge, in April they killed a French coureur de bois near Green Bay, and during the summer they infested the trade routes, causing havoc to French commerce in the west. In the fall a Fox war party raided near Detroit, killing three Frenchmen and six Hurons, and during the following winter they descended the Illinois River to attack a village of the Illinois confederacy located near Lake Peoria. Meanwhile, a war party composed of Fox refugees among the Senecas, aided by the Kickapoos and Mascoutens, struck again at the Hurons. Isolated French traders were waylaid in the forests, while French-allied tribesmen dared not run their trap-lines. In the summer of 1714 another Fox war party attacked a French boat carrying corn from Detroit to Michilimackinac. In the ensuing skirmish, three Frenchmen and three Fox warriors perished.[45]

The warfare paralyzed the fur trade. Both licensed traders and coureurs de bois feared to carry their wares into the west, while tribes such as the Ottawas, the Potawatomis, and the Miamis pleaded with the French for assistance. At Montreal, French merchants complained about "how little peltry has come down to Michilimackinac," while military commanders in the west reported that many of the French-allied tribes were in a "pitiable situation . . . dying of hunger in their cabins, not daring to leave them to go hunting on account of their well-grounded fear that the Reynards [Foxes] will destroy them all, one after the other."[46]

Inaction by the French caused consternation among their allies. The Ottawas and the Hurons continued to clamor for a major campaign while tribes such as the Menominees, Sacs, and Winnebagos, although officially "neutral," privately asked the French to take all "necessary measures" to restore the fur trade to their villages. At first the Potawatomis urged a policy of accommodation, but by 1715 they too had joined the growing chorus demanding French military action. Moreover, French traders warned that French prestige was waning. According to one official, it was "no longer possible to deal gently with that nation [the Foxes] without incurring the wrath of all the others," and if the Foxes continued to act with impunity, "some of these savage nations may . . . take the Reynards' side."[47]

While the French vacillated, the Foxes mounted a diplomatic offensive. First, to the surprise of the French and most of their allies, the Foxes negotiated a truce with the Sioux. Even a temporary peace with their age-old enemies was a bitter pill for many of the older members of the tribe to swallow, but their memories of kinsmen slain by the hated Dakota paled in comparison to their determination to seek revenge for the massacre at Detroit. The terms of this agreement remain unknown, but the Foxes may have promised to join the Sioux in a mutual campaign against the Chippewas, since the latter were allied to the French and also were extending their domain into former Sioux lands in northwestern Wisconsin.[48]

The Foxes also renewed their ties with the Iroquois. During the summer of 1714 Fox envoys from the Wisconsin villages visited their kinsmen among the Senecas and asked the Six Nations for assistance.[49] Although the Senecas refused to formally commit themselves, they encouraged the Fox resistance and assured the envoys that the Iroquois would at least follow a policy of "benevolent neutrality." Moreover, they also offered to intercede for the Foxes with the British, and in the following summer a mixed delegation of Foxes, Kickapoos, and Mascoutens journeyed to Albany, where they received the tenuous blessing of Governor Robert Hunter. Encouraged by their success, the Fox envoys returned to Wisconsin and boasted that both the British and the Iroquois were sympathetic to their cause.[50]

Jarred from their lethargy by the Fox diplomatic offensive, French officials finally were goaded into action. Soliciting the support of the coureurs de bois, Governor General Vaudreuil offered amnesty to all French traders accused of illegally trading with the western tribes if they would join an expedition to the Fox villages in Wisconsin. The expedition, to be led by Louis de La Porte de Louvigny, was to employ a dual strategy. Louvigny was instructed to first offer the Foxes a renewed membership in the French alliance, but if the Foxes remained recalcitrant, Louvigny intended to attack their villages. Meanwhile, French agents among the Miamis and the Illinois were instructed to settle a quarrel that had emerged between those tribes and to assemble them at Chicago, where they would be joined by the Potawatomis, the Ottawas, and the Hurons from the Detroit region. Other warriors would rendezvous at Michilimackinac. When his expedition arrived at the straits in the spring of 1715, Louvigny intended to provide these warriors with food, arms, and ammunition. Coordinating their approach, the parties from Michilimackinac and Chicago planned to arrive at the Fox villages during the last week of August 1715. Vaudreuil anticipated that the Foxes might abandon their homes, and in that case, Louvigny was instructed to "cut down their corn" and "burn their cabins," before dividing his expedition into several war parties who would "pursue and harass" the hapless Foxes as they fled through the forest.[51]

But the planned expedition failed to materialize. Louvigny became ill in the spring of 1715 and was bedridden at Montreal. Acting Governor General Claude de Ramezay appointed Constant Marchand de Lignery, already at Michilimackinac, to lead the campaign, but crop failures at that post and at Detroit prevented the French from securing sufficient provisions. They were forced to purchase corn from the Senecas, who eventually sold them almost 300 minots (bushels). But the delivery of the grain was delayed, and the corn and other supplies essential for the expedition arrived at Michilimackinac too late in the season. At Detroit the Hurons and the Potawatomis refused to leave their lodges, where they awaited a small contingent of Christian Iroquois en route from the mission at Sault St. Louis, near Montreal. Meanwhile, an epidemic of measles erupted among the Miamis. On August 17 Louis de Monnoir (Maunoir) de Ramezay, the second son of Claude de Ramezay, reached Chicago with almost 450 Illinois warriors, but when the other Indians failed to arrive, the Illinois retreated back to their villages. To add to the difficulties of the French, the Senecas surreptitiously sent messengers to the Ottawas at Michilimackinac, warning them that Louvigny only wished to lead them to Wisconsin so that another French expedition could fall upon their unprotected women and children.[52]

While the French expedition faltered, the Foxes made preparations of their own. Encouraged in their resistance by Pemoussa and the survivors of the massacre at Detroit, the Foxes rejected suggestions by some of their members that they flee toward Iowa. According to Pemoussa, the French and their allies had refused to attack the hastily fortified Fox camp at Detroit, and they would be even more reluctant to attack a heavily defended village in Wisconsin. Indeed, Pemoussa and his people had abandoned their village because of food and water shortages, not because of their enemies. If his kinsmen in Wisconsin stockpiled their provisions and strengthened their palisades, Pemoussa said, they could easily withstand the French.[53]

During the summer of 1715 the Foxes labored mightily at their fortifications. Anticipating that the French army would invade their homeland during late August or early September, the Foxes consolidated their outlying settlements at a large, fortified village constructed on a high bank overlooking the south shore of Big Lake Butte des Morts, on the upper Fox River in modern Winnebago County, Wisconsin. Using their trade axes, Fox warriors felled large oak trees from the nearby forests, and with the help of their women and children they dragged the massive trunks back to the village, where the logs were inserted into a ditch, forming a strong palisade. Inside the wall Fox women dug a trench designed to afford additional shelter for the Fox defenders, and the dirt from this excavation was piled around the base of the logs, further strengthening the breastwork. Meanwhile, other Fox women collected quantities of corn and dried meat, which they cached in storage pits inside the village. Fox warriors stockpiled their lead and gunpowder, and older men and boys worked day and night, fashioning an ample supply of arrows. Since a spring was located inside the village, the Mesquakies were assured of adequate water. If Lignery invaded their homeland, the Mesquakies were ready for him.[54]

Instead, the French and their allies attacked the Kickapoos and the Mascoutens. The mission Indians from Sault St. Louis arrived at Detroit in September, after both Lignery's campaign and the Chicago rendezvous had failed, but joined by Potawatomi and Huron warriors, they proceeded on to Starved Rock, on the Illinois River. There they enlisted the remnants of Maunoir's war party, and on November 20, 1715, they surprised a village of Kickapoos and Mascoutens hunting in southern Wisconsin. The Kickapoos and Mascoutens resisted valiantly, but they were overwhelmed, losing over one hundred warriors.[55]

When runners brought news of that attack to the newly fortified Fox village, Pemoussa led a large war party to his allies' relief. Although the Foxes arrived too late to provide any assistance, they pursued their enemies back toward Illinois and intercepted them on December 1. In a series of skirmishes that lasted throughout the day, they killed several of their enemies, while suffering seven casualties. Yet Pemoussa knew that the departure of his war party had left the Fox village virtually undefended, and late in the afternoon the Foxes withdrew from the engagement and retreated back toward Wisconsin. The oncoming winter precluded Lignery from attacking their village, but the Foxes feared that straggling war parties of other French-allied Indians might ascend the Fox River and fall upon their kinsmen in their absence.[56]

The Fox fears were unjustified. In November 1715 the French agents at Michilimackinac returned to Montreal. The ailing Louvigny spent the winter planning another expedition, but the costs of the aborted campaign, added to the expenses incurred in raising a second army, reached such figures that officials in Canada were reluctant to finance the campaign. Accordingly, they suggested that Louvigny combine his military expedition with a commercial venture. To recover the costs of the expedition, Louvigny and his associates would be allowed to carry an extensive supply of trade goods west, where they would trade with the western tribes. Since the Fox disruption of the fur trade had created a shortage of pelts at Montreal, such commerce offered the potential for considerable profits, and many entrepreneurs readily enlisted in the expedition.[57]

Louvigny left Montreal on May 1, 1716, accompanied by over two hundred merchants and soldiers and a large war party of mission Indians. En route he was joined by many coureurs de bois seeking both amnesty and profits, and he arrived at Michilimackinac early in the summer, where he enlisted other coureurs de bois and French-allied Indians. Now numbering over 800 men, Louvigny's army proceeded on to Green Bay, where they slowly ascended the Fox River. They reached the Fox village on Big Lake Butte des Morts in late June or early July.[58]

The Foxes were ready for them. The fortifications that they had prepared during the preceding summer remained intact, and the Foxes had purchased additional guns and ammunition from renegade coureurs de bois eager to obtain contraband pelts during a period of high prices. Moreover, almost all the Foxes who remained in Wisconsin were concentrated in the village overlooking Big Lake Butte des Morts, and they numbered about 500 warriors. In addition, their ranks were buttressed by almost 3,000 women, many of whom were eager to avenge fallen husbands, brothers, or other kinsmen. Most of these women had little experience in warfare, but they were embittered toward Onontio. Coureurs de bois familiar with the tribe warned Louvigny that the women would wield knives, war clubs, or trade axes with a frightening ferocity.[59]

But Louvigny's army also was well prepared. Anticipating a siege, the French had reinforced the bottoms and gunwales of three canoes, and had carried two small cannons and a grenade launcher from Michilimackinac to Wisconsin. On his arrival at Big Lake Butte des Morts, Louvigny positioned his artillery and opened fire on the Fox village. Yet, to his dismay, neither the cannons nor the artillery inflicted much damage upon the heavily reinforced oak palisade. Undaunted, he commanded his followers to dig a series of trenches that would shelter the troops as they advanced toward the Fox fortifications, and after three days and many casualties, the excavations had almost reached their destination. Louvigny planned to partially undermine the breastwork and place several mines against the base of the palisade. He hoped that the explosion from the mines would topple part of the wall. Then the French and their allies could emerge from the trenches and pour through the breach at the Fox defenders. The assault would be costly. Louvigny knew that the Fox warriors were prepared to resist to the death, and the coureurs de bois again cautioned that the Fox women would "fight like furies."[60]

Inside the palisade Pemoussa and his followers resisted valiantly. They poured a scathing fire in on the French soldiers who were digging the trenches, and although the artillery at first frightened them, the Foxes were heartened by the strength of their palisade. Advised by scouts of Louvigny's approach, Pemoussa had dispatched runners to the Kickapoos and the Mascoutens, and they had promised to send warriors to his assistance. The Fox supply of arms and ammunition was sufficient, and their food supplies certainly surpassed those of their adversaries. They obviously could survive a lengthy siege, and Pemoussa doubted that the French-allied Indians could be induced to storm the palisades. Yet the series of entrenchments had surprised him, and he realized that the ditches would provide adequate cover for large numbers of his enemies to approach the walls with impunity. If carefully planted mines destroyed part of the fortifications, his people would be hard pressed to keep the French from entering their village. Pemoussa and other Fox leaders were willing to die, but they remembered the slaughter in 1712, and they again feared for their women and children. Negotiations had proven fruitless at Detroit, but they might be successful in Wisconsin.[61]

On the morning of the fourth day the Fox leaders prepared a dual strategy. They sent a white flag to the French, offering a cease-fire and a series of peace proposals. Meanwhile, they also redistributed their supplies of arms and ammunition. If the negotiations failed, they planned to make a sortie, capture the French mines, and destroy part of the French entrenchments.[62]

To their surprise, Louvigny accepted their offer. Although his Indian allies protested that the terms of the agreement favored the Foxes, Louvigny and most of the coureurs de bois in his camp favored a quick solution. To placate his Indians, Louvigny replied that he feared the arrival of additional Kickapoo and Mascouten warriors, who might tip the scale in favor of his enemies. Moreover, he promised his allies that he would demand Fox hostages to ensure that the tribe honored its promises. Such a capitulation, he assured them, would bring "universal peace" to the west.[63]

Yet from the Fox perspective, the terms of the cease-fire were remarkably lenient. The Foxes agreed to make peace with all tribes allied to the French; to persuade the Kickapoos and the Mascoutens to do the same; to return all prisoners to their former tribes; to seek captives from hostile Indians in the "further districts," who would be offered as replacements to the French-allied tribes who had recently suffered casualties in the assault upon the Fox village; and to pay the cost of Louvigny's campaign through their participation in the French fur trade. In addition they acquiesced to Louvigny's demand that "six chiefs [including

Pemoussa] or children of chiefs" be surrendered to the French to be held hostage. In retrospect, the cease-fire saved the tribe considerable bloodshed, and with the exception of the immediate surrender of the hostages and a small goodwill payment of pelts, the rest of the Fox promises could be kept sometime in the future when Louvigny and his army would be gone from Wisconsin. After Louvigny departed, the Foxes would remain free. Of course, the French would hold the six hostages, but hostages had escaped at Detroit, and Louvigny would travel through many miles of lakes and forests before he could deliver his prisoners to officials in Canada. As the peace negotiations ended, the Foxes waited patiently while leaders among the French-allied tribes admonished them to keep the peace and obey Onontio. Their enemies were leaving. The People of the Red Earth could bide their time. Wisaka had not abandoned his children.[64]

After the negotiations Louvigny distributed the Foxes' payment of pelts to his Indian allies. The commander and his French colleagues were eager to leave the Fox village and continue their trade with the western Indians. Many of the coureurs de bois who accompanied the expedition stopped to exchange their goods with the tribes of the Green Bay region, and by the time the army had returned to Michilimackinac, what had begun ostensibly as a military campaign had deteriorated into a commercial venture. Heavily laden with western fur, Louvigny's expedition returned to Montreal in mid-October, and although special masses were celebrated in honor of the "success of French troops against the Fox Indians," cynics scoffed that "all that Louvigny reaped from his laborious journey, was . . . deserters . . . and their peltries." Vaudreuil defended the campaign against such charges, and the French court subsequently rewarded Louvigny with three thousand livres, but experienced traders such as Nicolas Perrot remained unconvinced. Charging that the expedition had failed, Perrot claimed that New France had consistently mismanaged her relations with the Foxes, and that French policies had goaded the latter into hostility. Moreover, Perrot asserted, French officials had foolishly yielded to pressure from traditional Fox enemies such as the Chippewas and the Hurons, and the subsequent "blood that has been shed, and which will yet be spilled," was as much their fault as the Foxes'. At best the new peace was tenuous; more likely, it was nonexistent.[65]

CHAPTER FOUR

BITTER
INTERLUDE

For Philippe de Rigaud de Vau-
dreuil, governor-general of New France, the winter of
1716–1717 seemed interminable. The snow that had blanketed the lower St. Lawrence Valley in early November
had remained throughout the winter months, and succes-
sive storms only added to the accumulation. In addition,
Montreal, Quebec, and the other isolated French settlements strung along the great inland waterway had been
inundated with a series of arctic cold fronts. The Canadian
winter, always severe, seemed unrelenting. To add to the
governor's woes, smallpox had erupted in the colony late
in October, and although the inclement weather had limited travel among the settlements, the disease advanced
with a will of its own. By Christmas it had spread to neighboring Indian villages, even infesting the Iroquois towns
south of Lake Ontario (which was, in Vaudreuil's opinion,
a positive aspect of the plague), and both French settlers
and tribespeople fell victim to the malady.

Not surprisingly, several of the Fox hostages and their
families whom Louvigny had carried back from Wisconsin

also contracted the disease. In January 1717 Pemoussa, Michiouaouigan, Okimaouassen, and other hostages fell ill, and although Vaudreuil and his subordinates took special pains to ensure their recovery, Pemoussa, Michiouaouigan, and one of the other hostage warriors perished. Okimaouassen survived the malady, but he was horribly disfigured, and a secondary infection left him sightless in his right eye. Fearful that the Foxes would blame the French for the death of the hostages, Vaudreuil ordered Louvigny to return to the west to explain the deaths to the dead warriors' kinsmen.[1]

Accompanied by Okimaouassen, the chief's wife and family, and a large party of traders, Louvigny left Montreal in late May. The party ascended the flooding Ottawa river, passed over the portage to Lake Huron, and arrived at Michilimackinac on June 29, 1717. There Louvigny ordered two interpreters and a handful of coureurs de bois to accompany Okimaouassen and his family on to the Fox villages in Wisconsin, where Okimaouassen promised to explain the cause of his companions' demise. The interpreters were instructed to cover the hostages' death with presents, request that the Foxes pay for Louvigny's campaign of the previous summer, and invite those Fox leaders remaining in Wisconsin to journey to Montreal to meet with Onontio.[2]

News of Okimaouassen's return preceded his arrival, and when the former hostage and his family arrived at the Fox villages, they found their kinsmen assembled to welcome them. Like other western tribes, the Foxes had learned of the smallpox epidemic in the St. Lawrence Valley, and rumors of the hostages' deaths also had reached Wisconsin. After accepting the trade goods to cover his kinsmen's death, Ouchala, who had emerged as the spokesman for the tribe, assured the French that his people did not hold them responsible for the hostages' demise. Indeed, according to Ouchala, the Foxes were grateful that Onontio had "laid them on his own mat" and had tried to prevent their deaths. He provided the French envoys with food and shelter and informed them that he would meet with them on the following day, after his people had performed the proper ceremonies and "dried the tears which is their wont to shed on the receipt of such news."[3]

Although Louvigny had instructed the interpreters to carefully monitor Okimaouassen's activities, they obviously failed, for on the next day, when the Foxes and the French again met in council, Ouchala and Okimaouassen had prepared a carefully orchestrated charade designed to convince the French that the Foxes really did intend to honor their commitments. When asked why they had not journeyed to Montreal to pay homage to Onontio, the Foxes replied that they had been afraid of the smallpox. Moreover, according to Ouchala, because his tribe had spent the previous summer preparing for Louvigny's campaign, they had completely depleted their stores of powder, lead, and other European commodities. Therefore, during the late winter and spring of 1717 their young men had been forced to trade all the pelts that they had hoped to amass as part of the payment for Louvigny's expedition to obtain necessities to feed and shelter their families.[4]

In a staged response designed to convince the interpreters of his loyalty, Okimaouassen then interrupted the speakers and denounced his kinsmen for their ingratitude. According to Okimaouassen, his fellow tribesmen "cover me with shame . . . for I see naught of what you promised." He reminded them that they were in Louvigny's and Onontio's debt for sparing their lives during the previous summer, and he asked them to remember that the French still held the remaining hostages.[5]

Ouchala's reply was both calculated and conciliatory. He agreed that Okimaouassen's protests were valid, but he asserted that his people "would never forget their father's kindness." Most certainly, Ouchala and his advisers would travel to Montreal "without fail next year," for according to the Fox leader, "it would be too much to lie twice to Onontio." The assembled tribesmen then murmured their assent, and convinced of the Foxes' sincerity, the French agents departed the Fox villages to return to Michilimackinac.[6]

Although Okimaouassen at first accompanied the agents, his family remained with their kinspeople, and as the French party passed through several Sac villages near Green Bay, the Fox hostage announced a change of heart. Declaring that he remained distressed over his people's failure to honor their commitments, Okimaouassen announced to the French that he had decided to return to the Fox villages "to make them remember their promises" and to ensure that they journeyed to Montreal during the following summer. The French continued on to Michilimackinac, where they informed Louvigny of Okimaouassen's decision. The French officer evidently believed Okimaouassen's protestations, for after returning to Quebec, Louvigny boasted that the French now could expect a permanent peace "among all the Nations."[7]

At first Louvigny's optimism seemed to be justified. Ouchala admitted that his people had failed to honor their previous agreements, and the Fox leader genuinely believed that peace was possible. During the summer of 1718 he sent Okimaouassen and four other Fox warriors, accompanied by several women, to Montreal to confer with Onontio. Ouchala did not accompany the delegation, but Okimaouassen was familiar with French politics at Montreal and the delegates accompanying him seemed committed to a lasting peace. They arrived at Montreal on July 20, 1718, and spent the next two weeks visiting the settlement and meeting with French officials. The Foxes were well received. French observers commented on the delegation's handsome physical appearance, but also remarked that the Foxes still remained on the periphery of the

French trade system, for unlike other delegations of western tribespeople, who were adorned in costumes fashioned from trade cloth, the Foxes continued to dress almost entirely in skins or leather garments.[8]

Since the French still held some of the hostages whom the Foxes had surrendered to Louvigny in 1716, Okimaouassen pleaded with Vaudreuil for their return. He informed the governor-general that the Foxes had refused to join with the Kickapoos and the Mascoutens in the latter tribes' recent attacks on the Illinois Confederacy, and he promised that Ouchala would visit Montreal during the summer of 1719.[9]

On August 4, 1718, Vaudreuil delivered his formal reply. Assembling Okimaouassen and his kinsmen before an audience of other western Indians, Vaudreuil chided them for failing to honor their promises, but he declared that "since they had come to prove their submission," he would "receive them as a good Father." He asked them to abide by the terms of Louvigny's agreement, to surrender all prisoners whom they had captured from other tribes, and to use their influence to persuade the Kickapoos and the Mascoutens to stop their raids against the Illinois. In return, he agreed to relinquish twelve of the remaining seventeen Foxes whom the French still held as hostages, and he promised to surrender the other captives during the summer of 1719 if Ouchala would escort the chiefs of the Kickapoos and the Mascoutens, especially the notorious Kickapoo chief Wabasaiya, or White Robe, to Montreal. Pleased with the conference, Okimaouassen assured Vaudreuil of the Foxes' compliance, and in mid-August the delegation and the twelve repatriated captives left Montreal for Wisconsin.[10]

Okimaouassen and his companions returned to their villages in September, and during the winter of 1718–1719 the Foxes met in council to debate the future course of their tribe. Although many of the young men remained

eager to prove themselves on the warpath and were reluctant to make peace, most of the village chiefs, including
Ouchala and Okimaouassen, argued that the People of the
Red Earth should walk Onontio's road. During 1718
increasing numbers of French traders ventured into the
Fox villages, and for the first time in decades trade goods
were not at a premium. Younger warriors could still vent
their anger against the Osages, but Ouchala counseled his
young men to abstain from striking the Chippewas, the
Sioux, and the Illinois. Indeed, during the spring of 1719
he met with the Kickapoos and the Mascoutens and even
convinced White Robe that he should accompany the
Foxes to Montreal to meet with Onontio.[11]

Honoring their promises, Ouchala, Okimaouassen, and
two other Fox warriors, accompanied by White Robe,
journeyed to Montreal during the summer of 1719. They
assured Vaudreuil that they had released all their captives
and "were disposed to maintain peace with all the Nations." White Robe complained that both the Kickapoos
and the Mascoutens had been repeatedly attacked by the
Illinois Confederacy, but he assured the governor-general
that both tribes would not retaliate, since Vaudreuil was
seeking a solution to the problem through French officials
in the Illinois Country. In response, Vaudreuil released the
remaining Fox hostages and the Indians boarded their
canoes and ascended the Ottawa River toward Wisconsin.
Self-satisfied, Vaudreuil reported to his superiors that as
soon as "the officer in command among the Illinois [Con-
federacy] is able to induce that Nation to make overtures
to obtain it . . . all would be peaceful on this continent."[12]

Yet peace, like Wisaka's favor, proved elusive. The warfare between the Kickapoos and the Illinois Confederacy
continued to fester, and not surprisingly, the Foxes soon
found themselves embroiled. True to his promise, Ouchala
initially attempted to avoid the confrontation. In the three
years following Louvigny's campaign Ouchala had suc-

cessfully persuaded his young men to refrain from the fighting, and when the Kickapoos and the Mascoutens had presented several Illinois captives to his kinsmen, Ouchala had returned the hapless prisoners back to their villages. Indeed, the Fox leader had even attempted to mediate between the two sides, although for decades the Foxes had been so closely allied with the Kickapoos and the Mascoutens that the Illinois refused to differentiate between the three tribes.[13]

During 1718, mistakenly accusing the Foxes of complicity in the warfare, small war parties of Illinois ambushed and killed several Fox warriors who were hunting alone in the forest. The Illinois depredations incensed many of the younger Fox warriors, and in 1719, while Ouchala, Okimaouassen, and the other members of the delegation were visiting Montreal, the warfare escalated. While hunting bison on the prairie near the Rock River in northern Illinois, a mixed camp of Foxes, Kickapoos, and Mascoutens was surprised by an Illinois war party which killed over twenty victims, including several women and children. A similar number were taken prisoner and carried back to the Illinois villages. When Ouchala returned to Wisconsin, he learned that many of his young men already had joined Kickapoo and Mascouten war parties, while others had foolishly killed a Miami warrior visiting in a nearby Sac village, accusing their victim of supporting the Illinois. In response the Sacs had withdrawn from their camp and had moved to the St. Joseph River, attempting to disassociate themselves from the killing. In addition, the Chippewas and some of the Potawatomis, always eager for Fox scalps, now asked the French for permission to join with the Illinois, the Miamis, and other tribes in a renewed campaign against the Fox villages. Bewildered, Ouchala still advocated patience, but his pleas for forbearance were ignored. Eager to avenge their relatives, young Fox firebrands denounced Ouchala as a stepchild of Onontio and vowed to follow their own counsel. In response, Ouchala dispatched a messenger to Vaudreuil, warning the governor-general that his "young men had lost their senses" and that the warfare with the Illinois would continue.[14]

In contrast, hostilities with the Sioux diminished. In the years following Louvigny's campaign, Canadian traders in increasing numbers had ventured into the Fox villages, and by 1721 the Foxes were accumulating a surplus of trade goods. Although they still opposed the passage of the coureurs de bois down the Fox-Wisconsin waterway, they now realized that the Sioux, their ancient enemies, offered economic opportunities that could be exploited. Moreover, following a decade of warfare against the French, many Fox leaders now envisioned Onontio as potentially more dangerous than the Sioux. Still threatened by the Potawatomis, the Chippewas, and the Illinois Confederacy, all close allies of the French, the Foxes sought a new alliance that would provide them with political and military advantages as well as economic opportunity. Peace with the Sioux would not only allow the Foxes to carry goods to the Sioux villages, it also might provide a safe haven if Onontio and his allies should force them from Wisconsin. In 1721 messengers were sent to the Sioux villages, ostensibly to invite Sioux warriors to join in the warfare against the Illinois and the Chippewas, and in the next few years relations between the two peoples markedly improved. By 1725 much of the Sioux fur trade was passing through the Fox villages and Lignery reported that the two former enemies had now formed an alliance.[15]

The Fox and Sioux warfare against the Illinois was inadvertently encouraged by a jurisdictional dispute between New France and Louisiana. In 1717 officials in France removed the Illinois Country from the political jurisdiction of New France and attached the region to Louisiana. Angered over the loss, and afraid that traders from Illinois would siphon the fur trade away from the St. Lawrence,

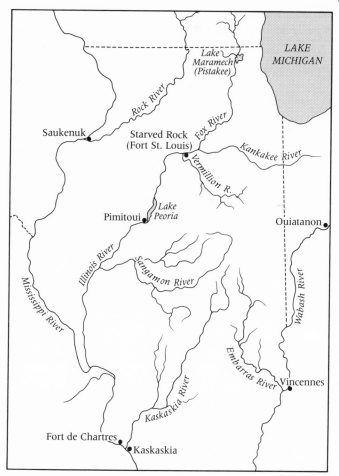

The Illinois Country, 1720–1740

Vaudreuil repeatedly charged his counterparts in Illinois
and Louisiana with mismanaging the region. In response,
officials in Louisiana accused Vaudreuil and other Canadian dignitaries of creating political and economic havoc
in Illinois by clandestinely encouraging the Foxes, the
Kickapoos, and the Mascoutens to attack the Illinois Confederacy. Such charges undoubtedly were exaggerated,

but Vaudreuil responded by placing the blame for the conflict on the Illinois, and by arguing that Fox attacks on residents of the Illinois Country were beyond his hegemony
and should be addressed by his counterparts in Louisiana.
Moreover, although he gave lip service to instructions from
officials in France that he restrain the Foxes and their allies,
Vaudreuil remained resentful over the transfer and refused
to prosecute such policies vigorously.[16]

Fueled by such bickering, the Fox-Illinois conflict bur-
geoned. In 1721 Fox war parties descended the Illinois
river valley to raid Illinois villages as far south as Kaskaskia, but they met with only limited success. Although
they surprised and killed a few Illinois tribesmen, the
Illinois mounted a counteroffensive and caught the raiders
before they could return to Wisconsin. In the ensuing skirmish the Foxes suffered many casualties, and the Illinois,
assisted by several coureurs de bois, captured over thirty
Fox warriors. Carrying the prisoners back to their villages,
the Illinois dispersed their captives among the Peorias, the
band of the Illinois Confederacy who had borne the brunt
of the Fox-Kickapoo-Mascouten warfare. Eager to avenge
themselves, the Peorias first tortured, then burned the Fox
captives.[17]

Among the victims was Minchilay, a nephew of Ouchala, and in response the aging village chief now joined in
the warfare. Organizing an immense war party, he struck
at the Peoria village at Pimitoui, at the outlet of Lake Peoria,
but found that his enemies had fled upstream to Starved
Rock, the site of La Salle's old Fort St. Louis, a towering
precipice overlooking the river. Since the Illinois position
seemed impregnable, the Foxes surrounded the Illinois
camp, limiting their enemies' access to food and water.
After several days the Illinois leaders asked for a truce, and
although Ouchala had difficulty in restraining his young
men, they reluctantly agreed. Informing the Illinois that
his mercy was motivated only by his loyalty to Onontio,

Ouchala agreed to spare their lives and withdraw if the Illinois would send back all their Fox, Kickapoo, and Mascouten prisoners. The Illinois eagerly agreed and Ouchala led his warriors back to Wisconsin.[18]

After returning to his village, Ouchala hurried on to Green Bay, where he explained his actions to French agents. He reminded them that he had tried first to mediate the dispute between the Kickapoos and the Mascoutens and the Illinois, and even though he had been forced to join in the attacks, he had treated the Illinois with mercy. Moreover, since his kinsmen's honor now had been restored, Ouchala proclaimed that "the wars are all ended today . . . and in the name of the whole nation, we will not go to war unless we are first attacked."[19]

Yet despite Ouchala's protestations, he did not speak for the entire tribe. After the old chief's speech, Elecevas, who Ouchala charged represented "the greater part of the young men [who] are absolutely worthless," also addressed the assemblage. Reflecting the younger, more-militant Foxes, Elecevas disdained Ouchala's pleas for mercy and boldly charged that Onontio had always "cherished the purpose of destroying us." He demanded that the agents inform him of official French policy and warned that if the French sent another military expedition to Wisconsin, they would find the Foxes awaiting them in their villages.[20]

In reply, Jacques Testard de Montigny, the French commander at Green Bay, warned Ouchala to keep the peace, but he praised him for his leniency toward the Illinois. Indeed, Montigny promised "to make known [Ouchala's actions] to your father Onontio," but his response to Elecevas was less sanguine. Informing the younger Fox warrior that he would carry his speech to Onontio, Montigny warned him that "unless his whole village comports itself as well as Ouchala . . . you shall indeed die."[21]

Despite Ouchala's efforts, the warfare widened. In 1720 warriors from Elecevas's village killed a Chippewa whom they encountered near Green Bay, and they captured two Potawatomis whom they delivered to the Kickapoos and Mascoutens. Ouchala attempted to cover the Chippewa's death with trade goods, and he persuaded the Kickapoos and the Mascoutens to return the Potawatomis to their village; but one of the Potawatomi captives was the son of Winimac (The Catfish), a powerful village chief from the St. Joseph River in Michigan, and the Potawatomi leader vowed vengeance. Winimac attempted to enlist support from his kinsmen at Detroit, but when they refused, he turned to the Chippewas. Still smoldering from their recent loss, the Chippewas readily joined in the warfare, and in the spring of 1723 they sent four war parties against the Fox villages. Since no lives were lost, Ouchala was able to prevent his warriors from retaliating, but in mid-July a war party of Chippewas from the Saginaw region fell upon a mixed party of Foxes, Sacs, and a few Winnebagos who were fishing on Lake Winnebago, killing twenty-two men, women, and children. In response, the Foxes sent four war parties against their enemies, and although Ouchala cautioned his young men to strike back only at the Chippewas, the Miamis and the Weas feared the Foxes would not discriminate in their retribution, and both tribes abandoned their plans to establish new villages in southwestern Michigan and northwestern Indiana. Meanwhile the fur trade again suffered, and officials in Canada feared that the warfare would soon spread to other tribes.[22]

They had ample cause for alarm. By the fall of 1723 the Fox-Chippewa conflict not only prevented Canadian merchants from trading with the Sioux, it also threatened to engulf the Abenakis. Oddly enough, since 1716 a growing relationship had developed between the Foxes and these former residents of Maine, now living at the French mission at St. François, near Quebec. In 1716 a party of Christian Abenakis accompanied the French army to Wisconsin, and after Louvigny had accepted the Fox terms, several of the Abenaki warriors settled in the Fox villages. Prominent among these exiles was Nenangouissik, a former village chief from St. François; Nessegambewuit, who had been to France; and Babamouet, a prominent war chief. Since all these Abenakis seemed loyal to New France, French officials believed they would exercise a positive influence on the Foxes and had not opposed their relocation in Wisconsin. Yet the Abenaki-Fox relationship progressed faster than the French had envisioned. The Abenakis were favorably impressed by the abundant cornfields and availability of game in Wisconsin, and in 1719 Nenangouissik returned to the St. Lawrence with a message from the Foxes to the Abenakis inviting the entire tribe to "go in great numbers to their country [Wisconsin] and . . . to pursue our Hunting, and make our abode there." French officials obviously opposed the move, and the Jesuits used their considerable influence to prevent the Abenakis from accepting the offer, but messengers repeatedly traveled between the two tribes and the ties between the Foxes and the Abenakis continued.[23]

During the summer of 1723, however, a Chippewa war party killed several of the Abenaki emigrés, including Nenangouissik's brother, and the Foxes again invited the Abenakis to move to Wisconsin, where they might share in the Fox bounty and also seek revenge against the Chippewas. Once again Vaudreuil and the Jesuits were able to restrain the Abenakis, but the prospects of a widening Indian war in the western Great Lakes did not bode well for the fur trade.[24]

Seeking to pacify the antagonists, Vaudreuil dispatched Lignery to Wisconsin to mediate a cease-fire between the Foxes and the Chippewas. Lignery arrived in August 1724 at Green Bay, where he met with the assembled leaders of the Foxes, the Sacs, and the neighboring Winnebagos. En route, the French officer had procured two Fox prisoners held by the Ottawas, and after returning the captives to their kinsmen, he persuaded the three tribes to cease their vendetta against the Chippewas. As a pledge of his good faith, Ouchala persuaded the more militant warriors to relinquish three Chippewa prisoners, whom Lignery promised to escort back to Michilimackinac.[25]

Lignery also requested the Foxes and their allies "to stay the war-club lifted against . . . the Illinois, upon whom you are waging a bitter war," but the Foxes adamantly refused. Although Ouchala had repeatedly repatriated Illinois prisoners, the Illinois had not reciprocated, and several Fox warriors captured by the Illinois either had been tortured and burned or were still held as captives in the Illinois villages. Embittered, the Foxes replied that "the Illinois have attacked us too often to allow of our staying our War-clubs. We hide it not from you, but we shall still have an arm lifted on that side."[26]

Lignery's request for a cessation of the Fox-Illinois warfare reflected the French court's response to the continued complaints about Fox incursions by French agents in the Illinois Country. Accordingly, since the Foxes officially remained within the jurisdiction of Canada, officials in France instructed Vaudreuil to restrain the tribe. Although Vaudreuil reported that he would "employ every means to attain this end, by ordering all the Commandants of the posts to work efficaciously for that object," he at best gave the requests only lip service, and indeed attempted to defend the Foxes. In a series of letters to officials in France and to French military commanders in the west, he placed the blame for the conflict on the Illinois Confederacy, charging that their refusal to relinquish the Fox captives left Ouchala and his people with no recourse. Interested primarily in Canada, and still resentful that the Illinois Country had been transferred to Louisiana, Vaudreuil continued to welcome the warfare because it disrupted the Illinois fur trade and prevented merchants among the Illinois from developing markets among the Sioux. From

Vaureuil's perspective, the lucrative Sioux trade belonged to Canada. A Fox-Chippewa peace would facilitate the Canadian penetration of the Sioux markets. Vaudreuil was relieved that the Foxes and the Chippewas had agreed to the cease-fire. He had little interest in preventing the Foxes from falling upon the Illinois Confederacy.[27]

Neither did the Canadian coureurs de bois. Also eager to tap the lucrative Sioux markets, French traders at Green Bay and along the Fox River encouraged the younger Fox warriors in their raids in the Illinois Country. Although Ouchala still urged caution, more militant members of the tribe secured arms and ammunition from the merchants and listened attentively as the coureurs de bois assured them that their loyalty was only to Onontio and Canada. Traders in Illinois were not Onontio's children, but were "other white men," outside Onontio's protection. According to the Canadian merchants, if Fox war chiefs such as Elecevas and his warriors took these "other white men's" scalps, Onontio would not punish them.[28]

Young Fox warriors needed little encouragement. Accompanied by war parties of Kickapoos, Mascoutens, and a few Winnebagos. they ranged across the Illinois Country, attacking both Illinois and French settlements with reckless abandon. During 1724 and 1725 they so harassed the French settlements in the American Bottom that the inhabitants were prevented from planting or cultivating their crops. As a consequence, French traders from the Illinois Country attempting to trade with the Sioux were forced to ascend the Missouri River to reach their markets. Hoping to intimidate their enemies, French officials in Illinois publicly burned several Fox warriors captured by the Illinois Confederacy, but the executions only enraged the Foxes, and their raids in the Illinois Country increased. Meanwhile, the fur trade collapsed and officials in Illinois reported that no pelts would be forthcoming "as long as the war with the Foxes lasts."[29]

The Illinois Confederacy reeled before the attacks. Claiming that they no longer held any Fox prisoners, Illinois leaders begged the French to intercede and stop the slaughter. They complained that Lignery's peace between the Foxes and the Chippewas had only turned the full force of the Foxes and their allies against them. In 1725, seeking refuge at Fort de Chartres, near the mouth of the Kaskaskia, Illinois leaders composed an extensive list enumerating almost one hundred of their kinsmen who had fallen to Fox raiders during the previous decade. Moreover, by 1725 the warfare had spread to the Missouri Valley as French traders from Illinois enlisted the support of the Otoes and the Missourias. Lured by the promise of inexpensive trade goods, warriors from those two tribes assisted the traders, but the Foxes then carried the warfare to their villages.[30]

Outraged by the burning of their kinsmen, and encouraged by the Canadian coureurs de bois, Elecevas and his followers killed a growing number of Frenchmen. Again Ouchala protested, but in June 1723 a small Fox war party first tomahawked a French soldier near the gates of Fort de Chartres, then, as they fled north toward Wisconsin, shot and scalped two traders on the Illinois River. In September another war party killed two Frenchmen hunting in eastern Missouri, and the following spring Fox warriors ambushed five other traders who were ascending the Illinois River, downstream from Lake Peoria. These victims also were scalped, and when the war party returned to their village, they danced with their trophies, proudly displaying the scalps to Ouchala. Meanwhile, during the following summer, Kickapoos allied with Elecevas attacked and killed five traders who were hunting on the lower Wabash. Although French officials at Green Bay and at Michilimackinac reprimanded the raiders, Vaudreuil took no action and the Illinois Country remained paralyzed.[31]

Ouchala renewed his attempts to end the bloodshed. He sent runners to Green Bay and Michilimackinac, reiterating his plea that, if the Illinois would only return their Fox prisoners, the carnage might be ended. But the Illinois answered that they held no Fox captives except those who remained by their own choice, and Sac emissaries sent south to retrieve the prisoners returned empty-handed. Finally, Ouchala admitted that he and other village chiefs could not control their young men, and asked that a priest and a French agent reside permanently in his village. Yet the war in the Illinois Country continued to enhance the Canadian fur trade, and Vaudreuil, Lignery, and François Amariton, the new commandant at Green Bay, did little to stop it.[32]

But other factors were working to the Foxes' disadvantage. By 1725 the continued complaints from officials in Louisiana had caught the attention of the French court, and ministers in Paris were determined to end the warfare. In addition, during 1725 a delegation of Illinois, Otoe, Missouria, and Osage chiefs visited France, where Chicagou, a chief of the Michigameas (one of the bands of the Illinois Confederacy) eloquently pleaded for French assistance. Reminding Louis XV that "the Fox are your enemies and ours also," he asked the king to send more troops, promising that "I, Chicagou, will myself lead the way and teach them how to . . . scalp our enemies." Frustrated by Vaudreuil's inaction, in June 1725 the Council of Ministers wrote to the governor-general, reprimanding him for allowing the Fox-Illinois warfare to continue. They also ordered him to relieve Amariton from his command at Green Bay, since French officials in Illinois were convinced that Amariton had openly encouraged the Fox raids into the Illinois Country.[33]

Ironically, Vaudreuil died on October 10, 1725, before the reprimand could be delivered, but the strongly worded message left little doubt that officials in France would no longer tolerate any procrastination. Vaudreuil earlier had made some desultory plans with Lignery and Amariton to meet again with the Foxes at Green Bay, and the message containing the reprimand and orders for Amariton's dismissal jarred both Lignery and Vaudreuil's temporary successor, Charles Le Moyne, baron de Longueuil, the new acting governor-general of New France, into action. Obviously frightened that their positions also were in jeopardy, Longueuil and Lignery now made a sincere effort to end the Fox raids in the Illinois Country.[34]

In June 1726, Lignery, although ill, journeyed to Green Bay, where he met with the chiefs of the Foxes, the Sacs, and the Winnebagos. His serious demeanor and the gravity of his message had a profound impact on the Indians. Lignery informed Ouchala and the other chiefs that his words came directly from the "Grand Onontio" (Louis XV), who was "not in the habit of speaking more than once to cause himself to be obeyed." The king, according to Lignery, had decreed that his children "absolutely terminate . . . the unjust war which [they] are waging against the Illinois." Those nations who disobeyed his orders would "rush to their own destruction." Moreover, Lignery left little doubt that officials in either Canada or France would accept any equivocation, for he demanded that the Foxes and their allies provide an answer: "Which shall come from the heart and not from the mouth only. . . . Reflect upon it seriously. It is of the highest consequence to you. Give me your reply, but remember that I expect it to be full of sincerity."[35]

Aware that Lignery's edicts no longer could be ignored, Ouchala attempted to placate the commander. Stating that he and the other village chiefs "still hold the French by the hand," the Fox patriarch admitted that they no longer could control their younger warriors. He reiterated his requests that a priest and a French agent reside in his village; only then could his young men be restrained. Moreover, he assured Lignery that, though several war parties of his young men currently were in the Illinois Country, he would speak with them upon their return and hoped "to gain them over." Otherwise, he admitted, the warfare would continue and the Foxes eventually would be "ruined."[36]

After the conference Lignery reported to Longueuil that he believed Ouchala and the chiefs of the Sacs and the Winnebagos truly wanted peace, but he was wary of their ability to control their younger warriors. He proposed that the French wait one year to see if the Foxes really would comply with the new policy. During that period they should exchange all prisoners with the Illinois Confederacy, and after a year-long armistice, both tribes, attended by their allies, would meet at either "Chicago" or Starved Rock to arrange for a permanent peace. Chiefs from all the tribes would then journey to Montreal for more formal peacemaking, and there, in the presence of all the assembled Indians, the French would grant Ouchala's request for a priest, and perhaps assign the Foxes an agent with a small force of soldiers. Meanwhile, French agents should use all their resources to detach the Sioux from the Fox alliance, so that if the Fox-Illinois armistice failed, the Foxes would be cut off from any retreat into Iowa or Minnesota. Then, if the armistice indeed was unsuccessful, the French and their Indian allies should wage a war of extermination against the Red Earth People.[37]

In August 1726, Charles de la Boische, marquis de Beauharnois, succeeded Longueuil as the governor-general of New France, and he was eager to implement Lignery's suggestions. Lignery already had taken some measures to disrupt the Fox-Sioux alliance, and in 1726 René Godefroy, sieur de Linctot, the commander at Fort La Pointe, on the shore of Chequamegon Bay, negotiated a peace between the Sioux and the Chippewas. Although the Foxes were not mentioned in the negotiations, the treaty worked to their disadvantage. The Chippewa-Sioux conflict had strengthened the Fox-Sioux alliance since it provided the two allies with a mutual enemy. Moreover, while their war

against the Sioux had continued, many Chippewas' attention had been focused toward the Sioux, who represented
a more numerous and powerful enemy. With the war
ended, however, the Chippewas could refocus all their
hostility toward the Foxes.[38]

Following Lignery's suggestions, Beauharnois also endeavored to strengthen French relations with the Sioux, At
Fort La Pointe, Linctot was instructed to dispense presents
to visiting Sioux chiefs and to promise them that many
Canadian traders would enter their villages if they would
end their alliance with the Foxes. In the spring of 1727 preliminary plans were formulated to establish a French post
among the Sioux villages on the upper Mississippi River,
and in June two Jesuits, Fathers Michel Guignas and Nicolas de Gonnor left Montreal for Wisconsin, accompanied
by a small party of traders led by René Boucher de La
Perrière. In August they passed over the Fox-Wisconsin
portage, where they were well treated by Ouchala's people, and in September they reached the Mississippi. There
they built a new post, Fort Beauharnois, near the site of
Perrot's former post on Lake Pepin. French traders and
missionaries now had direct access to the Sioux, and a
French post was reestablished on the periphery of the
Sioux heartland. The short-lived prosperity of the Foxes as
middlemen in the Sioux trade was ending.[39]

While the French were strengthening their ties to the
Sioux, Ouchala worked assiduously to convince his young
men to cease their warfare. The task was not easy. At the
Green Bay conference Ouchala had admitted to Lignery that
several of his warriors were absent on raids against their enemies, and in June 1726, when he returned to his village, he
learned that one party had struck the Chippewas, killing
one man and one woman, while suffering one dead and
three wounded. Yet Lignery intervened in the Fox behalf,
covered the Chippewa deaths with presents, and convinced
the Chippewa leaders that since the war party had left camp

Charles de Beauharnois, governor-general
of New France from 1726 to 1747. From a
painting by Henri Beau (1863–1949), after
R. Lournières (?), in the National Archives
of Canada (C-14594).

prior to the Green Bay agreement, they should not be held
accountable. Two other Fox war parties also had attempted
to attack the Illinois, but both had been intercepted by Illinois warriors, and the young men had been soundly defeated. Since the war parties against the Illinois had all been
killed, captured, or wounded, Ouchala argued that their
medicine was bad, and that Wisaka had turned his face
from those who warred in far places. Temporarily subdued,
the young men seemed more inclined toward peace, and
Ouchala informed French officials that these parties had
left the Fox villages before the new armistice; if the Illinois
would return the Fox warriors whom they had captured in
the recent skirmishes, the vendetta would be ended.[40]

The Foxes' cordial reception of the French party en
route to the Sioux also reflected Ouchala's efforts. In mid-
August 1727, when the cold, wet, and bedraggled mission-

aries arrived at the Fox village in the midst of a rainstorm, Fox elders and village chiefs marched out to meet them, their calumet lit as a sign of their good intentions. Although Father Guignas admitted that his party had approached the Fox village with considerable trepidation, he later reported that the Foxes were "in reality not very formidable." The Jesuit commented that the village seemed to be overrun with young boys "between ten and fourteen years of age," but he estimated that the tribe could muster no more than two hundred warriors. The French remained in the Fox village for two days and the tribespeople showered them with hospitality. After meeting with their guests in a formal council, the Foxes prepared a feast for the French, then provided them with dried meat and other provisions for their voyage to the Mississippi.[41]

Yet Wisaka, the Trickster, was inconstant in his affection, and in 1727 he again turned away from his people. Eager to expand their Indian trade, the British in 1724 had established Oswego on Lake Ontario, and two years later they strengthened the post as a permanent part of their commercial empire. Using Iroquois middlemen, officials in New York then clandestinely sent wampum belts to most of the Great Lakes tribes, inviting these western Indians to "cut the throats of the French in all the posts" and to trade with the British. Although most of the western Indians rejected the British offer, the tribes at Detroit used the threat of the British proposal to force the French to lower the price of trade goods at that post. They also reported that the Foxes had received the Iroquois envoys very favorably.[42]

Other circumstances also rendered the Foxes receptive to the British initiative. During the summer of 1727 Ouchala died, and with his passing the tribe's commitment to accommodation diminished. Still eager to enhance their prestige as warriors, young men again formed war parties and renewed their raids against the Illinois, killing or capturing several hapless French traders whom they chanced to encounter on the Mississippi. The elderly Okimaouassen ransomed the French prisoners and surrendered them to Nicolas-Antoine Coulon de Villiers, the commandant of Fort St. Joseph, on the St. Joseph River in Michigan, but Beauharnois accused the Foxes of violating the armistice and wrote to French officials in Illinois that since Ouchala's death the tribe no longer could be trusted. Although he earlier had informed his superiors in France that "all the tribes of the Renards (Foxes) and their allies, who earlier desired naught but war, now seem animated by quite opposite sentiments," by the fall of 1727 Beauharnois had abandoned his proposals of accommodation. Alarmed that the alleged Fox-British intrigue was only the initial step of a "fresh Enterprise of the English," the governor-general proposed "striking a Signal Blow" that would make an example of the Foxes. Otherwise, the British-Fox conspiracy might eventually alienate all of New France's Indian allies and "reduce this Colony to an Extremity."[43]

Without waiting for instructions from France, in late August 1727 Beauharnois met with his advisors and decided to attack the Foxes. Instructions were sent to French military commanders in the west to prepare for a major campaign during the summer of 1728, and messages also were sent to Charles Henri Desliettes (De Liette) de Tonty, commandant at Fort de Chartres in the Illinois Country, asking him to muster his troops and allied tribesmen at Chicago, where they too would join in the campaign. Since the French feared that the Foxes would learn of their plans and flee to the Sioux or the Iowas, the plans were supposedly kept secret, and officials at Green Bay and Michilimackinac were instructed to inform the Indians that Beauharnois was planning an expedition against the British post at Oswego. The French hoped that the Foxes would be surprised in their villages and soundly defeated.[44]

The Foxes learned of the enterprise. Although Beauharnois had intended to keep his preparations secret, the

Iroquois were informed of the campaign and sent messengers to the Foxes advising them of the French plans. Not surprisingly, the information again exacerbated the political split in the tribe. Convinced that Ouchala's policy of accommodation had failed, during the early summer of 1728 a war party of more militant warriors again struck at the Illinois. Meanwhile, Okimaouassen and Ouchala's successors counseled among themselves attempting to formulate a strategy to prevent the French from launching their invasion. In July 1728, while these tribal elders met in council, messengers brought the news that Perrière and some of the French who had wintered among the Sioux were descending the river toward Green Bay. Rushing from their council, the elders hurried to the riverbank and called to the French, inviting them to land and spend the night in the Fox village. Perrière and his companions beached their canoes at the village, but they were concerned for their personal safety. Although the village chiefs "seemed extremely peaceful," Perrière had learned of the recent Fox attacks in the Illinois Country, and his apprehension mounted when militant warriors proudly displayed four French scalps they had taken in the raids. Tribal elders assured the French that they would be safe in the village, but Perrière replied that he would not spend the night "in a place stained with the blood of Frenchmen." Proclaiming that the Foxes now were "dead men since our Father will not stop one night with us," Okimaouassen asked Perrière to allow one of their members to accompany the French party back to Montreal so that he might assure Onontio that most of the tribe wanted peace. Perrière agreed, and the warrior boarded the French canoe and rode with the French down the Fox River. But when Perrière refused to discuss the rumors of Lignery's impending invasion of Wisconsin, the Fox grew more apprehensive. The party crossed Lake Winnebago and made camp for the night several leagues downstream from the

Winnebago village, but shortly after consuming their
evening meal they were surprised by several Fox warriors
who had returned from northern Illinois and who reported that a large party of French and Illinois warriors
had attacked them near Chicago. Afraid that these enemies might be acting in support of Lignery, the Fox abandoned Perrière and returned to his village.[45]

The French party who surprised and attacked the large
hunting camp of Foxes near Chicago was led by Desliettes.
Originally they had planned to rendezvous with Lignery at
the Fox villages. Consisting of twenty French soldiers and
traders and several hundred Illinois warriors, Desliettes's
force greatly outnumbered the Foxes, and although the latter fought valiantly, they suffered twenty killed and fifteen
captured, including many women and children. The number of French and Illinois casualties remains unknown,
but the Illinois were so disheartened by the "victory" that
they refused to travel on to Wisconsin, and although Desliettes pleaded with them that their cowardice might allow
the Foxes to escape, they still abandoned the expedition
and returned to their villages.[46]

Unaware that Desliettes and the Illinois had withdrawn
from the campaign, Lignery led an army west toward Wisconsin. Leaving Montreal on June 5, 1728, the expedition
consisted of four hundred French soldiers and coureurs de
bois, and several hundred mission Indians. They ascended
the Ottawa River, passed over into Lake Huron, and arrived at Michilimackinac on August 1. There they were
joined by additional coureurs de bois and hundreds of
western Indians, including Ottawas, Potawatomis, Chippewas, and Hurons, who swelled Lignery's force to almost
1,650 men. But instead of sailing promptly to Green Bay
and ascending the Fox River, the French tarried at Michilimackinac for ten days. Then they were buffeted by contrary winds on Lake Michigan, which forced them to land
frequently as they proceeded on to Wisconsin. They ar-

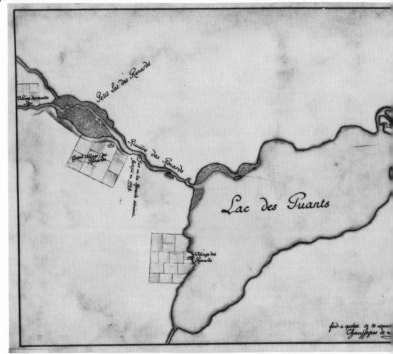

This map shows the Fox villages, fort, and cornfields near Lake Winnebago (Lac des Puants) burned by the French in 1728. The original map, drawn in 1730, is in the French Archives nationales, Paris (Colonies, C^{11} A,

rived at Green Bay on August 17, but hid their canoes behind some islands until nightfall, hoping to mask their approach from nearby Sacs and Winnebagos. Shortly before midnight Lignery sent several small parties ashore to warn the commander of the French fort (Fort St. Francis), and to keep any hostile Indians camped near the fort from fleeing to warn the Foxes and their allies.[47]

Lignery's attempts at subterfuge failed. The Winnebagos, the Sacs, and the Foxes all were aware of his approach, and although parties of Foxes and Winnebagos recently had been trading at the post, they fled shortly before his arrival. Unfortunately, however, four warriors

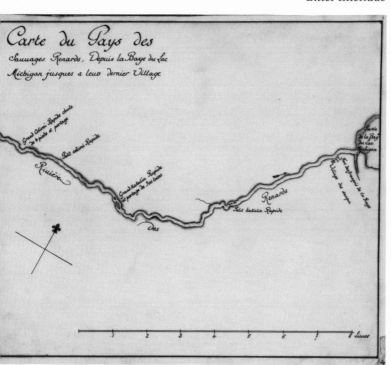

126: no. 13). Reproduced here is a version from about 1900 in the National Archives of Canada, NMC 24583.

(three Winnebagos and one Fox) had spent the previous two or three days carousing, and were still so intoxicated that the French and their allies discovered them asleep in an outbuilding. Although Lignery announced to friendly Potawatomis and Menominees that his intention was only to confer with "all the Nations, even the Renards," he delivered the hapless prisoners over to the Ottawas and the Chippewas, who spent the following day first torturing, then killing their victims.[48]

While Lignery was en route from Michilimackinac to Green Bay, the Foxes prepared to evacuate their villages. Although some of the younger warriors would have pre-

ferred to remain and fight, the older chiefs cautioned that
Lignery's army was large, and they remained uncertain of
the disposition of Desliettes's expedition. Afraid that other,
supposedly neutral tribes might feel compelled to also
enlist in the campaign, the Foxes were apprehensive that
they might be overwhelmed. Food, clothing, and ammunition were carefully wrapped in leather pouches, and
canoes were repaired to carry both those supplies and the
women and children up the Fox River toward the Wisconsin. Leaders of the Kiyagamohag society made plans for
some warriors to accompany the women and children in
the canoes while the majority of the fighting men followed
along the riverbank, protecting the retreat if the French
decided to pursue their enemies. Meanwhile, runners were
sent to the Iowas, asking for temporary sanctuary. In mid-
August, when scouts brought reports that Lignery's army
had landed at Green Bay, the Foxes abandoned their villages and retreated toward the Mississippi.[49]

Unaware that his enemies had withdrawn, Lignery spent
several days at Green Bay, evidently convinced that the
Foxes would sent representatives to parley. Finally, urged
on by his Indian allies, he proceeded up the Fox River,
where many of his canoes were damaged in negotiating
the rapids just downstream from the Winnebago village.
Like the Foxes, the Winnebagos also fled before the French
advance, and Lignery first burned their abandoned lodges,
then crossed Lake Winnebago to the Fox villages, where
he arrived on August 24, 1728. Although Lignery was
impressed by the large fields of "Indian corn, peas, beans,
and gourds which they had in great abundance," he was
disappointed that the only Foxes whom he encountered
were one old woman too ill to travel, who was attended by
her granddaughter, and one elderly Fox warrior who had
stubbornly vowed that the French would never force him
from his homeland. Lignery first interrogated the prisoners, then surrendered the old warrior to the Chippewas,

who "burned [the Fox warrior] by a slow fire, without manifesting the least repugnance for committing so barbarous an action." Lignery's canoes were damaged, his men "had no shoes and no food other than corn," and Desliettes and the Illinois tribes had failed to appear. Lignery therefore was reluctant to pursue the Foxes. After dispatching several messengers to the Sioux, advising them against giving assistance to his enemies, Lignery burned the Fox villages, cut down their cornfields, and retreated back to Green Bay. Fearing Fox and Winnebago retribution, he ordered the small garrison at Fort St. Francis to abandon their post and withdraw with his expedition. Early in September, after burning Fort St. Francis, Lignery and his followers returned to Michilimackinac.[50]

Although Lignery boasted that his expedition had been "advantageous to the glory of the King and the welfare of both Colonies," he knew the campaign had ended in failure. He had destroyed the Fox cornfields and he assured Beauharnois that "one-half those people will die of hunger," but his destruction of Fort St. Francis bore mute testimony to his realization that the military power of the Foxes and their allies remained unbroken. Moreover, in the same report in which he boasted of his success, Lignery complained about the "unwillingness" of his "Canadians" to pursue the Foxes toward Iowa, and also carped that if Desliettes and the French from the Illinois Country had honored their promises and "marched toward the Ouisconsin with the southern people, the Renards would have been surrounded." Seeking sympathy, Lignery complained that he had been ill and had "never had so much trouble in my life as during the past four months." He knew that both the Canadians and the Indians participating in his expedition considered the campaign to be a failure, and he pleaded with Beauharnois to protect him from the wrath of "the [French] minister."[51]

But Beauharnois also was worried about censure. His arbitrary decision to initiate the campaign reflected his propensity for ill-advised, rash action as governor, and the expedition had surprised officials in France, who "had reason to believe that . . . peace between the Illinois and Fox Indians was on the eve of being concluded." Although the logistics of time and distance precluded their prevention of the campaign, in May 1728 French officials informed Beauharnois that "His Majesty . . . wished that such a step, the success whereof is problematical, should have been postponed until his orders had been received." If the expedition failed, they warned, the Foxes might seek refuge among the Sioux, "from which point they will cause more disorder in the Colony than if they had been allowed to remain quiet in their village."[52]

Anxious to shift the blame from his own shoulders, Beauharnois replied that the threat of a spreading Fox-British conspiracy had forced him to authorize the campaign; otherwise, the French would have suffered "the loss of all the posts in the Upper Country." Moreover, according to the governor-general, the expedition had failed due to Lignery's mismanagement. Beauharnois charged that Lignery had wasted supplies, had used the expedition as a personal trading venture, and had spent entirely too much time at Michilimackinac before proceeding on to Green Bay, where he again procrastinated before marching against the Fox and Winnebago villages. He also criticized Lignery for not pursuing the Foxes over the Fox-Wisconsin portage, stating that the Canadian and Indian members of the expedition were eager for such action, but Lignery had stubbornly refused. In closing, Beauharnois admitted that the Foxes had escaped, but assured his superiors that he was providing them with "the truth of the matter," even if such information was unpleasant."[53]

While French officials scrambled to affix the blame for the failure, the Foxes returned to their homeland. They had taken temporary shelter on the Mississippi near the mouth of the Wapsipinicon, and when scouts brought news

that Lignery had retreated, they returned to their burned
villages and broken cornfields. Short of food and facing the
oncoming winter, most of the tribe followed the old pat-
tern of scattering through the forest in small camps, planning to provide for their families through hunting. Some
traveled down the Fox River to the Green Bay region, hoping to solicit assistance from kinsmen intermarried among
the Sacs, but when they arrived at the bay, they found that
the Sacs, fearing they might be swept up in the warfare,
had abandoned their village and had fled to the St. Joseph
River in Michigan. Other Foxes retreated into northern
Illinois or returned to western Wisconsin, where, ironically, they sought refuge near Fort Beauharnois, the newly
established French trading post on the upper Mississippi.[54]

The months following Lignery's campaign were a period
of soul-searching for the Red Earth People. Although the
French had failed to surprise them in their villages, the
expedition illustrated that they remained vulnerable to
well-organized, large-scale French military operations, and
Beauharnois's willingness to undertake such measures
reflected an inclination toward action lacking in the vacil-
lating Vaudreuil. No longer would the Foxes and their
allies be able to walk the jurisdictional tightrope between
Canada and Louisiana. The new Onontio seemed ready to
forget such petty quarrels, and indeed had enlisted the aid
of Desliettes and the Illinois tribes against them. More
ominous, the Iowas and the Sioux had not denied them
temporary refuge on the Mississippi, but they had informed the Foxes that they would oppose any permanent
relocation of the Red Earth People in their homelands. If
the French sent another expedition and these western
tribes refused to give them sanctuary, where would the
Foxes flee? With the exception of the Winnebagos, the
Kickapoos and the Mascoutens, most of the neighboring
tribes had either joined with Lignery or remained neutral,
and the Foxes knew that many of the French-allied In-

dians, especially the Chippewas, the Potawatomis, and the Menominees, were intent upon renewing their warfare against them. Predicting disaster, some of the tribal elders still urged that the Foxes ask Onontio for mercy, but others, led by the younger war chiefs, remained defiant. Had not the Mesquakies always stood alone? Were they not a race of warriors? Assuredly the French had invaded Wisconsin, but had not the Red Earth People readily evaded them? Their villages had been burned and their crops had been devastated, but the Mesquakies had survived. In 1712, at the siege of Detroit, Pemoussa had stood on the ramparts and warned the French that the Foxes were "immortal." Undaunted, many members of the Kiyaga-mohag still believed in Pemoussa's protestations. They were certain that the Red Earth People eventually would triumph.[55]

CHAPTER FIVE

ARMAGEDDON

On September 7, 1728, the small party of coureurs de bois and Menominees dispatched by Lignery reached Fort Beauharnois, on Lake Pepin in western Wisconsin. It had not been a pleasant voyage. Although they arrived safely, they had passed down the Wisconsin River in a state of constant alarm, afraid that Fox war parties might ambush them at every bend of the river. Carrying news of Lignery's failure, they informed Pierre Boucher, sieur de Boucherville, who commanded at the post, that the Foxes had fled into northwestern Illinois or eastern Iowa, but that they might seek retribution against any Frenchmen whom they encountered. Boucherville and Father Michel Guignas, the Jesuit at the post, were much alarmed and sent the Menominee guides and several traders on to the Sioux villages near the Falls of St. Anthony, seeking assurances that the Sioux would protect the garrison from any assault by Fox war parties.[1]

The Sioux provided scant assurance. Although Sioux village chiefs treated their visitors hospitably and promised the traders that they would never tolerate any permanent relocation of the Foxes in their homeland, they remained equivocal about military assistance, and the Menominees reported back to Boucherville that the Sioux could not be trusted; they had "Renard [Fox] hearts." Afraid that the Foxes "would employ their usual stratagems to seduce our allies," Boucherville reported that "it would be unwise to confide in these inconstant tribes." Claiming that Fort Beauharnois held insufficient provisions to sustain his garrison through the upcoming winter, on September 18 he met with Guignas and the traders and announced that the fort should be abandoned. The priest and traders would load their property into canoes, descend the Mississippi, and seek refuge in the Illinois Country.[2]

Not all the traders at Fort Beauharnois shared Boucherville's sentiments. On October 3, when Boucherville, Guignas, and ten companions boarded their canoes for the voyage down the Mississippi, the remaining traders (about half a dozen) refused to accompany them. Complaining that Boucherville had overestimated the Fox threat and that they "would be unable to sell their goods elsewhere," the traders decided to remain at the fort. Lured by the prospects of the lucrative Sioux trade, the merchants realized they would hold a virtual monopoly over trade goods on the upper Mississippi during the coming trapping season. And if the Foxes established villages in the region, they too would need lead and powder. Some coureurs de bois had always benefitted from the Fox trade, and for these merchants the risks were far outweighed by the potential for profits.[3]

In contrast, Boucherville, Guignas, and their companions withdrew from the fort and descended the Mississippi past the mouth of the Wisconsin, where they found the scattered ashes of several recent Fox campfires. Proceeding on to the mouth of the Wapsipinicon, they discovered several canoes beached by a Fox hunting party who had just gone ashore in Iowa. Traveling at night, Boucherville and his companions silently passed the mouth of the Rock River, watching from the darkness as children played around the campfires of a Fox village. By the morning of October 16 they had reached the mouth of the Skunk River in eastern Iowa, but before they could beach and conceal their canoes they were discovered by a party of Kickapoos and Mascoutens, who forced them ashore and carried them to their village.[4]

Fearing for their lives, Boucherville prayed that God would be merciful and allow them "just to be plundered." When the Kickapoos took them to the lodge of Ouiskouba (He Who Likes Sugar), a village chief who recently had lost his wife and children in Desliettes's attack on the mixed hunting camp of Kickapoos and Foxes near Chicago, the Frenchmen believed they were doomed. To their surprise, however, they remained unharmed. The tribesmen deposited all their possessions with them in Ouiskouba's wigwam, then sent runners to find the chief, who was hunting with several companions in central Iowa.[5]

For several days the lives of the Frenchmen hung in the balance. Awaiting Ouiskouba's return, the Kickapoos and the neighboring Mascoutens debated among themselves over the fate of their prisoners. Many of the tribal elders argued that the captives be put to death. Traditional allies of the Foxes, they were especially suspicious of Father Guignas, whose breviary contained a text partially printed in red ink, which the old men claimed was the blood of their fallen kinsmen. Yet several younger warriors intervened, warning the "old babblers" that Ouiskouba had been deemed "the arbitrator" of the Frenchmen's fate and no action could be taken until he returned. To the Frenchmen's relief, when Ouiskouba arrived he declared that his "heart was good"; although he still grieved for the loss of his family, he did not blame Boucherville and his companions. Moreover, according to the chief, two years previously he had been to Montreal and visited Onontio,

who he declared still "governed his thought and actions."
Boucherville could "rely on his word; no harm would come
to them."[6]

In the weeks that followed Boucherville met with White
Robe, The Shawnee, and other Kickapoo leaders, plying
them with presents and cajoling them to release his party
before any Foxes might arrive and "cause trouble." But the
Kickapoos answered that since "Onontio is angry with us,"
they feared the French-allied Indians more than the Foxes.
To preclude any attacks on their village, they decided to
hold all the Frenchmen hostage. Although Boucherville
protested, the Kickapoos advised him to "prepare yourselves to spend the winter with us and begin to build your
cabins."[7]

Following their captors' orders, the French settled in for
the winter. Then, in early November, they were alarmed to
learn that a party of ten Fox warriors, led by the war chief
Kansekoe, had arrived in the village and was demanding
that the Kickapoos surrender the Frenchmen. Although the
Kickapoos refused Kansekoe's demands, the Foxes seemed
to intimidate them, and Boucherville distributed more of
his trade goods in an effort to retain the Kickapoos' protection. In response, Kansekoe attempted to bribe Pe-
chicamengoa, a Kickapoo war chief married to a Fox
woman, to murder Father Guignas, but other Kickapoos
learned of the plot and sequestered the Frenchmen in a
heavily defended camp on an island in the river. His plot
discovered, Kansekoe again met with the younger Kickapoos and accepted a large present of trade goods offered by
Boucherville to cover the death of the Fox warrior at
Green Bay and to make amends for other Fox hardships
suffered during the recent invasion. Now willing to allow
the Frenchmen to remain among the Kickapoos, Kansekoe
left peacefully, but warned that a large party of Foxes and
Winnebagos had recently passed through southwestern
Wisconsin and would soon arrive at the Kickapoo village.[8]

Kansekoe's threats frightened the French, and although the Kickapoos had refused to surrender them, Boucherville and his companions remained apprehensive about their safety. In the confusion following Kansekoe's departure, three of the French captives managed to escape and eventually reached the French settlements in the Illinois Country. Although Boucherville initially had advised against such flight, the escapes worked to his advantage. Now certain that French officials knew they held the captives, the Kickapoos treated their "visitors" with increased hospitality. They still refused to relinquish the hostages, but they redoubled their efforts to protect them.[9]

The French needed such protection. As Kansekoe retraced his route back toward the Rock River, he met the approaching Foxes and Winnebagos, among whom was the father of the hapless Fox warrior whom the Chippewas had tortured and burned when Lignery had landed at Green Bay in August. Kansekoe offered the old man part of his recently acquired trade goods, and although the old man was willing to accept the merchandise as payment for his son's death, many of his companions refused. After a lengthy discussion, the Foxes divided into two parties. Seventy warriors returned with Kansekoe and the old man to their winter camps, while thirty others, primarily younger warriors, continued on to the Kickapoo village.[10]

Still seeking the French hostages, the Foxes brashly entered the Kickapoo village, arrogantly ignoring the time-honored traditions of protocol and restraint. "Contrary to the custom of the savages," the younger war chief who led the party first harangued the Kickapoos to surrender their captives, then presented The Shawnee and Black Bull, influential Kickapoo chiefs, with a bloodstained buffalo robe and wampum belt to signify the seriousness of his mission. His face painted black, the Fox war chief offered the assembled Kickapoos a calumet adorned with bloody feathers, also an indication that he was asking for the lives

This watercolor, painted in Quebec about 1730, bears the following legend: "Fox Warrior. Feared by all nations for their valor and speed, capable of going 25 to 30 leagues [60 to 72 miles] a day without any food other than plants and leaves from the woods. There are about 400 to 500 men bearing arms divided into three or four villages. Ever since they have been at war with the French, almost all the nations have been doing their hair Fox-style. If they have a shirt, they wear it as a breechcloth when they have to fight." The warrior depicted had been the Foxes' courier to other nations. He was captured by the Miamis and given to Beauharnois, who sent him to France, where he died in prison in 1732. Photograph from the Bibliothèque nationale, Paris (cliché 82C113155).

of the Frenchmen. Some of the older Kickapoo men accepted the pipe, but again Ouiskouba and the younger warriors rallied in the prisoners' behalf. Despite considerable intimidation, they refused to smoke the calumet, informing the Foxes: "We had no evil design in stopping the French. We wish them to live. . . . We will die together rather than give up a single one of these Frenchmen."[11]

Angered, the Foxes stormed out of the council meeting and withdrew from the Kickapoo village. Threatening vengeance, they returned toward their homes, still determined to make the Kickapoos pay for their refusal. After traveling three days, they encountered two warriors, one Kickapoo, the other Mascouten, hunting in the forest. Although neither of these warriors were residents of the village that held the Frenchmen, the thirty Foxes fell upon them with a vengeance, and in an act of monumental stupidity they butchered the hapless hunters and carried their scalps back to the Fox village.[12]

News of the attack had a profound impact on both the Kickapoos and the Foxes. Dumbfounded, Fox leaders, both war chiefs and village chiefs, condemned the action and berated the war party, reminding them that the Kickapoos and the Mascoutens were much intermarried with the Foxes and had always been their staunchest allies. Indeed, when many of the other tribes either had wavered or had joined the French, both the Kickapoos and the Mascoutens had refused Onontio's offerings. Did these "foolish young men" not remember that Kickapoo and Mascouten warriors also had fallen with Pemoussa's people at Detroit and that French fear of Kickapoo reinforcements had contributed to Louvigny's willingness to negotiate with their fathers in 1716? Had these young warriors completely lost their senses? Meeting in hurried council, Fox patriarchs demanded that these firebrands explain why, in addition to "raising up against us all the nations that have sworn to destroy us; you must likewise massacre our kinsmen?"[13]

In a desperate attempt to "atone for this murder," the
Fox elders sent five men to the winter camp where the
hunters had resided, and two of the warriors stripped
naked and lay upon a white robe, offering their lives to the
Kickapoos in exchange for the dead men. But the hunters'
relatives refused, stating that they already had sent runners to the other Kickapoo and Mascouten villages, informing the tribes of the Foxes' perfidy. According to the
bereaved tribesmen, "the matter is no longer in [our]
hands; the matter rests with the young Kickapoo chiefs"
back on the Skunk River.[14]

The Kickapoos now faced a series of decisions critical
both for themselves and for the Foxes. Although some of the
older, pro-Fox Kickapoo warriors first argued that if the
Kickapoos had given up the French, the murders would not
have been committed, Boucherville reminded his captors
that he had warned them against the Foxes; and when the
Kickapoos and the Mascoutens replied "we are between
two fires; the Renard [Fox] has killed us, the Illinois has
killed us, the Frenchman is angry with us. What are we to
do?" Boucherville offered to intercede in their behalf and to
"make peace" between his captors and the French and Illinois. After some discussion the Kickapoos and the Mascoutens each agreed to send one warrior (both born of Illinois mothers) to accompany Boucherville to the Illinois.[15]

Accompanied by the two warriors, Boucherville reached
the Peoria village on the lower Illinois River on January 5,
1729. After learning of his mission, the Illinois lavished
hospitality on their guests, seating them upon a pallet of
mats and bearskins and providing them with "the most
palatable food in the village." Eager to enlist the Kickapoos
and the Mascoutens against the Foxes, Illinois war chiefs
promised the newcomers they would "help you avenge
your dead," and they assured the Kickapoos and the
Mascoutens that they would return all of their kinsmen
held prisoner in the Illinois villages. Suffering from frost-

bite, Boucherville could not proceed on to Fort de Chartres, but he sent a message to Desliettes from the Kickapoos and the Mascoutens, asking the French for a formal alliance. As an indication of their tribes' sincerity, the two warriors accompanying the Frenchman also sent Desliettes the bloodstained wampum and calumet originally offered to them by the Foxes.[16]

Much encouraged by the Kickapoo and Mascouten defection, Desliettes sent a quantity of trade goods to Boucherville, which he carried back to the Kickapoo village. Boucherville was joined by Étienne d'Outreleau, a Jesuit from the French settlements, and when they arrived on the Skunk River, they were greeted as heroes. Readily embracing Desliettes's promise of an alliance, the Kickapoos quickly dispatched two war parties to strike at the Fox winter camps. Although the first party returned empty-handed, the second initially attempted to attack a Fox camp through subterfuge and, when that failed, they enticed two Fox war chiefs, Chichippa (The Duck) and Pemoussa (a son or nephew of the Fox war chief at Detroit), to return to the Skunk River to meet with Kickapoo leaders. Eager to mend the rift between their people and the Kickapoos, the Fox chiefs carried calumets and white wampum belts, but en route to Iowa the Kickapoos murdered them, carrying their scalps back to the Kickapoo village. Meanwhile, a war party of Illinois also arrived on the Skunk River, bringing additional gifts from Desliettes at Fort de Chartres. In March 1729, Boucherville, Guignas, and the remaining French "prisoners" were escorted by about three dozen Kickapoo warriors to the Illinois Country. After the Kickapoos presented Chichippa's and Pemoussa's scalps to the Illinois Confederacy, "a thousand attentions were lavished upon them," and they concluded a formal alliance with their former enemies.[17]

Frightened by the defections, some of the older Fox chiefs desperately sought an accommodation with Onontio.

Shortly after Boucherville's departure, about sixty lodges of Foxes and a few Winnebagos arrived in western Wisconsin, where they spent much of the winter camped near Fort Beauharnois. Wary lest they offend the neighboring Sioux, the Foxes traded peacefully with the merchants who remained at the post, even interceding on behalf of the French when the Winnebagos attempted to seize traps and other French property. In the summer of 1729 Fox warriors from this village persuaded Christophe Dufrost de La Jemerais, one of the traders at the fort, to accompany them to the rebuilt Fox village on the Fox River in central Wisconsin. The Foxes treated Jemerais hospitably, and he remained in the village for almost three weeks before accompanying three older chiefs and a small party of warriors to Fort St. Joseph, in southern Michigan. There they met with Nicolas-Antoine Coulon de Villiers and again pledged their loyalty to Onontio.[18]

Both Villiers and Jemerais believed in the Foxes' sincerity, and when Jemerais traveled on to Montreal, he urged Beauharnois to honor the Fox request. Beauharnois ignored Jemerais's recommendations. Earlier in the summer he already had assembled representatives from many of the western tribes, and after referring to the Foxes as "demons," he had exhorted the assembled tribesmen to exterminate them. In addition, he had dispatched Paul Marin de la Malgue and a small party of soldiers to Green Bay, where Marin fortified and reoccupied an old French trading post near the Menominee village, reasserting the French presence in eastern Wisconsin. Tragically, Beauharnois's exhortations proved persuasive; for in the months following the Fox chiefs' return from Fort St. Joseph, Onontio's allies again attacked the Fox villages.[19]

As news of the Kickapoo and Mascouten defection spread to other tribes in the Great Lakes region, many were emboldened to join in Onontio's campaign. During Jemerais's brief tenure in the Fox village the settlement had been raided by a small war party of Menominees, and although the Kiyagamohag had pursued the fleeing Menominees through the forest, the Foxes had been ambushed and defeated. In the fall of 1729 they suffered losses of a much more serious consequence. Informed of the Kickapoo and the Mascouten defection, the Winnebagos now believed that the Fox cause was lost, and they too sought to mend their French fences. Attempting to prove their change of heart, some Winnebagos previously hostile to Onontio now joined with Ottawas and Chippewas from the Michilimackinac region and, assisted by a few Menominees, they struck at an outlying Fox village, killing thirty men and almost seventy women and children. Encouraged by their success, warriors from the same tribes then joined to surprise a large party of Fox villagers who were returning from a buffalo hunt in Iowa. Although the Foxes fought back valiantly, their enemies numbered almost two hundred warriors, and in the ensuing melee the French-allied Indians again inflicted heavy losses. Many Foxes were killed, others were taken captive, and the victors distributed both their prisoners and the scalps of the fallen to neighboring tribes in Michigan and Wisconsin, inviting them also to join in the renewed campaign against the Foxes.[20]

Responding to the attacks, in November a group of older village chiefs sent an emissary to Fort St. Joseph to again meet with Villiers. Pleading his kinsmen's cause, the Fox spokesman informed Villiers that the village chiefs realized the extent of their tribe's political and military isolation. He admitted that if his people had been killed, "it has only been done after repeated warnings to us to preserve the peace." Now his kinsmen's "hearts were quaking"; they "considered themselves dead." Now even the most militant of the young warriors had been cowed. Now the village chiefs currently possessed "more influence over their young men" than at any time in their memory. The season was late, and the Fox emissary feared that the road to Onontio's lodge still was infested with those nations who opposed them, but if the "good heart of their father, Onontio," would restrain their enemies, in the spring when the ice melted, the Fox chiefs would go to Montreal and throw themselves at his mercy.[21]

But the village chiefs' "influence over their young men" continued to be limited. Angered by the recent attacks, the Kiyagamohag lashed out at the Fox enemies. Small war parties made futile, if determined, raids against the Kickapoos, the Chippewas, and the Menominees, but their greatest vehemence was focused on the Winnebagos. Unlike the Kickapoos and the Mascoutens, the Winnebagos had no reason for defection; moreover, they too had suffered the humiliation of burned villages and wasted cornfields during Lignery's campaign. And indeed, those Foxes who had wintered on the Mississippi near Fort Beauharnois had shared their meager rations with several lodges of Winnebagos who had camped in their midst. Now some of those same Winnebagos had guided the Ottawas, the Chippewas, and the Menominees in the attack on the Fox hunting party. The Kickapoo and Mascouten defections may have been more critical, but the Winnebago treachery was more perfidious.[22]

Even those Foxes who favored Onontio called out for vengeance. In October 1729 the Winnebagos who had participated in the massacre established a new village on a small island in Little Lake Butte des Morts, near modern Neenah, Wisconsin. Fox scouts brought news of the settlement, and during February 1730 large numbers of Foxes assembled along the Fox-Wisconsin waterway, then joined together to march on the Winnebago village. Envisioning a prolonged siege, the Foxes brought their families and food caches, determined that the Winnebagos responsible for the slaughter should be punished. They first attacked and killed two Winnebagos fishing on the lake, then surrounded and besieged the Winnebago village. After two days of fighting the Winnebagos requested a truce, claiming that "from the olden times of our forefathers . . . we have always been your true brothers." "Why," asked the Winnebagos, "should you attack us today without saying anything?" Although they admitted that they had "dipped our hands in your blood," the Winnebagos claimed that they had been forced to join in the recent attack by the Ottawas and the Menominees. They also admitted to capturing two Fox warriors whom they recently had delivered to the Menominees, but they attempted to appease the Foxes by offering them four Menominees who had been visiting in their village. Two of these hapless visitors were decapitated, and their heads were presented to Fox war chiefs, while the others were bound by the Winnebagos and surrendered to the Foxes as live captives.[23]

Still angered by the Winnebago treachery, the Foxes accepted the Menominees, but they also demanded that their enemies surrender the Winnebagos who had guided the Ottawas and the Chippewa to the Fox hunting party. When the Winnebagos refused, the Foxes renewed their firing. Although the Winnebagos could not break the siege, they had a large quantity of corn stored in their village, and they believed the Foxes would tire of the attack and eventually retreat back up the Fox River. Yet the Foxes were determined, and they too possessed adequate stores of corn. Moreover, both sides believed they could supplement their food supplies by fishing. The siege continued.[24]

At Green Bay, Marin was unaware of the siege, but after several weeks the Menominees sensed something was amiss when small parties of Winnebago warriors failed to make their usual appearance to trade in the Menominee village. In addition, the party of Menominees visiting in the Winnebago village had failed to return (some had already been killed by the Winnebagos or handed over to the Foxes), and their kinsmen became alarmed for their safety. Menominee leaders dispatched scouts to Little Lake Butte des Morts who returned and reported that the Foxes were besieging the Winnebago village. They also informed the Menominee chiefs that the beleaguered Winnebagos desperately needed reinforcements.[25]

The chiefs promptly notified Marin, who agreed to lead a war party to the Winnebagos' assistance. After moving their families to the small French fort, about three dozen Menominee warriors, accompanied by Marin and five French soldiers, left Green Bay for the Winnebago village. They arrived at the lake on March 19, 1730, but found they could not penetrate the Fox lines to reach the Winnebagos. While Marin was attempting to fortify his camp, the Foxes discovered the newcomers and rushed toward the French and their allies. Marin's warriors repulsed the attack and drove the Foxes back toward their original positions. The Foxes then ceased firing and called to the Menominees, asking why the latter were attempting to rescue the Winnebagos, a "treacherous people" who had already sacrificed the four Menominee visitors in a futile effort to escape the Foxes' retaliation. The Fox strategy at first seemed successful. Since the Menominees had no previous knowledge that the Winnebagos had either surrendered or killed their kinsmen, they were incensed over the treachery. They vowed that they now perceived the Winnebagos as no better than the Foxes. Although hard pressed, Marin eventually persuaded the Menominees to at least postpone any quarrel with the Winnebagos until after the Foxes had been defeated.[26]

Angered over their failure to seduce the Menominees, the Foxes renewed their assault on Marin's encampment, but when the French and the Menominees again repulsed their attacks, they asked for another parley. Bowing to Menominee pressure, Marin reluctantly agreed, and when the Fox spokesmen entered the French camp, they again tried to convince the French and the Menominees that the

Fox siege of the Winnebago village was justified. Assuring Marin that the quarrel was a personal vendetta between themselves and the Winnebagos, Fox spokesmen argued that the warfare had little to do with Onontio. Why, they asked, should Marin and his followers "display such ardor on behalf of people who are so little worthy of thy protection?" According to the Foxes, the Winnebagos, their former allies, now were "cowards" who had delivered "into our hands thine own children [the Menominee visitors] that we might drink their blood." But Marin replied that since their defection from the Foxes, the Winnebagos had become "the true children of Onontio," and if they had unjustly killed two of the Menominees in their village, he would punish them himself; he did not want nor need the Foxes' assistance.[27]

Frustrated, the Foxes withdrew from the French camp, and there was desultory sniping from both sides. But the advantage now passed to the French and their allies. During the following night Marin and his reinforcements were able to cross the lake and reach the Winnebago village. The Foxes again attempted to persuade Marin and the Menominees that their quarrel was only with the Winnebagos, but Marin refused further negotiations and the Foxes remained reluctant to storm the Winnebago palisade. Since the siege had now continued for over a month, both sides had exhausted their food supplies. Disheartened, the Foxes decided to withdraw. They first evacuated many of the women, children, and older tribespeople who had accompanied them to the lake; then, late in March, the warriors abandoned their positions under cover of darkness. When Marin and his allies awoke on March 25, 1730, the Foxes were gone.[28]

Although both the Foxes and the French-allied Indians suffered similar casualties (about twelve to fifteen killed or seriously wounded) during the siege, the outcome of the battle proved to the Foxes' disadvantage. Not only had they failed to adequately punish the Winnebagos, they also had been unable to exploit the potential quarrel between the Winnebagos and the Menominees. Moreover, their fate was sealed. They now were completely isolated, surrounded by tribes loyal to Onontio. For once even the Kiyagamohag realized that the Foxes could no longer maintain their position of independence. No longer were they masters of the Fox-Wisconsin waterway. Now most Foxes agreed that their redemption lay in either flight, or accommodation.[29]

During May 1730, Fox leaders from all the villages assembled on the Fox River, in the center of the Fox homeland, to discuss their options. Although they reached a general consensus that they no longer could defy the French if they remained in Wisconsin, Wisaka's people still disagreed among themselves over what actions should be taken. Again, many of the older chiefs argued that their attack on the Winnebago village had satisfied the requirements of the vendetta against that tribe, and that they could rely upon Onontio's goodwill to understand that the siege had been justified. If they would lay down their arms and travel to Montreal, they would receive Onontio's mercy and could remain at peace in Wisconsin.[30]

Many members of the Kiyagamohag disagreed. Unwilling ever to make peace with Onontio, the more-militant Foxes preferred to abandon Wisconsin in favor of a new home that would offer them independence. Runners were sent to the Sioux and the Iowas to ascertain if they would renew their offers of refuge, but Onontio and the French traders had plied their trade well, and those tribes replied that the Red Earth People no longer would be welcome west of the Mississippi. The Kickapoo and Mascouten defection obviously precluded any relocation in northern Illinois, and the Foxes were surrounded on all other sides by tribes whose animosity they had nurtured for generations. From only one people was there any chance

of succor, and this sanctuary lay far to the east, a journey
of eight hundred miles. And yet for many Foxes there was
no alternative. They refused to accept Onontio's yoke.
They could not remain in Wisconsin.[31]

Runners were sent to the Iroquois. During the first week
of June 1730 those Foxes seeking a new sanctuary dispatched messengers to the Senecas, asking for permission
to resettle in the Iroquois homeland. The Fox emissaries
carried two red stone axes that they gave to the Senecas.
They also asked both the Iroquois and some Mohican
tribesmen currently settled in Pennsylvania to rise up and
strike the French. Indeed, several younger Fox war chiefs,
who earlier had spent some time in the Iroquois villages,
instructed the messengers to ask the Senecas living near
Niagara to dispatch a war party westward to meet the
Foxes as they emigrated toward the east. In addition, other
Fox runners were sent among the Weas and the Miamis,
tribes living along the upper Wabash, a region through
which the Foxes would be forced to pass. Since these tribes
recently had quarreled with the Potawatomis and other
pro-French Indians, and since they occasionally traded
with British merchants from New York or Pennsylvania, the
Foxes asked for permission to pass through their villages.[32]

The Foxes received a mixed reply. Ironically, the Weas
and the Miamis, tribes ostensibly closer to the French, responded favorably and informed the Foxes that they would
not oppose their emigration. Indeed, they even promised
to supply them with provisions as they passed through
their villages. In contrast, though the messengers to the
Iroquois were cordially received, the latter were noncommital in their response. They accepted the red stone axes,
but after the Fox messengers left for Wisconsin, French
Jesuits and Jean Coeur, a renegade French trader among
the Senecas, convinced the Iroquois to remain neutral and
to surrender the axes to Beauharnois. In retrospect, it
seems that the Senecas were reluctantly willing to accept

the Foxes into their homeland, but they refused to create any diversionary action or otherwise assist the Fox emigration.[33]

Assuming that the Iroquois would welcome them with open arms, the Foxes had made plans for their departure. Although the young men boasted that they soon would be dwelling among the longhouses of the Senecas, more-seasoned warriors knew that the journey would be a long and arduous one. Burdened by their women, children, and old people, the emigrants would be forced to travel slowly, hunting for food as they trekked eastward. Some Fox warriors suggested that they skirt the southern tip of Lake Michigan, then proceed through the St. Joseph Valley toward Detroit, but others warned that such a direct route would expose them to powerful enemies: the Potawatomis, the Ottawas, and the Hurons. Why not journey south to "the Rock," the site of La Salles's old fort on the Illinois River, then turn east across the Grand Prairie of the Illinois? There they might encounter the Illinois Confederacy, but better to risk a confrontation with these demoralized "women" of the south than the more warlike tribes from the lakes. Moreover, once on the prairie, they would be isolated from the more highly traveled trade routes. If Wisaka was smiling, they might reach the Wea villages along the Wabash undetected.[34]

But Wisaka turned his face from his people. Several Fox women had married Kickapoo and Mascouten husbands, and when these learned of the Fox exodus, they warned their respective tribes. At first French officials in the Illinois Country discounted the disclosures, and in early June 1730, when approximately three hundred warriors and six hundred women and children left their villages along the Fox-Wisconsin waterway, their enemies were unaware of their departure. Traveling slowly, they crossed out of the hardwood forests of southern Wisconsin into the parklands of northern Illinois, where they followed the gentle uplands between the Rock River and the Fox River of

Illinois. Here the Foxes passed through a region of prairies interspersed with small woodlands where towering groves of oaks, maples, and elms clustered wherever the creeks or sloughs provided sufficient water. In early July they reached the Illinois River, just downstream from its juncture with the Fox, and because the water was relatively low they crossed to the southern bank with little difficulty. Pausing in their journey, the Foxes established a temporary settlement. While tribal elders and children recuperated around the campfires, women repaired clothes and sewed new moccasins. Meanwhile, hunters scoured the surrounding prairies, hunting meat for their trek to the Wea villages along the Wabash.[35]

Unfortunately, however, while stalking bison on the prairie southeast of their camp, Fox warriors also encountered hunting parties from the Illinois Confederacy. Emboldened by the recent Kickapoo and Mascouten defections, late in the spring part of the Cahokia tribe of the Illinois Confederacy had reestablished a village adjacent to the Rock, just fifteen miles downstream from the temporary Fox encampment. Unaware of the new Cahokia village, the Foxes were surprised to find their enemies north of Lake Peoria, and the initial encounter between the two hunting parties resulted in a brief skirmish. Neither side suffered serious casualties, but the Foxes captured seventeen of their enemies. The prisoners were carried to the Fox camp, but other Illinois hunters escaped and brought news of the skirmish back to the Cahokia village.[36]

In the Fox encampment reports of the encounter triggered considerable consternation. The Foxes had hoped to reach the Wea villages undetected, but now the Cahokias knew their location and might send runners to the French and their allies, bringing additional enemies to oppose the migration. Meeting in hurried council, Fox leaders sent a small delegation of warriors to the Cahokia village to assure their enemies that they would return the captives and only wanted to continue their journey in peace. The envoys hastened to the Cahokia encampment, but on their arrival they were received with ill-concealed hostility. Although the Cahokias agreed to meet with them in council, decades of resentment boiled over, and in the midst of the negotiations an Illinois warrior sprang forward and stabbed one of the Fox delegates with his hunting knife. The wound was not serious, and the Cahokia elders sent their kinsman from the council house, but the act was such a flagrant violation of intertribal protocol that it incensed the visitors. Breaking off the negotiations, the Fox delegation stormed from the village and returned to the Fox camp. Before leaving, however, they learned that the Cahokias already had sent runners to several villages of Kickapoos and Mascoutens who also were hunting in the region. Any hope of a peaceful emigration to the Iroquois ended.[37]

Enraged by the Illinois attack, the Foxes enacted a terrible and ill-conceived vengeance. Most of the Cahokia prisoners captured in the recent skirmish, including the son of a prominent Cahokia village chief, were first tortured, then burned to death. Meanwhile, scouts dispatched to ascertain the locations of the Kickapoos and Mascoutens returned to report that these former allies—now enemies—were approaching from the northeast. Aware that their warriors would be outnumbered, the Fox war chiefs decided to lead their people away from the river onto the vastness of the prairie. They were still encumbered by their children and old people, but if the Foxes first turned south, then east, they still might elude their converging enemies.[38]

Late in July the Foxes abandoned their camps near the Illinois River and trekked due south onto the Grand Prairie. Here they left behind the pleasant blending of grasslands and hardwood groves that they had encountered north of the Illinois River, and entered into a seemingly endless sea of high prairie grasses interrupted only rarely by the small "islands" of trees whose green profiles broke the horizon's monotony. Indeed, the manitous had so flattened this region that the summer rains which fell on these grasslands drained very poorly, and the prairies were interlaced with numerous shallow, muddy sloughs that markedly impeded the Foxes' progress. In addition, the tall grasses swarmed with clouds of green and black flies whose bites were painful and which seemed particularly to harass the children. Their war chiefs urged them on toward the Wabash, but the women and old people were exhausted by the heat and humidity. The Foxes traveled slowly.[39]

Cahokia scouts monitored their journey. The Cahokia village near the Rock could not muster sufficient warriors to seriously threaten the emigrants, but they had sent runners to the Kickapoos, Mascoutens, and other villages of the Illinois Confederacy, and they were aware that the Foxes' progress was slowed by their elders and children. If Cahokia war parties could harass the Fox column and further impede their flight, they might retard the emigrants until additional Kickapoos, Mascoutens, and other Illinois warriors could arrive and completely cut off their retreat. Accordingly, in early August, Cahokia war chiefs from the village near the Rock led a large party who intercepted the Foxes early in the morning of August 4, 1730, as the latter were fording a small river that traversed the prairie in east-central Illinois. Although the Cahokias posed little threat to similar numbers of heavily armed Fox warriors, Fox war chiefs realized that as long as their families were straggling across the prairie or fording the stream, they would be vulnerable to their enemies. In response, they herded their women and children into a small grove of trees that overlooked the river, and the Kiyagamohag rushed forward to meet the Cahokias. Most of the younger Fox warriors remained confident. In the past, their fathers often had routed these servants of Onontio. If their medicine was good, the Foxes would carry additional Cahokia scalps to their new home among the Senecas.[40]

But their medicine proved empty. Instead of confronting the Foxes in pitched battle, the wily Cahokias skirmished, then retreated, yet when the Foxes in turn withdrew back toward the grove, the Cahokias again advanced, engaging the Foxes from a distance. Again the Foxes charged, and again the Cahokias fell back, but they refused to leave the scene of the battle, and like wolves around a bison herd, they forced the Fox warriors to maintain their defensive perimeter. The skirmishing continued throughout the morning until shortly before noon, when from the shelter of the grove several of the Fox women noticed additional Indians advancing south across the prairie. To the Foxes' dismay, the Cahokias had been joined by the Potawatomis, the Kickapoos, and the Mascoutens.[41]

For the Foxes, a bad situation immediately grew much worse. The Cahokias had been a nuisance, a harassing enemy who prevented the Foxes from mounting an orderly march, but they had posed no serious threat to the survival of the emigrants. In contrast, the large war party of Potawatomis, Kickapoos, and Mascoutens numbered almost two hundred warriors and were led by Maudoche and Okia, Potawatomi war chiefs infamous for their hatred of Wisaka's people. Abandoning their attack on the Cahokias, the Fox warriors now joined their women and children in the small grove and hurriedly prepared to defend themselves. They did not wait for long. Emboldened by the arrival of their allies, the Cahokias advanced in strength on the Foxes' southwestern perimeter, while the northern Indians attacked from the opposite direction. Sheltered by the trees, the Fox warriors repulsed the initial assaults, but their enemies pressed forward, firing indiscriminately at the women and children crouched down behind the trees for protection. The fighting continued throughout the afternoon, and at nightfall, when both sides ceased their firing, the Fox war chiefs learned that had lost seven killed and thirty wounded, including many women and children. The Cahokia casualties remain unknown, but the northern Indians sustained losses similar to the Foxes', including the death of Okia.[42]

Yet Okia's death was a Pyrrhic victory. His comrades still surrounded the grove. The Fox route to the Wea villages was blockaded. Aware that they now faced a prolonged siege, Fox war chiefs conferred through the night. They had carried a considerable supply of lead and powder with them from Wisconsin, and since their hunting parties had returned with several deer and bison before their initial encounter with the Cahokias, the Fox chiefs believed they could withstand a lengthy siege. They were more concerned about providing their women and children with adequate protection from the musket balls and arrows of their enemies. Accordingly, during the next several days, they worked diligently at fortifying their position. At night, under the cover of darkness, Fox warriors felled many of the smaller trees in the interior of the grove, trimmed the logs, and then erected them into a loose palisade with which they enclosed the grove, except on the south side where the stream's embankment formed a natural barricade. Meanwhile, the women dug a series of shallow trenches along the palisade's perimeter and piled the branches trimmed from the fallen trees into screens designed to shield the interior of the Fox fort from their enemies' observation. The women and children also excavated shallow "burrows" about four feet deep, which were first covered with reed mats, then topped with two feet of soil, providing the Foxes with bulletproof dwellings. In addition, a series of shallow ditches were dug from shelter to shelter, connecting the dwellings with another covered trench leading from the perimeter of the fort down to the small river. From the Fox perspective, they might be surrounded, but their fortified position seemed to assure them that they would not be overrun. Moreover, Fox leaders were confident that neither the Cahokias nor their

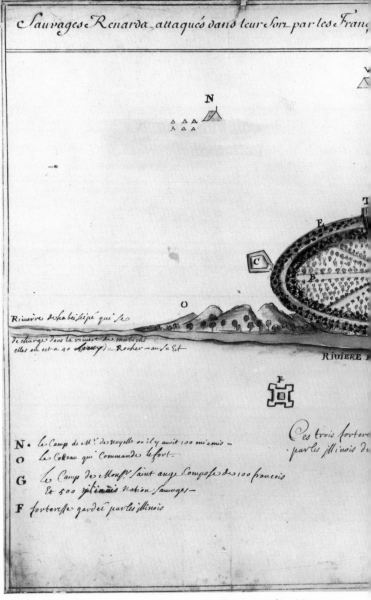

Map of the great siege of the 1730 Fox fort on the Illinois Grand Prairie before the battle on September 8–9, 1730. Drawn by an anonymous member of the Canadian contingent, this map places the fort one hun-

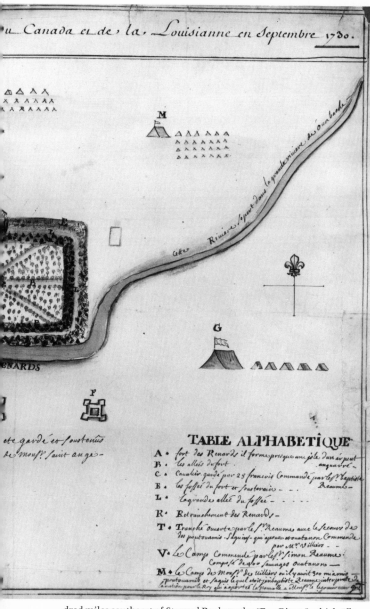

TABLE ALPHABETIQUE

A • fort des Renards il forme presque une isle dun ne peut
B • les allées du fort.   anquervé .
C • Cavalier gardé par 28 francois Commandé par le S.t Baptiste
E • les fossés du fort et souterain - - - .   Reaume .
L • la grande allée du fossé - - - - -
R • Retranchement des Renards -
T • Tranché ouverte par le S.t Reaume avec le secours de
    les poutouamis Saquis qui ayant et ouatanon Commandé
    par M.r Villiers - -
V • le Camp Commendé par le S.t Simon Reaume
    composé de 200 sauvages ouatanons -
M • le Camp de Mons.r des Villiers où il y avoit 300 miamis
    poutouamis et saquis lequel etoit jn baptiste Reaume interprete
    canadien pour le Roy qui a aporté la nouvelle a M.r le gouverneur

dred miles southeast of Starved Rock on the "Fox River," which "flows into the great Wabash River." From the Bibliothèque nationale, Paris, cliché 62C19303.

Potawatomi, Kickapoo and Mascouten allies had the stomach for a prolonged siege. The Fox exodus might be delayed, but it would not be terminated.[43]

But again they miscalculated. On August 6 or 7 runners from the Cahokia village near the Rock brought news of the Fox migration to the other towns in the Illinois Confederacy that were clustered around Fort de Chartres, in southern Illinois. After listening to the messengers, about three hundred Illinois warriors from these villages formed a huge war party and immediately set out to assist their kinsmen, who now were in pursuit of the Foxes. Meanwhile, Robert Groston de St. Ange, the French commander at the post, rallied almost one hundred French soldiers and Creole traders residing near the fort, and on August 10, 1730, after enlisting about one hundred other Illinois warriors, he too marched forth to join the campaign. En route up the Illinois river valley St. Ange's followers joined with the large Illinois war party who had preceded them, and on August 17 the combined army of almost five hundred French and Illinois arrived at the site of the battle.[44]

St. Ange's forces were not the only French reinforcements. The Potawatomis, Kickapoos, and Mascoutens who had arrived at the battle on the afternoon of August 4 had also sent runners to French posts in Michigan and Indiana. On August 6 an exhausted Mascouten messenger had stumbled into Fort St. Joseph to inform Nicolas-Antoine Coulon de Villiers of the impending battle. After dispatching couriers to Detroit and to the Miamis, Villiers assembled approximately three hundred Sacs, Potawatomis, and Miamis, and on August 10 he too marched forth to wage war on the Foxes. Although Villiers's force temporarily became lost on the prairie, they arrived at the battle site before noon on August 17, 1730. Later in the day they were joined by twenty-eight French and four hundred Weas and Piankashaws led by the grizzled old Simon Réaume, the senior resident trader at Fort Ouiatanon.[45]

The arrival of the Weas and the Piankashaws boded particularly ill for the Foxes. On August 4, when they first had been confronted by the Cahokias, the Mascoutens, the Kickapoos, and the Potawatomis, the Fox war chiefs had dispatched two younger warriors east across the prairies to ask the Weas for assistance. The Weas initially had agreed, but when Réaume learned of the request he met with the Wea chiefs, "gave the war chant," and through "his influence and authority stirred blood against blood, and relatives and friends though they [the Foxes and Weas] were, he made them enemies." Now, instead of coming to the Foxes' assistance, the Weas and their Piankashaw kinsmen seemed to be allied with their enemies.[46]

And yet not all of the manitous had turned from Wisaka's people. Although the Sacs and the Weas ostensibly had joined the French and their allies, both tribes still were bound by numerous blood ties to the Foxes, and the bonds of kinship transcended more-recent political alliances. The Illinois, the Potawatomis, and the Mascoutens earlier had rebuffed Fox offers of negotiations, but with the arrival of the Sacs and the Weas, the Foxes redoubled their efforts. They achieved some temporary success. Meeting under a flag of truce, the Foxes returned almost all of their remaining Illinois prisoners and pleaded with St. Ange, Réaume, and Villiers to allow them to continue on to the Senecas. When the Frenchmen refused, Fox leaders offered to surrender and proposed that their people should be divided among the Sacs, the Weas, the Piankashaws, and other tribes where their captors "could teach them of Onontio's peace." Villiers was almost persuaded, but Réaume and especially St. Ange refused any compromise. Reflecting the steadfast enmity of the French in the Illinois Country, they argued that the second proposal only masked a Fox escape attempt. Rather than diminish Fox influence, it would permit them to spread their "corruption among those with whom they would be living." The request was denied. No quarter would be given.[47]

Meeting secretly with the newly arrived Sacs and Weas, other Fox envoys were more successful. In a series of clandestine councils, the Foxes persuaded these newcomers to surrender a small quantity of their surplus food and ammunition. In addition, Fox spokesmen pleaded with the Sacs to honor their kinship obligations, and after considerable discussion those Sacs who had relatives within the Fox camp agreed to provide sanctuary for many of their kinsmen's children. When the councils ended, the Sacs carried these Fox children back to their encampment. Although many of the Fox parents were reluctant to give up their sons and daughters, at least the children would be spared if the French and their allies overran the Fox position. Moreover, while the children were in their enemies' camp they would not further deplete the Foxes' rapidly diminishing supply of provisions; and finally, if the Foxes escaped their enemies, the children eventually would be reunited with their parents. The decision to relinquish the children was difficult, but it was a wise one.[48]

The Sac acquisition of the Fox children did not go unnoticed. Suspicious of the Sac intentions, the Illinois warned both St. Ange and Réaume that the Sacs and the Weas were plotting to facilitate a Fox escape, and Réaume immediately stormed to the Sac camp and denounced them for accepting the Fox children. To prevent any further contact between the two tribes, St. Ange announced that he and the contingent of French and warriors from the Illinois Country would now maintain a sporadic fire upon the Fox fort. The Sacs or other tribes would risk their own lives if they ventured too close to the Foxes.[49]

Although they remained reluctant to risk a frontal assault, St. Ange and Villiers tightened their siege of the Fox position. They fortified the separate camps of all the tribes present at the siege to protect their occupants from any Fox sortie, and Villiers ordered his men to excavate a trench to approach the Fox fort on its northeastern perimeter. Villiers intended to use the ditch to gain access to the Fox palisade, which he hoped to set ablaze with torches, but the Foxes showered the workers with arrows and musket balls, and the trench eventually was abandoned. Meanwhile, Villiers also constructed two "cavaliers," or fortified gun towers, on the northern perimeter, which allowed the French and their allies to fire down into the Fox position.[50]

Inside the Fox fort, conditions deteriorated. Although their heavily fortified palisade and maze of trenches protected the Foxes from the French gunfire, the prolonged siege exacted a toll of a different nature. When the blockade had first begun, Fox leaders had collected and distributed the game that their warriors recently had killed on the prairie, but none of the war chiefs had foreseen a siege of such duration. Unlike their enemies, the Foxes could not send out hunting parties to periodically replenish their larders, and although Fox envoys had been able to secure small quantities of provisions from the Sacs and the Weas, as the blockade continued, their food supplies diminished. Moreover, the heat and confinement also plagued their old people and children. Several trees left standing within the fort provided shade to part of the trenches, but as the August humidity bore down across the prairie, the other burrows steamed like misshapen sweat lodges. Sequestered in these earthworks, the elders and children suffered accordingly.[51]

Again the Foxes attempted to negotiate, and again the French rebuffed their efforts. Late in August, Fox leaders persuaded the Sacs again to intercede for them, and although Villiers and St. Ange agreed to another parley, the Frenchmen refused any compromise. To these final councils the Fox envoys brought several of their infants, hoping that the French and their allies would be moved by the children's suffering, but both Villiers and St. Ange informed them "that all their words were in vain, and that they were not to come back again." Indeed, to emphasize their point, the French violated the flag of truce and fired on the hapless envoys and their children as they retreated toward the Fox palisade. None of the Foxes were injured, but the volley reinforced the hopelessness of their position. Fox promises or pleas no longer were accepted. This time their enemies were determined.[52]

If it was possible, on September 1, 1730, the Fox position worsened. At midday Fox observers reported that an unidentified party of warriors was approaching the French encampment from the east, and at first spirits within the palisade began to rise. The French obviously were surprised by the intrusion, and Fox warriors watched in exhilaration as the French and their allies began to form a skirmish line in anticipation of the newcomers. Rumors circulated amidst the trenches that the Senecas finally had sent a large war party to the Foxes' rescue, and even the old people peered over the top of the embankments, hoping to catch a glimpse of these potential allies. But Wisaka was ever a trickster, and he often tantalizes his people before frowning upon them. As the warriors drew nearer, the Foxes watched in dismay while the French and their allies threw down their arms and shouted cries of welcome. The newcomers were not the Iroquois; they were a party of almost two hundred Hurons, Potawatomis, and Miamis who had come to reinforce the besiegers. Led by Nicolas-Joseph des Noyelles, the French commandant at Fort Miamis, the Hurons also carried specific instructions from Governor General Beauharnois forbidding any negotiated settlement. The Fox enemies had increased, and the uncompromising decisions of Villiers and St. Ange now had official sanction.[53]

And still the Foxes persisted. By the first week of September the cicadas singing in the grove above their heads reminded them that summer soon would be over. Desperately short of food, their women were forced to supplement their meager supplies of corn by boiling their spare clothing and moccasins. On September 8, 1730, the Fox war chiefs met in council, and after conferring with tribal elders they decided to make one last plea to Wisaka not to forsake his people. Sacred clan bundles were brought forward, medicine drums were unwrapped, and while tribal shamans and other people with powerful medicine chanted, the drumbeats carried their message to the manitous. Mamasa, a medicine man from the Bear clan, led in the singing, and when the drumming stopped, two young warriors from the Wolf clan carried their sacred wolf skin down through the trenches to the river, where they miraculously were protected from the French musket balls that fell around them. Following the instructions of the shamans, when they reached the riverbank the two warriors attempted to sweep the wolf skin lightly over the river's surface, which their medicine people promised would cause part of the water to ascend into the air and create a fog. But to their dismay one of the warriors stumbled and immersed the skin beneath the water, and when they retracted it and brought it back into the fort, the elders found it was saturated.[54]

At first their medicine seemed impotent. Early in the afternoon the Foxes learned that some of the Illinois had abandoned the siege and were returning to their homes near Fort de Chartres, but the Fox war chiefs knew that the recent arrival of Noyelles's contingent more than compensated for these French losses. Meanwhile, their grandfather the sun beamed down upon the prairie, and although the weather remained humid, the manitous sent no fog to hide the Foxes. But late in the afternoon the breeze subsided, and a shaman still looking for a sign of Wisaka's favor watched as a long line of dark storm clouds arose across the northwestern horizon. The wolf skin had been soaked: Wisaka was sending more than fog. Assisted by the Thunderers, he drove the storm clouds south across the prairie, and an hour before sunset the Foxes and their besiegers were inundated in a storm so intense that it turned the twilight as dark as midnight. First rain, then hail fell in roaring torrents, and both the Foxes and their enemies sought sanctuary in any available shelter.[55]

Fearing that the Foxes might use the storm to mask an escape attempt, the French commanders urged their Indian allies to man the picket lines that surrounded the Fox camp, but the storm was so severe that the warriors refused. Meanwhile, within the palisade Fox war chiefs made preparations for a final dash toward freedom. Scouts sent out through the falling rain reported that their enemies had abandoned the picket lines, and gathering up the remainder of their meager possessions, the Foxes congregated on their fort's southern perimeter, planning to use the access trenches that led down to the river as the initial routes for their escape. At midnight, with the rain still falling, they moved silently through the trenches, then formed in small groups and crossed the river toward freedom. The initial exodus was led by Mamasa. Other leaders led other families or kinship groups, but they planned to reassemble a few miles southwest of the fort, then flee west across the prairie. Undoubtedly the Thunderers would hide their flight, and perhaps the heavy rain might even obliterate their trail. Seasoned warriors remained pessimistic, but they had little choice. To remain in the fort meant certain destruction.[56]

The night, the wind, and the rain both served and betrayed them. The storm and the darkness masked their withdrawal, and almost half their number successfully negotiated the French lines and passed onto the prairie, but the very conditions that facilitated their escape also precipitated their capture. The rain was cold, and the night held shadows, and shortly after midnight, as Fox parents carried their hungry, frightened children through the darkness, some children cried out in fear and bewilderment. The cries alerted the French, who had suspected an escape attempt, and they quickly raised their allies. Meanwhile, the remainder of the Fox refugees hurried through the trenches, but in their haste individuals became separated in the darkness. A Chippewa woman married to a Fox warrior lost her way, and in her confusion stumbled into one of the French outposts. Carried to Villiers, she divulged the plans for the evacuation.[57]

Within the French camp, all was chaos. Villiers and St. Ange wanted to send their forces in immediate pursuit, but the grizzled old Simon Réaume wisely counseled against such a decision. In the darkness it would be easy for converging forces of French and allied Indians to mistake one another for the Foxes, and they might kill more of their friends than their enemies. In addition, Réaume knew that many of the northern tribes still bore considerable enmity toward the Illinois Confederacy, and he feared that Potawatomi and Sac warriors might use the enshrouding darkness to settle old vendettas. Better to wait, he argued, until daybreak, when friend and foe could be distinguished. Meanwhile he again chided the Sacs for their lukewarm support of the French and for their friendship with the Foxes. If they really were Onontio's children, perhaps the Sacs should send out scouts to monitor the Fox retreat. If they took some of the Foxes as prisoners and reported the Fox escape route, they could truly prove their fidelity. Chagrined by Réaume's comments, small parties of Sacs followed in the Foxes' wake, and during the early morning hours they captured several scattered groups of Foxes. Some they brought back and surrendered to the French, but others they sequestered in the Sac encampment. Yet the scouts continued to report on the Fox retreat, and by sunrise the French were well apprised of their enemies' location.[58]

At daybreak, about twelve miles southwest of their abandoned fort, the remaining Foxes straggled westward

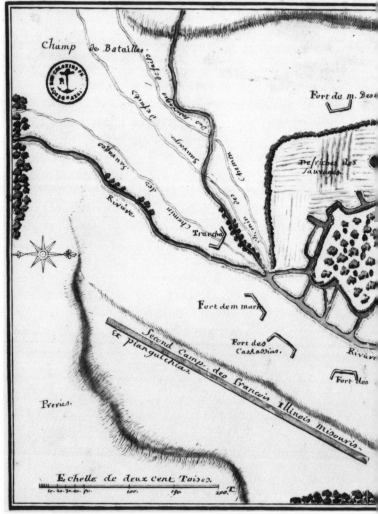

Map of the battlefield and Fox fort, September 8–9, 1730, on the Illinois Grand Prairie. It was drawn in New Orleans six months after the Fox defeat from the French officers' field reports and their post-battle conference. North is on the right. Note the Foxes' escape route to the

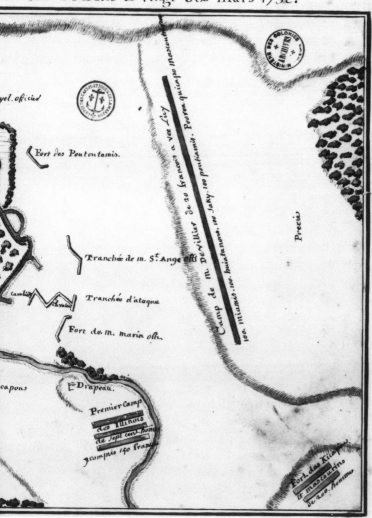

southwest, where they were defeated at one day's distance from the fort, on September 9. Archives nationales, Outre-mer, 1731 (Dépôt des fortifications des Colonies [Louisiane], 46C).

across the prairie. Before sunrise they had assembled all of their separated parties, and the war chiefs had urged them on toward safety. The storm had passed, but the grasslands were partially flooded and the Foxes were weakened by hunger and exhaustion. Expecting pursuit, the chiefs had placed the women, children, and elders at the head of their column, while the Kiyagamohag brought up the rear. In addition, several of the younger men trailed the main party, serving as scouts to warn the chiefs of any approaching enemies.[59]

They did not wait for long. Late in the morning the scouts reappeared and reported that the French and their allies were approaching from the northeast and would soon overtake the column. Bone-weary, the Fox war chiefs now formed their warriors into a skirmish line and hurried the women and children westward across the prairie. Much of the Fox gunpowder had become dampened during the flight through the rainstorm, but the remainder was distributed among those warriors who still retained their muskets. Other defenders bedecked themselves with fresh paint and tightened their bowstrings. Grim-faced, some watched in silence as the French and their allies also formed a long skirmish line, then advanced rapidly toward their position. Other Foxes sang their death song. At least they would die as warriors.[60]

The ensuing battle was brief and bloody. The Fox skirmish line contained no more than three hundred men and boys, while their attackers numbered almost twelve hundred warriors. Undaunted, the Foxes stood their ground, and they fought, and they died. In his official report, Villiers reported that the battle, while momentarily fierce, was a "rout." Another French officer boasted that since "our savages were fresher and more vigorous, . . . their [the Fox] ranks were at once broken and defeated." And with the warriors "broken," the French and their allies then turned on the old people, women, and children. Although

This war club, constructed of wood, a metal spike, and animal hair about 1830, is similar in design to weapons carried by the Mesquakies in their warfare against the French and their allies. Field Museum of Natural History, Chicago (neg. A111009, cat. 92029).

the fallen warriors had hoped that their stand would purchase an enlarged opportunity for their families' escape, in
this instance they gave their lives in vain. Weakened by
hunger and exhaustion, the Fox women and children fell
easy prey to their pursuers. When the slaughter ended,
over two hundred warriors and approximately three hundred women and children lay dead upon the prairie. The
remainder of the women, children, and other noncombat-
ants were taken as prisoners. About fifty warriors escaped,
but in their flight they discarded all their food and even
their weapons. Pursued by the Potawatomis, Kickapoos,
and Mascoutens, some of these individuals fled singly, rac-
ing back toward the forests that covered the Illinois river
valley, while others attempted to elude their pursuers by
hiding among the willows that blanketed the sloughs on
the prairie. Some were successful. Others were not. Those
who were hunted down were carried back to their enemies' camp, where in addition to many of the captured
women and children, they first were tortured, then
burned to death. Armageddon had ended. The Fox exodus
was over.[61]

In the aftermath of this massacre French officials exulted
in what they described as the "almost total destruction" of
the Foxes. In the following months Beauharnois estimated
that only 450 Foxes remained alive and that the majority
of those were held captive by French-allied Indians.
Several remnant hunting camps still clung to their ances-
tral homeland in Wisconsin, but those remnants numbered no more than thirty lodges, and Beauharnois reported that many of their inhabitants were "old women
without children, wandering without food or ammunition." Beauharnois admitted that the military action had

cost the French King almost 22,000 livres, but he assured his superiors that "peace and tranquility . . . now reign in the upper Countries." Moreover, other officials boasted that the volume of the fur trade would markedly increase and that "the routes to the Mississippi, as well as to the Sioux settlement will now be open. The Green Bay country will be tranquil, and we will be able to build a good settlement there. The farmers of Lake Erie's Detroit will cultivate their gardens in complete safety . . . this is a general peace whose authors deserve to be rewarded." For French officials in Canada, those few Foxes who had survived the holocaust no longer were a threat. It was time to bask in the king's favor. They believed the Fox wars were over.[62]

GENOCIDE

In the months that followed the great battle on the prairie, officials in Canada and the Illinois Country gloated over the French victory. Describing the massacre as a "brilliant action," Beauharnois boasted that he had "succeeded in almost totally destroying that nation" and had "reestablished tranquility in Canada, and communication with Louisiana." Regions such as Green Bay, the upper Mississippi Valley, and the Sioux Country, "where our Indians did not dare to hunt before," would again be open to trade. Even the Iroquois would be cowed, and French farmers at Detroit could now "cultivate their gardens in complete safety."[1]

In contrast, the surviving Foxes faced a barren future. About fifty warriors, accompanied by a handful of women and children, had escaped the slaughter on the prairie, and as these refugees made their way back to Wisconsin, they learned that many of their captured kinsmen (primarily women and children), who initially had been spared by the French and their allies, had been carried back to their enemies' home villages, where many of these captives had been tortured and killed. Others had been dispersed among the victors' camps, where instead of being adopted by their captors (the traditional fate of most prisoners whose lives had been spared), they had been relegated to slavery.[2]

The Fox refugees who had eluded capture were welcomed back to their old homeland by those members of the tribe who had chosen not to make the ill-fated emigration. Numbering about three hundred and fifty individuals, primarily older people, women, and children, this remnant was composed of those who were too old, infirm, or conservative to risk the journey. They had established a new village on the north bank of the Wisconsin, in modern Richland County, and were led by a war chief, named Kiala, who opposed the French but believed that Wisaka had chosen his people to remain near the Fox-Wisconsin waterway. Not surprisingly, the news of the massacre had a profound impact on Kiala and his followers. Devastated by the magnitude of the defeat, they met in hurried council and concluded that their only recourse now lay in accommodation. Kiala's village contained only fifty warriors, some of whom were little more than boys, and even if their ranks were buttressed by a similar number of warriors who had survived the recent holocaust, they could not hope to withstand additional attacks. Within Kiala's village were two warriors who had accompanied La Jemerais and the old chiefs to Fort St. Joseph, where they had met with Villiers in the summer of 1729. In addition, one of these warriors was married to a Potawatomi woman whose brother, Meguesiliguy, maintained a lodge near the French post. In desperation, the Foxes decided to send the two warriors to again plead their case before Villiers.[3]

In midwinter the two emissaries journeyed to the St. Joseph River, where they asked the Potawatomis to intercede in their behalf. Meguesiliguy agreed, and on January 19, 1731, the two Foxes met with Villiers, reminding him that during the past decade they both had personally intervened to save several captured Frenchmen. Pleading for Onontio's mercy, they admitted that other Fox warriors had not always honored their promises, but they placed the blame on former leaders such as Okimaouassen, the Kickapoo war chief White Robe, and other individuals who now were dead and safe from any French retribution. Pledging that the remaining Foxes were "resolved to yield to the will of Onontio, their father," the emissaries offered to remain as hostages with Villiers until the latter could arrange for Fox chiefs to meet with Beauharnois.[4]

Villiers was conciliatory in his reply. Although he asserted that their past deceptions had "caused the destruction of your villages," Villiers now believed that the remaining Foxes had "a good heart" and he was willing to grant them mercy. If they would remain at peace and trust "in the kindness that this good father [Beauharnois] has for all his children," they could be assured that Onontio's clemency would "save the rest of your nation." In addition, Villiers instructed one of the emissaries to return to Wisconsin and inform Kiala that he and several of his counselors must also journey to Fort St. Joseph, where they would be taken prisoner and sent to Montreal as hostages to ensure their people's continued cooperation.[5]

The two Foxes returned to Wisconsin, where they relayed Villiers's instructions to Kiala. Wary of Onontio's clemency, Kiala was reluctant to surrender, but he promised to keep his remaining warriors in their village and at peace. Meanwhile, the two warriors who initially had met with Villiers returned to the St. Joseph and accompanied the commander to Montreal. Arriving in September 1731, they were paraded before an assemblage of French officials, whom they petitioned for mercy. No longer a threat to New France, the Fox envoys pleaded with Beauharnois "to grant us peace in order to use it to atone through our submission for the enormous crimes that our unfortunate stubbornness made us commit." Echoing the requests previously made by Ouchala, they asked Onontio "to give us someone to govern us who, in representing your illustrious person, will inspire in the rest of our young men the respect and submission that they owe you."[6]

For Beauharnois the Fox submission was a personal triumph, and he was scathing in his reply. He denounced the Foxes for their efforts to form an alliance with the Senecas and informed the envoys that "all the reasons that you could bring to lessen the magnitude of your perfidy could never include anything which could be used as justification." According to the governor-general, the envoys were "unworthy" even to appear before him, but because of his "exceeding kindness," he would condescend to grant them their lives. He demanded, however, that they provide "other guarantees and additional security for your faithfulness." One of the envoys would be held hostage in Canada while the other was ordered to return to Wisconsin, where he would repeat French demands that Kiala and four other prominent Foxes journey to Montreal and throw themselves at Onontio's feet. If Kiala and his advisers failed to appear during the summer of 1732, Beauharnois vowed absolutely to destroy the remaining Foxes.[7]

Assuring the assembled officials that Kiala would comply, the lone Fox emissary left Montreal and started home toward Wisconsin. Meanwhile, Beauharnois broke his promises. Although the governor-general had informed the two Foxes that he would take no action until the following summer, the Fox messenger had hardly left Montreal before Beauharnois entertained a mixed delegation of Hurons from Detroit and Christian Iroquois from the Jesuit mission at the Lake of Two Mountains. Led by La Forest, a Huron war chief, these "domiciled" allies of New France requested Beauharnois's permission to mount a surprise attack against the remaining Foxes in Wisconsin. Envisioning the proposed campaign as an opportunity (at

The manuscript summarizing the 1731 Fox surrender terms. The importance of the surrender is indicated by the unusual red, white, and black decorative border on this official report. Photograph from the Bibliothèque nationale, Paris (Fonds français, nouvelles acquisitions, liasse 2551, f. 136).

little or no cost to the Crown) to absolutely annihilate his former enemies, Beauharnois gave the venture his tacit approval. Although he initially responded that he "could not *give* them such permission because he had granted the Renards their lives," he later admitted, "I fully believed that if I did not expressly *forbid* them, they would carry out their design." Thus Beauharnois hypocritically added that although he could not *approve* of the proposal, he also would not *oppose* their campaign and would "remain neutral in any disputes that might arise" between the two sides.[8]

Unaware of Beauharnois's betrayal, the Fox emissary carried the governor-general's promises back to Wisconsin. There he learned that in his absence Kiala had labored diligently to rekindle Fox bonds with their former allies. Utilizing the blood ties that still existed between the Foxes, and the Sacs, the Kickapoos, the Mascoutens, and even the Potawatomis, Kiala sent runners to those tribes' villages, pleading with them to remember their kinship obligations and to relinquish their Fox prisoners. He also played on their sympathies, reminding these tribes that they had played a major role in the Fox demise and asking that they take pity on his shattered nation. Chagrined by the accusations, many of the tribespeople acquiesced to Kiala's pleas and allowed their remaining Fox captives to return to Wisconsin. Moreover, some of these tribes, especially the Sacs, the Kickapoos, and the Mascoutens, seemed to nurture a growing doubt about French policies. If Onontio could annihilate the Foxes, what would keep him from turning his armies against their villages?[9]

But not all their neighbors were susceptible to Kiala's petitions. Fox lodges still held many Cahokia and Kaskaskia scalps, and the Fox-Illinois vendetta was bitter and of long duration. Illinois chiefs refused to meet with Fox emissaries, and after a village of Mascoutens, encamped near the southern shores of Lake Michigan, agreed to relinquish their Fox prisoners, an Illinois war party am-

bushed the freed hostages and their escorts as they journeyed back to Wisconsin. In the resulting melee, some of
the Foxes escaped, but the Illinois killed three Fox women
and took fifteen prisoners, including five warriors.[10]

Although the Illinois attack saddened the other captives'
homecoming, the Foxes still despised the Illinois and
believed that they had neither the strength nor the courage
to mount a major offensive. Yet a much more serious
threat loomed on the Fox horizon. Disaster followed in the
wake of the Fox warrior who recently had returned from
Montreal. Other enemies were approaching Kiala's village.[11]

Neither the Fox envoy nor Kiala were aware of Beauharnois's meeting with the Hurons and Christian Iroquois,
and they had no knowledge that in early October 1731
forty-seven Iroquois warriors had accompanied the Hurons
back to Detroit, where they made preparations for a winter attack on Kiala's village. Both the Hurons and the Iroquois hoped to solicit additional warriors, but when they
approached Ottawa and Potawatomi villagers living in the
Detroit region they received, at best, a noncommittal answer. Ottawa and Potawatomi chiefs informed them that
most of their young men already had left for their winter
hunt and advised them to wait until the following spring
when more warriors would be available. But the Hurons
and the Iroquois refused, and well supplied by Henri-Louis
Deschamps de Boishébert, the commander at Detroit, on
October 17, 1731, seventy-four Hurons, forty-seven Iroquois, and four Ottawas left the French fort en route to the
Wisconsin.[12]

They planned to enlist other allies as they passed
through southern Michigan and northeastern Illinois, but
they received only a lukewarm reception. Potawatomi villagers along the St. Joseph River abandoned their wigwams at the Huron and Iroquois's approach, pleading that
their young men were engaged in their winter hunt and
could not join the expedition. Indeed, according to the

Potawatomis, the Hurons and the Iroquois should turn back and wait until spring, when the Potawatomis grudgingly agreed that they would accompany them. By the time the expedition had reached the Chicago River winter had arrived and they were forced to build a permanent winter camp, where they left several members of their party who had become ill or injured. Proceeding to the Fox River of the Illinois, they encountered a village of Kickapoos, who also were frightened at their approach, and who reiterated the Potawatomi position. The Hurons and the Iroquois then turned west toward the Kishwaukee River, where they found a large encampment of Mascoutens who also were suspicious of the Iroquois. The Hurons attempted to assure them that the Iroquois were friends, but when they asked the Mascoutens to join their expedition, the latter replied that a winter campaign "would be too risky" and that the Foxes, who again "were very numerous," could not be destroyed. After a series of threats and promises, the Hurons and the Iroquois were able to coerce a party of ten Mascouten warriors supposedly to guide them to the Fox village, but after proceeding a day's march northwest into the driftless region of southern Wisconsin, the guides refused to go any farther. They informed the Hurons that they now had passed beyond "the boundaries that enclosed the children of Onontio" and had entered the Fox homeland. If the Hurons and the Iroquois journeyed on to the Wisconsin River, they "would meet nothing but Foxes."[13]

Trudging on toward the Wisconsin River, the Hurons and the Iroquois were buffeted by a blizzard that spilled almost a foot of snow across southern Wisconsin, piling up huge drifts where the forests were interspersed with small prairies. Weakened and disheartened, about forty of the party turned back to seek shelter with the sick and injured at the winter camp near Chicago, but forty Hurons and thirty Iroquois continued on, fashioning snowshoes to facilitate their passage through the forest. On a morning in mid-December they reached a small creek that flowed into the Wisconsin, and as they followed the stream they encountered three Fox warriors tracking deer across a small prairie.[14]

The Foxes were completely unaware of the approaching enemy. The warrior who had returned from Montreal had brought Beauharnois's promises that he would "grant them their lives" at least until the following summer when Kiala and his advisors were to journey to Montreal and meet with Onontio. Moreover, the winter of 1731–32 had been a time of rejoicing for the return of the former captives, who had increased the Fox ranks to over one hundred warriors and about three hundred women and children. The recent hostages had been welcomed back amidst a round of feasts and ceremonies. In addition, the thick snow that blanketed the region also seemed to provide a measure of protection. When the three deer hunters burst from the forest sounding the war cry and warning that the Hurons and the Iroquois were approaching, the village erupted into confusion. Some warriors immediately seized their muskets and struggled through the snow toward the village's periphery, attempting to establish a defensive position. Others, who had been visiting with friends, hurried back toward their lodges to search for weapons and warn their families. Some seemed surprised that the alarm included the Iroquois. For indeed, had not the Senecas traditionally extended the white wampum of friendship? The Hurons had always been treacherous, but Wisaka's people had long counted the Iroquois among their friends. Bewildered, Fox mothers gathered their children and sought refuge within the uncertain sanctuary of their lodges while the remaining warriors, now armed, stumbled through the snowdrifts in an attempt to join their kinsmen.[15]

Although the Hurons and the Iroquois were slightly outnumbered, they possessed some marked advantages. The Foxes mustered about ninety defenders, but many of these warriors were untried adolescents or older men who ordinarily would no longer have participated in intertribal warfare. In addition, the Hurons and the Iroquois still wore their snowshoes, while the Foxes were forced to trudge forward through snow that reached almost to their knees. And finally, the attackers were battle-hardened veterans who had the advantage of surprise and organization.[16]

The Hurons and the Iroquois quickly seized the upper hand. Although the slowly assembling Foxes began to fire at their attackers, the Hurons and the Iroquois advanced rapidly, mounting two volleys in prompt succession. Then, following the examples of their war chiefs, they discarded their muskets and fell upon the disorganized Foxes with their knives and tomahawks. In this hand-to-hand fighting, their snowshoes gave the attackers a marked advantage. Kiala's warriors were forced back into their village, where the retreat became a rout as Fox men, women, and children fled from burning lodges and struggled through the snow attempting to evade their pursuers. When the carnage ended, 70 Fox warriors, along with 80 women and children lay dead or bleeding in the snow. Approximately 140 women and children and an additional 14 warriors were taken as captives. Only 5 Hurons and no Iroquois were killed in the battle. Kiala and a handful of warriors escaped, but they fled without food or adequate clothing into the forest. To add insult to injury, the victors spared one wounded Fox war chief and six women, whom they sent to a smaller Fox village on the Mississippi with the message that "the Hurons and Iroquois had just eaten up their chief village where they would remain for two days; that if the Renards [Foxes] wished to follow them, they were free to do so but that as soon as they would see them they would begin by breaking the heads of all their women and children; that they would make a rampart of their dead bodies and afterward would endeavor to pile the remainder of the nation on top of them."[17]

After waiting two days, the Hurons and the Iroquois herded their prisoners together and marched them, via the Chicago encampment, back toward Detroit. But, as they proceeded around the southern tip of Lake Michigan, the victors became impatient with the slow pace dictated by some of the Fox elders and children. When it became apparent that these prisoners were having difficulty maintaining the desired pace, the Hurons and the Iroquois first tomahawked, then scalped them. In February 1732 approximately one hundred Fox prisoners, escorted by their captors, arrived at Detroit, but they left the bodies of fifty-six of their kinsmen, mostly women, children, or elderly, scalped and dead along their trail.[18]

Yet the killing had not ended. Afraid that the Hurons, like the other tribes, might eventually weaken their resolve and relinquish the Fox prisoners, Jean-Charles d'Arnaud, an officer at Detroit, warned the Hurons that if they permitted the Fox captives to live, they would be "nourishing snakes in their bosom." Inspired by such advice, the Hurons killed most of the remaining Fox prisoners. Delighted by such slaughter, Beauharnois praised D'Arnaud as "that quick-witted and very wise little man," and promoted him to the command of the French post at Fort Miamis. In addition, the governor-general also awarded medals to the Iroquois and Huron chiefs who commanded the winter expedition.[19]

While their relatives were marching and dying en route to Detroit, the seven Foxes released by the Hurons and Iroquois, accompanied by Kiala and the other refugees, arrived at the small Fox settlement on the Mississippi. There they found the remainder of their nation lodged in two camps: nine wigwams near the mouth of the Wisconsin, and three others on the Mississippi, at the site of Perrot's old wintering post, near modern Trempealeau. Unaware of Beauharnois's treachery, the smaller settlement of Foxes had provided shelter to René Godefroy de

Linctot and a small party of Frenchmen who were en route to reestablish a new French post among the Sioux. When news of the Huron-Iroquois attack reached these three lodges, warriors from the settlement disarmed the Frenchmen and accused Beauharnois of complicity in the massacre. In response, Linctot and his companions assured them that the attack had originated at Detroit "without their Father being informed of the expedition." Desperately wanting to believe that the Huron-Iroquois raid did not signal a renewed French campaign against their villages, the Foxes granted Linctot and his companions their lives, but the warriors did force the Frenchmen to return with them to the site of the recent battle. There they provided one of Linctot's companions with their entire winter store of furs and sent him after the Hurons and the Iroquois in a pathetic and futile attempt to ransom members of their families. Although the Frenchman, a Sieur Dorval, eventually overtook the war party and their prisoners, he simply kept the pelts and made no effort to retrieve the captives.[20]

In the following months the remaining Foxes reached the nadir of their existence. Reduced to about fifty warriors, including untried adolescents and men past their prime, and about ninety women and children, the Foxes withdrew from the Mississippi and returned to their old homeland. Now vulnerable to any tribe who hoped to curry favor with Onontio, the Foxes feared attacks by the Illinois Confederacy or the Winnebagos, who still nurtured a vendetta from the Fox siege of their village during February 1730. Some sought sanctuary among the Kickapoos and Mascoutens, but although those tribes expressed sympathy for the Foxes' plight, they refused them refuge because they were fearful of French retribution. The warrior whose wife was related to Meguesiliguy, the Potawatomi chief on the St. Joseph River, led two lodges of refugees to southern Michigan, but the Potawatomis too were afraid to anger Onontio, and although they provided the Foxes with corn, they turned them from their village. In desperation, twenty warriors and about forty women and children journeyed to Green Bay, where Villiers had reestablished a French post, and pleaded with him for mercy. Villiers remained noncommital, and the Foxes withdrew, finally joining with the rest of their kinsmen to establish a small village near "Lake Maramech" (probably Lake Pistakee, part of the Fox River drainage in modern Lake and McHenry counties), in northeastern Illinois.[21]

Desperately attempting to defend the remnants of their families, Kiala and his remaining warriors spent the summer of 1732 fortifying their village. Located on a narrow spit of land between the lake and a marsh, the camp was surrounded with an earthen wall and a palisade. Inside the walls Kiala's warriors constructed a blockhouse that served as both a firing position and a watchtower. Meanwhile, the Fox women and children planted small patches of corn, beans, and squash on the fertile land where the narrow spit containing their village adjoined the prairie.[22]

The French duplicity continued. Masking his treachery, Beauharnois released his remaining Fox hostage during the spring of 1732. He sent him back to Kiala with the message that "the attack just made upon them by the Hurons and the Iroquois was apparently the sequel of an old quarrel . . . ; [and] that I [Beauharnois] had not been informed of their expedition." Yet according to the governor-general, since Kiala and his advisers (who had spent the spring and summer trying to recover from the attack) had not journeyed to Montreal, they had "failed to observe the conditions that had induced me to grant them their lives." Consequently, the returning envoy was instructed to inform his kinsmen that they no longer enjoyed Onontio's (dubious) protection. In reporting his actions to officials in France, Beauharnois boasted, "I left their fate to the discretion of the other savages. We may consider that it is in good hands judging from the ardor they display, and I do not think there will be a question of any [live] Foxes next year."[23]

Beauharnois had every reason to believe his policy of genocide would be successful, for he knew that another expedition already had been launched against Kiala's village. In September 1732 another large war party of Hurons, accompanied by a scattering of Ottawas and Potawatomis, left Detroit intent on annihilating the remaining Foxes. En route across Michigan they passed through Potawatomi villages along the St. Joseph River where the tribesmen also reluctantly agreed to participate in the campaign. Yet the Potawatomis and Ottawas urged the Hurons to proceed on alone while they journeyed to Mascouten villages in northern Illinois to enlist those warriors in the expedition. Once the Mascoutens had been raised, the Potawatomis and the Ottawas would join with them and march to the Fox village. Agreeing to the Potawatomi proposal, the Hurons sent additional runners to the Illinois Confederacy, inviting them to participate in the proposed attack also. Then the Hurons, accompanied by a few Ottawas, journeyed on to the Fox village.[24]

This time the Foxes were prepared. Scouts hunting along the Des Plaines River brought news of the Huron approach, and when the invaders arrived at Kiala's village, they found the Foxes ensconced behind the fortifications. A small party of Huron scouts killed a Fox woman who left the palisade at daybreak to gather firewood, but the Foxes sent out a sortie, a skirmish occurred, and both sides sustained casualties. The Hurons then proposed a truce, promising to spare Kiala's people if they would only surrender. Inside the fort the Foxes played for time. Distrusting the Hurons, Kiala replied that he would accept the Huron proposal but preferred to wait for the arrival of the Potawatomis and the Mascoutens—tribes who still maintained important kinship ties to the Foxes. Meanwhile, Fox women and children strengthened the stockade and sharpened stakes to use as weapons in any final defense of the village. Trenches were dug to protect children and the elderly from arrows launched over the palisade, and the experienced warriors collected and dispensed the tribe's limited supply of lead and gunpowder. If this was to be their final stand, they planned to die like Foxes.[25]

But Wisaka, saddened by their plight, finally smiled upon his people. Three days after the Hurons' arrival the remainder of the Ottawas, the Potawatomis, and the Mascoutens reached the Fox village, and they were immediately joined by a large party of Peorias from the Illinois Confederacy. Although the Potawatomis and the Mascoutens still seemed unwilling to attack the Foxes, the Peorias nursed a host of old quarrels, and joining with the Hurons, they urged the other Indians to assault the Fox village. The Potawatomis and the Kickapoos reluctantly agreed, but when the besiegers moved forward, firing at the stockade, the Foxes repulsed the attack, then struck back, sending out a small party of hardened veterans who overran their retreating enemies, killing three of the Hurons and wounding several Peorias.[26]

Although the Hurons and the Peorias had pressed forward, the Potawatomis and the Mascoutens had only followed in their wake, and they had taken little part in the fighting. Now eager to secure a truce, Meguesiliguy, the Potawatomi chief from the St. Joseph River, called the other Indians into council and proposed to meet with the Foxes. Convinced that the Potawatomis, the Mascoutens, and most of the Ottawas would now render no further assistance in the siege, the sulking Hurons and Peorias agreed. On entering the Fox village, Meguesiliguy was welcomed by his wife's kinsmen. He then met with Kiala, who informed him that the Foxes distrusted the Hurons, and although they previously had agreed to surrender, they now were convinced that such an action would only result in their annihilation. He informed Meguesiliguy that his followers, though outnumbered, were prepared to fight to the death. They would not surrender. In response, Meguesiliguy assured him that the Potawatomis, the Mascoutens, the Sacs, and many other neighboring tribes now secretly sympathized with the Foxes and questioned Onontio's policy of genocide. Heartened by the Potawatomi's revelation, Kiala promised that if the besiegers withdrew, the Foxes would seek no retribution. In addition, in the spring of 1733 he would bring his people to Fort St. Joseph, Detroit, or one of the other French posts such as Green Bay or Ouiatanon.[27]

Pleased by the agreement, Meguesiliguy returned to his "allies" and convinced them to accept Kiala's terms. The Potawatomis, the Mascoutens, and the Ottawas eagerly abandoned camp and withdrew to their villages, while the sullen Illinois retreated to Lake Peoria. Also resentful, the Hurons marched back to Detroit, where they complained of their losses. Assuring Boishébert that if the Foxes failed to honor the agreement, he would "not fail to return to attack them," La Forest, the Huron chief who had led the winter campaign, sought more reliable allies. He again made plans to recruit the Christian Iroquois.[28]

At Lake Maramech Kiala spent the winter of 1732–33 meeting with his people and discussing their future. Huddled around their lodge fires, the Foxes were encouraged by Meguesiliguy's counsel of friendship, for they realized that they no longer had the strength to stand on their own. Reduced to just fifty warriors (forty adults and ten boys of twelve or thirteen years of age), Kiala and his advisors knew that if the French, the Hurons, the Illinois, and the Christian Iroquois came back in sufficient numbers, Wisaka's people would be destroyed. Their only hope now lay in a close alliance with some of their former friends.[29]

But to whom should the Foxes turn? Some of Kiala's advisers argued for a new alliance with the Kickapoos or the Mascoutens, traditional allies of Wisaka's people, who only recently, in 1728, had been seduced by Boucherville and the black robe held captive in their village. But other Foxes reminded their friends that these tribes recently had denied them refuge. Meguesiliguy's kinspeople suggested that they accept his invitation and join the Potawatomis along the St. Joseph River. Meguesiliguy was a proven friend, and during the previous spring his people had provided Fox refugees with corn. Fort St. Joseph, the French post near Meguesiliguy's village, was commanded by Nicolas-Antoine Coulon de Villiers, and although Villiers had led their enemies in the great battle on the prairie, in the aftermath he had interceded with Onontio in the Foxes' behalf. Other warriors argued that the St. Joseph Valley was too near Detroit, accessible to both Boishébert and the Hurons. They also reminded the council that Villiers had recently left Fort St. Joseph to reestablish a French post at Green Bay. In addition, the Sacs had rebuilt their village at that location. Survivors of the prairie battle recalled that during that encounter the Sacs had saved several Fox children and had provided their embattled parents with food and ammunition. Finally, like the Potawatomis, the Kickapoos, and the Mascoutens, the Sacs also had intermarried extensively with the Foxes. After careful deliberation, Kiala and his advisers reached their decision. In the spring of 1733 they abandoned their village on the shores of Lake Maramech and sought shelter among the Sacs in Wisconsin.[30]

At first things seemed to go well. The Sacs welcomed them into their village. Located near the rebuilt French post, the Sac village lay on the south bank of the Fox River at its juncture with Green Bay. Protected by a palisade, the village housed over 150 Sac warriors, many of whom had important kinship bonds with Kiala's people. The river and adjoining bay offered excellent fishing, and the Sac women were willing to share the bottomlands along the Fox River so that Kiala's followers could plant their cornfields. French merchants were active in the region, and the Foxes had their winter cache of pelts to trade. Honoring their truce with the Hurons, the Foxes remained at peace.[31]

Also honoring his pledge, Kiala surrendered to Villiers. In late April 1733, Kiala met with the French commander and informed him that he and three of his advisers were willing to offer themselves as hostages for the continued good conduct of their people. Delighted with his coup, Villiers quickly made plans to accompany the Fox warriors and two of their wives to Montreal, and in early May the Foxes, Villiers, and a small party of Frenchmen left Green Bay for Canada. In late June they arrived at Montreal, where a gloating Beauharnois divided the captives, sending Kiala, whom he described as "the instigator of all their misdeeds," with two of the men and the two Fox women, on to Quebec, where he ordered them imprisoned in preparation for deportation to the French West Indies. Villiers, the other Fox warrior (who earlier had been held hostage at Montreal), and the small party of Frenchmen were sent back to Wisconsin.[32]

Yet the French treachery continued. Before Villiers left for Green Bay, he met privately with Beauharnois, and the governor-general ordered him to continue the campaign against the Foxes. Although Kiala and the other chiefs had surrendered, and the Foxes had remained peacefully in the Sac village, Beauharnois instructed Villiers to return to Wisconsin, assemble a large war party of "the Nations which are faithful to us," and force all of the remaining Foxes to come to Montreal, where they would be divided into small groups and scattered among the Christian Iroquois and other "villages of settled savages." If the Foxes refused to leave Green Bay, Beauharnois ordered Villiers to "destroy them, . . . kill them without thinking of making a single prisoner, so as not to leave one of the race alive in the upper country."[33]

Villiers's initial response to those orders remains unknown. Unquestionably, Kiala and many of his counselors believed that among all the French commanders in the West Villiers was probably the most sympathetic to the Foxes. Yet Villiers also was well acquainted with the Sacs, and he knew that the two tribes had often intermarried. His familiarity with the Sacs, the Potawatomis, and the Kickapoos convinced him that those peoples had grown suspicious of Beauharnois's policy of genocide, and he knew that the Sacs would be reluctant to relinquish their Fox kinsmen. Anticipating trouble, Villiers returned to Green Bay via Michilimackinac, where he and Jean-Baptiste-René Legardeur de Repentigny, the French commander at that post, raised a large war party of Ottawas, Chippewas, and Menominees. Accompanied by about sixty French traders, the officers and warriors reached Green Bay in mid-September.[34]

They were not unexpected. Sac warriors, trading among the Chippewa villages on the northern shores of Lake Michigan, brought news of the force assembling at Michilimackinac, and as Villiers approached Green Bay, his scouts reported that both the Sacs and the Foxes had retreated into the fortified Sac village. Halting his expedition about one and one-half miles away from the village, on September 16, 1733, Villiers dispatched his eldest son, Ensign Nicolas-Antoine Coulon de Villiers, Jr., with about ten Frenchmen and fifty warriors to proceed around the Sac camp and block any escape up the Fox River. The rest of his party remained in camp while Villiers, two other sons, and about ten other French officers and soldiers proceeded on to the village.[35]

Aware of Villiers' intentions, the Sac chiefs refused to allow Villiers and his party to enter their village. Instead they met with him outside the gates of their stockade, where Villiers relayed Beauharnois's orders that the remainder of the Foxes must be surrendered. The Sac leaders withdrew a short distance to discuss the French request, but they came to no immediate conclusion. Growing impatient, Villiers informed the Sacs that all escape routes were blocked and that Repentigny and the remainder of the expedition were encamped just half a league from their village. Assuming he had intimidated the Sac chiefs, he instructed them to reenter their stockade and send out the Foxes; otherwise, "he would go and get them himself." Meanwhile, he ordered Repentigny and his men to advance and surround the village.[36]

The Sac chiefs withdrew into their village, but they did not surrender the Foxes. Inside the stockade the Sac village chiefs counseled caution, but they were angered by Villiers's role in these events. He long had lived in close association with their tribe, and he initially had given permission for the Foxes to settle in the Sac village. Now he seemed to be betraying them. Asserting that both Villiers and Onontio had broken their promises, younger warriors seized their weapons and rushed forward to the gate, vowing that neither Villiers nor any member of his party would enter the Sac village. The Fox participation in the initial phase of these affairs seems to have been minimal, but unquestionably they were encouraged by the Sac resistance.[37]

Still confident that he could intimidate his former friends, Villiers again approached the Sac village. Villiers was accompanied by two of his other sons; his son-in-law, François Regnard Duplessis; and by eight other Frenchmen. Most of the party were known to the Sacs, and Villiers obviously believed that the Indians would not fire on these acquaintances. He was wrong. He was unaware of the magnitude of the Sacs' resentment, and he grossly underestimated the ties that had been rekindled between the Sacs and the Foxes during his absence. At the gates of the Sac palisade Villiers encountered a party of young Sac warriors who both refused his demands to surrender the Foxes and barred his entrance. Several Sac chiefs advised him to withdraw, but Villiers persisted and attempted to force his way past the warriors into the village. Some of the warriors brandished their weapons, and as the French pushed forward, three shots were fired and one of Villiers' sons fell dead at his feet. Enraged, Villiers fired back and a general skirmish resulted. In the midst of this pandemonium, Makautapenase (Black Bird), a twelve-year-old Sac boy, raised a rust-flecked musket, took careful aim, and shot Villiers through the heart.[38]

Responding to the gunfire, Repentigny and his companions rushed forward to Villiers's assistance, but the Sacs at the gate now had been joined by others of their tribe and by most of the Foxes. As Repentigny approached, accompanied by the other French and their Indian allies, the Sac and Fox warriors surged forward to meet them, firing as they advanced. Repentigny and six of the other Frenchmen, including several officers, were killed. The Sacs and Foxes then retreated back into their village, and although the remaining French and Indians fired upon the palisade, they did little damage. Informed of the death of his father and brother, Ensign Nicolas-Antoine Coulon de Villiers abandoned his position on the Fox River and joined the forces besieging the Sac village, but the Sacs and Foxes defended themselves admirably, and their enemies gained no entrance.[39]

Inside the village Sac and Fox leaders met and pondered their future. For the Foxes, the scenario was distressingly familiar—within the past three decades they often had been besieged by the French and their allies—but for the Sacs it was an unfamiliar and frightening experience. Moreover, even their wisest elders could not remember any military engagements in which the Indians had killed two French commanders and such a large number of officers. Surely Onontio would exact a terrible revenge. After careful deliberation, Sac and Fox leaders decided to withdraw completely from the territory under Onontio's hegemony. Three days later, during the early morning hours of September 19, the Sacs and the Foxes abandoned their village and fled up the Fox River. They planned eventually to cross the Mississippi and seek sanctuary in Iowa.[40]

Informed of their flight, Ensign Nicolas-Antoine Coulon de Villiers mustered the remaining French and their allies and followed in the Sac and Fox wake. Eager to avenge the deaths of his father and brother, Villiers pushed his men forward, and late in the afternoon of September 20, 1733, he overtook the refugees at Little Butte des Morts, near modern Appleton, Wisconsin. Expecting pursuit, the Sacs and Foxes were well prepared, and while the women and children hurried on toward Lake Winnebago, the warriors took defensive positions along the banks of the river. The battle, which began at about four in the afternoon, was fought with considerable intensity. Well armed, the Sacs and the Foxes were determined to protect their fleeing families, and they repulsed repeated sorties by the French and their allies. By nightfall, when both sides disengaged, the Sacs and Foxes had lost between twenty-five and thirty warriors. But they had taken a heavy toll on their enemies. Almost all of the remaining French officers, including Cadet Louis Coulon de Villiers, another of Villiers's sons, had been wounded. Two other French officers had been killed. The Ottawas lost nine men, including their principal war chief; the Menominees counted six dead; and the Chippewas suffered two killed and several warriors wounded. Dispirited, the French and their allies withdrew to Green Bay while the Sacs and Foxes continued their exodus up the Fox River toward the Wisconsin.[41]

Villiers's death and the subsequent flight of the Sacs and Foxes caused considerable consternation in both Montreal and Paris. Previously assured by Beauharnois that the Foxes no longer posed a serious threat to New France, the French court informed the governor-general that Louis XV had received reports of the recent debacle with "surprise and distress," and he now considered "the peace as troubled as ever by the joining of the Sacs with what remains of the Foxes." Attempting to shift the blame, Beauharnois replied that the recent disaster "should be attributed less to the remnant of the Renard nation, than to the slight precautions observed by the sieur de Villiers." Lying through his teeth, Beauharnois stated that he had warned Villiers "to adopt only the gentlest measures to secure the subjugation of the Renards" and that "the misfortune that happened . . . was impossible for me to foresee owing to the measures that I had taken." Meanwhile, the governor-general assured his superiors that he would attempt to split the Fox-Sac alliance and would punish those (the Foxes) responsible for the catastrophe.[42]

Tragically, the immediate retribution for Villiers's death fell upon Kiala. Accompanied by one other Fox hostage, Kiala had been imprisoned at Quebec awaiting the outcome of events in Wisconsin. His wife, also detained by Beauharnois, subsequently had been surrendered to the Christian Hurons, who kept her a prisoner in their village at nearby Lorette. During the winter of 1733–34, Kiala and his fellow prisoner at Quebec contracted some unnamed malady. Kiala recovered, but his companion died, and in the spring when the French court decided "to make an example of them," only Kiala remained. Although the French ministers at first favored putting Kiala to death, they finally decided on a more practical solution. Instructions were sent to both Canada and to the Indies, and during the summer of 1734 Beauharnois ordered the shackled Fox chief to be led aboard the *St. François* and shipped to Martinique, in the West Indies. There the Marquis de Champigny, governor of Martinique, was ordered to sell Kiala into slavery.[43]

Ironically, Kiala's reputation already had preceded him. French officials and planters in the West Indies were well aware of the Fox resistance, and Beauharnois's warnings that "this man was considered intrepid in his nation which is our enemy, . . . he must be watched closely," only added to their apprehension. Meanwhile, on learning of her husband's deportation, Kiala's wife attempted to escape from the Hurons, but was recaptured and also sent to Martinique, where she too was to be sold into slavery. But when both Kiala and his wife were put upon the block, none of the planters could be persuaded to buy them. Afraid that the Foxes, "who are accustomed to making war upon the whites, would encourage their slaves, whom fear alone restrains, and would incite them to some kind of revolt," the planters clamored that Kiala and his wife be removed from the colony. Admitting that the planters' "fear is not groundless," Champigny at first kept the Fox couple imprisoned in the French fort, but he also did not want Kiala loose upon his island. Finally, after explaining to officials in France that "no *habitant* wants to take charge of them, even though we would give them away for nothing," Champigny ordered the Foxes deported to the northern coast of South America. There, in the spring of 1735, near the mouth of the Orinoco River, "this intrepid man named Kiala" and his wife were either put ashore or finally sold into slavery.[44]

While Kiala and his wife were being carried to Martinique, their kinsmen were en route to Iowa. Accompanied by the Sacs, they stopped first near the mouth of the Wisconsin and sent runners to the Sioux and the Iowas, asking for refuge in their villages. Eager for French trade, both tribes denied them sanctuary, but the Iowas informed them they would not oppose the establishment of a separate village west of the Mississippi. So the Sacs and the Foxes continued their trek, paddling their canoes down the broad river and following the Mississippi to the mouth of the Wapsipinicon. They then turned westward, ascending this small but picturesque river about thirty miles to where they established two adjoining but separate villages, one Fox, the other Sac, near the juncture of modern Cedar, Jones, and Clinton counties in Iowa. Temporarily secure, the remnants of Wisaka's people settled in for the winter.[45]

Beauharnois already was planning his retribution. Eager to recoup his declining reputation, the governor-general spent the early months of 1734 mustering his forces at Montreal and meeting with those western tribesmen who still harbored hostility toward the Foxes. In the spring he greeted a delegation of Ottawas from Michilimackinac who had lost several warriors in the recent battles at Green Bay. They presented Beauharnois with strings of black wampum and asked for French assistance in another expedition against the Sacs and Foxes. Seeking Beauharnois's approval, French commanders at Detroit, Ouiatanon, and other western posts also sent questionable assurances that Indians near their forts were eager to participate in such a campaign, and the governor-general spent the summer "conferring with the Sieur Hocquart and the most experienced officers in the Colony" making final preparations for the venture. Finally, on August 14, 1734, Nicolas-Joseph des Noyelles was dispatched from Montreal with "a party of eighty-four French, consisting of seven officers and the remainder of the Cadets, Sergeants, Soldiers and some settlers," accompanied by approximately two hundred Christian Iroquois and Hurons. They were to proceed to Detroit, enlist the Hurons and the Ottawas, then rendezvous with Ottawas and Chippewas from Michilimackinac and march to Iowa. Still convinced that the Sacs could be weaned from the Fox alliance, Beauharnois instructed Noyelles "to grant peace to the Sakis if they consent to give up the Renards; if not, to destroy both nations and to let your savages eat them up."[46]

Such a feast was easier to plan than to serve up. Noyelles first traveled to Detroit, where he was joined by some Hurons and Potawatomis. Then he went on to Ouiatanon, where he encountered a party of Kickapoos. The Kickapoos accompanied Noyelles to their village in Illinois, and reluctantly agreed to guide him to the Sacs and Foxes, but they also informed him that a small village of Sacs (six lodges) had returned from Iowa to the St. Joseph River in southern Michigan, where they had asked the French for asylum. Since Noyelles wished to separate the Sacs from the Foxes, he no longer considered these Sacs to be hostile; but the Hurons from Detroit, accompanied by a few Potawatomis, announced that they saw no reason to make the long journey to Iowa when they could more easily attack these refugee Sacs, who now were located near their villages. Noyelles pleaded with them to remain with his expedition, but in February 1735 about seventy Hurons and ten Potawatomis abandoned the campaign and turned back "to eat up those six cabins."[47]

Noyelles had planned to rendezvous with the Chippewas and the Ottawas from Michilimackinac, but after returning from Montreal these tribesmen had undergone a change of heart and refused to join Noyelles in the Illinois Country. They informed French officials at Michilimackinac that they no longer wanted to make war upon the Sacs, "whom they looked upon as brothers," and only "wished to live in peace and hunt for the subsistence of their wives and children." Although the Kickapoos had agreed to guide Noyelles to the Sac and Fox villages, they led him onto the Grand Prairie of the Illinois, and then proceeded to lead him in circles until some of his Iroquois scouts captured five Sac warriors who were en route to the St. Joseph to inquire about the possibility of French clemency. The prisoners informed Noyelles that the Sacs and the Foxes already were aware of the expedition, had abandoned their towns on the Wapsipinicon, and had retreated to new villages on the Des Moines River in central Iowa. No longer trusting the Kickapoos, Noyelles threatened to "have them [the Sac prisoners] tied to the stake to be burned" if they did not lead him to their new villages.[48]

Fearing for their lives, the Sacs agreed, but they were aware that Noyelles's position was rapidly deteriorating. The Ottawas and the Chippewas from Michilimackinac had failed to appear, the Hurons and the Potawatomis had turned back toward Michigan, and the French and their allies were plagued by intertribal squabbles and a shortage of provisions. Beauharnois originally had chosen Noyelles to lead the expedition because he "is very efficient and is greatly loved by the Savages, and he adds to these qualities a Constitution capable of Enduring the fatigues of an Expedition which can be undertaken only in a very inclement season," but by late February 1735 Noyelles was hard pressed to keep his command together. Early in March they crossed the Mississippi, but they were desperately short of food. Although Noyelles encouraged his allies to stop and hunt, they refused. Convinced that they soon would encounter the Fox village, the Christian Iroquois boasted that they would take what they needed from their enemies. But on March 12, when they reached the sites of the Sac and Fox villages on the Wapsipinicon, they found these settlements deserted. Now forced to hunt, Noyelles dispersed his men into small parties who scattered throughout the region looking for game while he remained on the Wapsipinicon. Yet game was scarce and the weather was bitterly cold, and after two days many of the parties failed to rejoin the expedition. Determined to push forward, Noyelles left a small party of men in camp with instructions for the stragglers to follow in his wake. Then he forged westward, following a trail that he hoped led toward the Des Moines Valley. Finally, after fording the icy Cedar, Iowa, and Skunk rivers, Noyelles and his companions arrived, after dusk, on the Des Moines, "wrapped up in our robes, greatly fatigued, wet through, and very hungry."[49]

The Sacs and the Foxes were aware they were coming. When Noyelles's scouts had captured the five Sacs in Illinois, a Fox warrior accompanying them had escaped and brought news back to Iowa of Noyelles' approach. In response, the Sacs and Foxes had consolidated their scattered winter camps into one large village and had constructed a fortified position on an island in the Des Moines River. Noyelles and his men had expected to find many small winter camps dispersed along the east bank of the river, and when dawn broke they divided into several parties to search for these settlements. But instead of finding small campsites they returned with reports that the large Sac and Fox village was located on the opposite side of the Des Moines, "a very wide and rapid river full of floating ice."[50]

Some of the Christian Iroquois wanted to swim across the river immediately, but Noyelles wisely advised against such folly. He reminded them that the water was so cold that many might drown in the attempt, and those who reached the opposite shore would have soaked their powder, rendering their muskets useless. Instead, Noyelles urged them to wait until all his remaining men arrived. Then they should proceed upstream until they found sufficient driftwood to construct rafts so that they could float down the Des Moines and cross in safety. But the Iroquois war chief accused Noyelles of cowardice and a quarrel ensued, after which twenty-three Iroquois, accompanied by seven Frenchmen, left Noyelles's position and marched upstream looking for a place to make an immediate crossing.[51]

On the opposite bank the Sacs and Foxes monitored Noyelles's activities, and as the French and Iroquois proceeded upstream, Sac and Fox warriors followed along the west bank of the river, prepared to oppose any crossing. They knew they would be forced to fight. About three miles upstream from their village a massive logjam had caught in the river, and the Sacs and Foxes themselves had used the fallen trees to pass over to the eastern bank. They were not disappointed. When the French and Iroquois found the logs they scrambled across them, and a skirmish occurred in which the invaders were momentarily successful, pushing the Sacs and Foxes back from the riverbank. Yet the defenders rallied and forced the French and Iroquois back toward the logjam, attempting to annihilate them before they could be reinforced.[52]

Unfortunately, they failed. Informed of the encounter, Noyelles sent the remainder of his party forward, and these additional forces crossed the logjam, reinforcing the French and Iroquois position on the western bank. Meanwhile, many of the French and allied stragglers from the Wapsipinicon arrived, and during the afternoon Noyelles led these additional men across the logs to the opposite shore. The battle continued sporadically throughout the afternoon. As night fell, the Sacs and Foxes retreated into their fort and Noyelles's forces sought scanty shelter in the river bottom.[53]

Although the remainder of Noyelles's army had now crossed the river, he remained in a precarious position. He had been accompanied on his journey by about forty Kickapoos, many of whom had served as dubious guides as the expedition crossed Illinois. As dusk fell the latter withdrew from the French position. Forming their own encampment on a small hill, overlooking both the French camp and the Sac and Fox fortress, they informed Noyelles that they were leaving the battle. The French commander conjectured that they were waiting to see if the tide of battle might turn in the Sac and Fox favor. Then, he believed, they would join ranks with the Sacs and Foxes. Moreover, the French and their allies remained desperately short of food. The hunting parties on the Wapsipinicon had found scarcely enough game to fill their own stomachs, and although the French shot and killed a stray horse and several dogs that had wandered from the Sac and Fox encampment, this meat provided but meager rations for the entire expedition.[54]

On the following morning Noyelles asked for a truce and the Iroquois invited the Sacs to send a delegation of spokesmen to their encampment. Carrying a white flag, a lone Kickapoo warrior, married to a Fox woman, emerged from the Sac and Fox fort and met with Noyelles and his allies. After listening to Noyelles's pleas for the Sacs to abandon the Foxes, he asked for Noyelles to surrender one of the Sac prisoners he had captured in Illinois. Noyelles agreed, and both men went back into the Sac and Fox fort. The Sacs soon returned with wampum, pelts, and other presents, but informed Noyelles that since the Iroquois were the Sacs' ancient enemies, "they had every reason to fear that when they were separated from the Renards . . . the Iroquois would put them [the Sacs] in the kettle." Noyelles attempted to assure him that the Indians enlisted in his expedition were under his control, but the Sac spokesman remained skeptical. After informing the commander that the hour had grown late, and the weather was cold, he returned to the fort to consult with his advisers.[55]

Inside the Sac and Fox fort, leaders from both tribes met in council. Both the information supplied by the Kickapoos and their own observations indicated that their besiegers had exhausted their food supplies. The Sac and Fox war chiefs believed that Noyelles would not risk an assault on their fortified position. In contrast, the Sacs and Foxes were well supplied with corn, dried meat, and other foodstuffs, and they knew they could withstand a siege more easily than their enemies. Although they were in the minority, the Foxes were adamant in their refusal to surrender, but they urged the Sacs to promise anything if it would deter their enemies. Why not agree to return to Green Bay during the following summer if the French and their allies would abandon the siege and leave Iowa? In response, on the following morning the Sacs sent word that, although they preferred to surrender, it was temporarily impossible. If they attempted to leave the stockade, the Foxes would attack their women and children. Therefore, they suggested that Noyelles and his men withdraw. After they left, the Sacs would return to Wisconsin.[56]

Noyelles realized that his enemies were stalling, but he had exhausted his options. He remained on the Des Moines two days longer, then withdrew to the Illinois Country. Although most of his Indian allies had assured him earlier that they would join in a new campaign against the Chickasaws, they were hungry and exhausted. Some of the Iroquois attacked the Kickapoos because, they said, "We have come to seek enemies; here are some already found since by their conduct they are as much Renards as the others." But most of the Indians straggled dejectedly back to their villages. The last grand campaign against the Foxes had ended in failure.[57]

As in the past, Beauharnois refused to assume any personal responsibility for the fiasco. Although he admitted that the Iowa expedition "had not succeeded," he defended Noyelles and placed the blame on the Kickapoos, Ottawas, and Hurons, who he charged "manifest much ardor towards the French, yet act quite differently" when called "to encounter our enemies." Moreover, he asserted that the campaign also had been sabotaged by certain voyageurs who "secretly dissuaded them [the French-allied Indians] from it for their own interests." Yet Beauharnois assured officials in France that the expedition still had "produced a good effect on the mind of the savages," for it had proved that French power could be extended beyond the Mississippi. According to the governor-general, rumors subsequently had reached Montreal that the Sacs now planned to abandon the Foxes, and if such were the case, the Foxes would be "completely exterminated." But other Frenchmen were not so sure. Jesuit priests among the Iroquois reported to their superiors that the western Indians now sympathized with the Foxes, and that Beauharnois would never again "muster sufficient numbers to destroy them."[58]

In Iowa, the Sacs and Foxes fostered a growing optimism. Noyelles's retreat left them relatively unscathed, and although the Iowas and the Sioux had informed the French that they would not offer these refugees any sanctuary, they privately assured the Sacs and Foxes that they could remain in the Des Moines Valley as long as they wanted. During the spring of 1735 French officials in the Illinois Country encouraged a large war party of Kansas and Missourias to march against the Sac and Fox village, but Sac warriors living among the Iowas informed their kinsmen of the expedition, and the Sacs and Foxes abandoned their camps on the Des Moines and fled to safety in northeastern Iowa. There they separated into two camps. Part of the Foxes accompanied the Sacs back to the Rock River Valley, in northwestern Illinois, while other Foxes journeyed up the Mississippi and formed another village near the mouth of the Wisconsin. Moreover, as news of Noyelles's failure permeated the region, neighboring tribes sent white belts of friendship. During the summer of 1735, while Wisaka's people erected new wigwams, planted their cornfields, and settled into their daily routines, they also welcomed back almost all of their kinspeople previously held as captives by the other western tribes. When the corn was harvested in the fall of 1735, they could again muster over one hundred warriors.[59]

Many of their former enemies also interceded with Onontio in their behalf. During the summer of 1736, White Cat, a Sac chief from the villages on the St. Joseph River, accompanied a delegation of Ottawas and Chippewas to Montreal, where they pleaded with Beauharnois to pardon both the Sacs and the Foxes. The Senecas also asked Beauharnois to cease his campaign of annihilation, and in the following summer a large party of Ottawas, Chippewas, Potawatomis, Menominees, and Winnebagos returned to Montreal, assuring Beauharnois that "all the evil hearts had been destroyed." If Onontio would grant them his mercy, both the Foxes and the Sacs would "grasp closely, the white wampum of peace."[60]

At first Beauharnois remained reluctant. In the spring of 1737 a series of minor skirmishes occurred between hunting parties of Foxes and Illinois near Lake Peoria, and Beauharnois feared that old vendettas might again spark intertribal warfare. But leaders from both tribes interceded and the impending conflict was defused. Meanwhile, French commanders in the west were beset with a growing number of other problems. In 1736 some of the Hurons at Detroit left Michigan and established a new village at Sandusky Bay, a migration that Beauharnois feared would put them in contact with British traders. During the same year the Chickasaws defeated expeditions from New Orleans and the Illinois Country, capturing Pierre d'Artaguiette, commandant of Fort de Chartres, in the Illinois country; François-Marie Bissot de Vincennes, commandant at Fort Wabash; Pierre de St. Ange; Father Antoine Sénat; and sixteen other Frenchmen. On March 25, 1736 (Palm Sunday), the Chickasaws burned all but two of these captives at the stake. During the following summer warfare flamed anew between the Sioux and the Chippewas, and in the spring of 1737 the French were forced to abandon their post on the upper Mississippi, which was about twenty-five leagues upstream from Trempealeau, Wisconsin.[61]

Fearful that the Foxes might take advantage of such disruption, Beauharnois now condescended to offer a pardon to the Sacs and to spare the Foxes' lives if the Sacs would surrender the refugees so that the French could "disperse" the remaining Foxes "among the nations." Not surprisingly, both the Sacs and the Foxes rejected the offer, but in 1737, when delegations of western tribesmen journeyed to Montreal to plead again for the Sacs and the Foxes, Beauharnois moderated his position. He instructed the Winnebagos to inform the Sacs and the Foxes to come to Montreal in the summer of 1738, when he would grant them the king's peace. Meanwhile, as an indication of his sincerity, he instructed French officials at Green Bay to send presents to his former enemies.[62]

The Foxes remained divided. During 1737 those Foxes who had separated from the Sacs and had formed the village near the mouth of the Wisconsin recrossed the Mississippi to establish a new settlement in northeastern Iowa. Cultivating their ties with the Sioux, they sympathized with these western tribesmen in their renewed quarrel with the Chippewas, and although Fox warriors were hesitant to join in the conflict, they remained reluctant to renew their ties with Onontio. In contrast, those Foxes living with the Sacs were much more willing to come to terms with the French, and during the late spring of 1738 they accompanied a delegation of Sacs to Green Bay, where Claude Antoine de Bermen de la Martinière, the commandant of the French post, assembled a mixed party of western tribesmen and voyageurs for the journey down to Montreal. Leaving Wisconsin in early June, the Foxes and their companions arrived in Montreal seven weeks later.[63]

Led by Mekaga (the Eagle), a village chief from the Rock River, the Foxes formally petitioned Beauharnois for a pardon. They assured the governor-general that they would remain as attached to the French as Beauharnois's "true children" (the other western tribes) and requested that the governor-general send an officer to help them keep their young men at peace and to "rekindle the fire in their village." In response, Beauharnois granted the pardon, promised that the Sacs and the Foxes would "be harassed no longer," and dispatched Paul Marin de la Malgue as the new officer to be located in the Sac and Fox village. Beauharnois instructed Marin to consolidate the Sacs and the Foxes into one settlement at the site of their former village at Green Bay, where, according to Beauharnois, Marin should "be very attentive as to their actions in order to know . . . whether they have dissimulated the repentance that they displayed."[64]

Mekaga and the other Fox leaders accompanied Marin back to the Rock River, where he met with leaders from the Fox settlement in northeastern Iowa. Mekaga and Marin persuaded these expatriates to rejoin their kinsmen in Illinois, but most of the Sacs and Foxes were reluctant to return to Wisconsin. Unfortunately, while Mekaga had been absent in Montreal, a small party of young warriors from his village had killed a Frenchman in northern Illinois, and although the dead man was a French deserter and a fugitive from French justice, the Foxes were afraid that Beauharnois still might seek retribution. Moreover, during 1738 rumors reached the western Great Lakes that another large French expeditionary force had been assembled at Montreal. Marin assured the Foxes that the army was destined to descend the Ohio and join in the French campaign against the Chickasaws, but Mekaga and other Fox chiefs remained wary of Beauharnois's intentions and refused to relocate their people any closer to Montreal.[65]

Other factors also strengthened the Sac and Fox resolve to remain on the Rock River. During the late 1730s the fish population in Lake Michigan, and especially in the Green Bay region, had undergone a periodic decline, and the spring spawning runs up the Fox River had diminished considerably. Moreover, the region surrounding the mouth of the Fox River had sustained a relatively large Indian population for almost a century, and the rock-strewn cornfields, never particularly fertile, had been depleted of many of their nutrients. In contrast, the Rock River Valley held an abundance of fish and game, and the black prairie loams that abutted the river valley produced bumper crops with little effort. More important, however, was the growing conflict that again had erupted between the Sioux and the Chippewas. Many of the Foxes remembered that their old nemesis, the Sioux, had recently extended refuge to them in Iowa. Most secretly favored the Sioux, but they still wished to remain neutral in the conflict. If they reestablished a village near Green Bay, they would place themselves astride a major route used by Chippewa war parties venturing west to attack Sioux villages. Intent upon remaining apart from such warfare, the Sacs and the Foxes refused to return to Wisconsin.[66]

Unfortunately, their villages in the Rock River Valley proved vulnerable to the lure of Sioux war parties en route south to attack the Illinois Confederacy. Although Mekaga and the other village chiefs counseled against such actions, young Fox warriors, still eager to prove their mettle, listened readily to the promises of Sioux war chiefs and joined Sioux parties who descended upon Illinois villages in the Lake Peoria region. At first these small parties proved more a nuisance than a threat, but during May 1741 about twenty Fox warriors joined with a large Sioux war party led by Wabasha, and attempted to attack Pimitoui, the Peoria town near Lake Peoria. Afraid of the French reaction, other Sacs and Foxes clandestinely warned the Illinois, and the Peorias remained within their fortified village, but Wabasha's war party surprised a French traveler en route down the Illinois River and hacked him to pieces.[67]

The attack caused considerable consternation among those Sacs and Foxes who had remained on the Rock River. Fearing French retaliation, Mekaga and other chiefs reminded Marin that they had warned the Peorias of the impending attack, and assured him that most of their warriors had opposed the action. Moreover, when those Fox warriors who had accompanied Wabasha returned to the Rock River villages, they were not treated as returning heroes, but were subjected to so much ostracism that many of them withdrew from the Rock Valley and formed a small, separate village near the Sioux, at the mouth of the Wisconsin River. And finally, still hoping to convince both Marin and Beauharnois that they wanted no part of the Sioux-Illinois warfare, in late fall 1741 the remaining Sacs and Foxes reluctantly abandoned their homes in the Rock River Valley. About ten lodges journeyed to the Chicago River, three lodges went to Milwaukee, but the rest returned to the site of the old Fox village at Little Lake Butte des Morts, one day's march above Green Bay, on the Fox River in Wisconsin.[68]

Both Marin and Beauharnois responded favorably to the Sac and Fox emigration. When Beauharnois initially had earned of the Fox participation in Wabasha's raid, he began preparations for a new campaign against the Sac and Fox villages, but Marin's explanations and the Sac and Fox emigration convinced Beauharnois to abandon the expedition. In addition, during the summer of 1742 a delegation of Fox warriors accompanied Marin and many other western Indians to Montreal, where they met with Beauharnois and further assuaged his anger. Mekaga did not join the delegation, but the Foxes were represented by Pemaho (The Swimmer), a warrior from the Fox River village, and Pemoussa (son or nephew of the patriot of the same name who fought the French at Detroit), who represented the small village at Chicago.[69]

Pemoussa reported that shortly before his departure his village had been surprised by a large war party of Illinois seeking revenge for the recent Sioux-Fox raid against Pimitoui, and in the skirmish the Illinois warriors had killed four Fox women. Pemoussa and his followers had pursued the Illinois back down the Illinois River Valley, killing ten and taking five prisoners. But as a gesture of their goodwill, they had released their captives, informing them, "You are fortunate in being Children of Onontio; otherwise, we should burn you." Pemoussa readily admitted his part in the affair, but explained to Beauharnois that none of the Fox or Sac warriors from his village had joined in the raid against Pimitoui; and indeed, since Wabasha

and his raiding party had killed no members of the Illinois
Confederacy, the Fox leader argued that the Illinois should
not have sought retaliation.[70]

Beauharnois was surprisingly conciliatory in his reply.
Currently alarmed about British trading activity in the
upper Ohio Valley, the failure of the Chickasaw campaigns, and the growing hostility between the Sioux and
the Chippewas, the governor-general was eager to accept
any Fox explanation that would keep his old nemesis the
Foxes from adding to his difficulties. He assured Pemoussa,
"I could not blame you for defending yourselves. . . . I am
pleased with you for sending back the captives." Beauharnois promised to write to French officials in Illinois and
order them to "prevent the Illinois from picking any further quarrel with you," and he praised the Foxes for their
forbearance. As a token of his appreciation, he awarded
medals to Pemoussa and Pashpoho (He Who Touches in
Passing), a Sac chief, and he provided all the Sacs and
Foxes in Montreal with presents. Finally, as an additional
indication of his favor, he released four Sac and Fox women
whom the French had held as hostages in Montreal for
almost a decade. Three of the four women had become
so acculturated that they preferred to remain in Canada,
but the fourth, the daughter of Ouchala, welcomed her
repatriation.[71]

Following the conference, Pemoussa, Pashpoho, and the
other Sacs and Foxes returned west, but the peace to
which they now aspired still proved elusive. Although
Mekaga, Pemoussa, and the other village chiefs, like their
fathers before them, counseled tolerance, the Sacs and
Foxes were hard pressed to remain apart from the growing
warfare between the Sioux and the Chippewas. The Foxes,
particularly, were distrusted by the Chippewas, the Ottawas, and other long-standing French allies, and although
Wisaka's people had once warred for decades against the
Sioux, their more recent association with these western

The Sac warrior Massika and the Fox Wakusasse, as painted by the Swiss Karl Bodmer. Although Bodmer painted Wakusasse, *right*, in 1833, the warrior's scalp lock, deerskin roach, jewelry, and facial paint were characteristic of Mesquakie adornment in the eighteenth century. From the Joslyn Art Museum, Omaha, Nebraska.

tribesmen and their history of anti-French resistance continued to make them the objects of suspicion. Beauharnois no longer envisioned them as a threat, but the Chippewas and their allies accused the Foxes of providing covert aid and information to the Sioux, and relations between the Foxes and many of their neighbors slowly deteriorated. As the Sacs and the Foxes earlier had feared, Chippewa war parties passing up the Green Bay–Fox–Wisconsin waterway continued implicitly to threaten the Sac and Fox villages, and in 1742 a small Menominee war party attacked one of the outlying Fox hunting camps. The Foxes did not retaliate, and the Menominees eventually apologized and surrendered those warriors responsible for the assault, but the events only confirmed Fox fears that they remained exposed in the Green Bay region. Late in the summer of 1742, while Pemoussa, Pashpoho, and Marin were returning from Montreal, a war party of Chippewas and Ottawas killed a Fox hunter in northern Wisconsin, and during the following year the Chippewas again attacked a Fox hunting camp, carrying three men and two women into captivity. Once again the Foxes sought no immediate retribution, but when Fox leaders met with Marin at Green Bay in April 1743, they warned that unless the French intervened, they would seek vengeance.[72]

In response, Marin promised to again accompany a delegation from both tribes to Montreal, where they could repeat their pleas to Onontio. In July 1743 a delegation of Sacs and Foxes, accompanied by Marin and a few Menominees and Winnebagos, met with Beauharnois and pleaded for his assistance. Cataloging the abuses they had suffered, Pemoussa and other leaders pointed out, "We have encamped where Monsieur Marin indicated that you wanted us to and . . . have not made a move because you have forbidden us to do so," but, they reminded Beauharnois, "Among us Indians, when we kill each other, we fear nothing because we avenge ourselves." Unless the depredations ceased, new vendettas would be initiated.[73]

Again, Beauharnois was conciliatory in his reply. After "cleansing their hearts" with brandy, he praised the Sacs and the Foxes for their restraint and for "having listened to what Monsieur Marin told you on my behalf." A small delegation of Chippewas also was visiting Montreal, and he scolded them in the Sac and Fox presence. Informing the Chippewas that they had "plunged into evil acts," he ordered them to stop their warfare against the Sioux and to cease their harassment of the Sac and Fox hunting camps. Presenting the Chippewas with a wampum belt, Beauharnois informed them, "I bar you, as well as all your brothers from the road which led you to them [the Sacs and Foxes], and I remove any discord that may exist between you." Gifts of trade goods were lavished on Pemoussa and his companions, and late in July the Sacs and Foxes left Montreal for Wisconsin temporarily satisfied.[74]

But the problems at Green Bay continued. Although the Chippewa-Sioux warfare decreased in intensity, the Sacs and the Foxes remained wary of the Chippewa intentions, and their association with the Sioux grew stronger. Moreover, in 1743 Marin was replaced at Green Bay by Paul-Louis Dazemard de Lusignan, a commander noted for his cultivation and charm but a stranger to the Sacs and the Foxes. Meanwhile, the French trade system collapsed into a morass of expensive licenses and monopolies. Short of funds, in April 1741 the French government decreed that new licenses were needed to trade at the western posts, then auctioned off such licenses at Montreal, authorizing the successful bidders to establish trade monopolies at the western locations. Not surprisingly, the prices of trade goods appreciated, while their quantity decreased. Attempting to circumvent the trade restrictions, coureurs de bois conducted an illegal trade in the region, but their rivalries degenerated into lawlessness, and in 1746 the licensed traders' warehouse mysteriously caught fire and burned to the ground. During the following year Lusignan was replaced by Jean Jarret, sieur de Verchères, but the shortage of trade goods continued. In addition, British traders were able to establish trading bases among the Hurons, the Miamis, and the Piankashaws in Ohio, and discontent among all the western tribes simmered.[75]

Discouraged by those events, the Sacs and the Foxes turned increasingly westward. Although the majority of both tribes continued to reside at their village on the Fox River, growing numbers of families began to leave the town and establish a series of small settlements along the lower Rock River, near its juncture with the Mississippi. Younger Fox warriors again joined Sioux war parties, descending the Mississippi to harass the Illinois Confederacy, and French commanders at Fort de Chartres, threatened by the British expansion in the Ohio Valley, seemed powerless to prevent such raids. Meanwhile, in 1747 Beauharnois, the Foxes' old antagonist, was recalled to Paris, and Roland-Michel Barrin, marquis de La Galissonière, was appointed as the acting governor-general of New France. The Foxes' response to the Beauharnois departure remains unknown, but for those tribespeople who had survived Beauharnois's policy of genocide, his return to France must have been welcome.[76]

Yet most of the Sacs and Foxes were more concerned with events in Wisconsin, and in this instance their focus remained upon Paul Marin, their great friend and the former commander at Green Bay. Although Marin had been replaced by Lusignan in 1743, he had retained his ties with many of the western Indians, and when Sac and Fox leaders had journeyed to Montreal, they had continued to meet with him. Marin, in turn, was eager to reestablish himself in the west. Familiar with intertribal trade and politics, he realized that the Sioux and the tribes of the upper Mississippi Valley now offered greater trading opportunities than the native peoples crowded around Green Bay. In 1749, when Galissonière was replaced by a new governor-general, Jacques-Pierre de Taffanel, marquis de La Jonquière, Marin met with the new Onontio and offered to build a new post, Fort Marin, to be located on the upper Mississippi, near modern Frontenac, Minnesota. The focus for the fur trade would be shifted westward, and as part of Marin's scheme, the Sacs and Foxes would be encouraged to return to the Rock River, in northwestern Illinois.[77]

At Green Bay the remaining Sacs and Foxes received news of the plan with jubilation. Many abandoned their villages on the Fox River in the spring of 1750, moving to the lower Rock River Valley in April so that their women could plant corn. Others, learning that Marin would go up the Fox River en route to his new post, waited to greet their old friend, and in August, when his party approached their village, they met him with much feasting and ceremony. Marin continued on, but the remaining Sacs and Foxes lingered at their village until the fall, when they too harvested their corn. Although several lodges from both tribes decided to remain near Green Bay, the majority of the tribespeople still residing on the Fox River now also abandoned their lodges and proceeded up the river toward the west. When the snow fell in December 1750, almost all the Sacs and Foxes were living on the lower Rock River, near modern Rock Island.[78]

And Wisaka, no longer fickle, smiled his broadest smile, for his people now occupied a new heartland. At the confluence of the Rock and Mississippi rivers they built a new village, and they planted their corn, and for four generations life would be good, and the People of the Red Earth would prosper. Young men would go forth to war against the Illinois, or to strike the Osages, and they would return in triumph, and the sounds of the people's celebrations would echo off the oaks and maples that towered along the river bottom. And old men would sit by the winter fires telling their grandchildren of the days when their grandfathers had stood alone and had defied Onontio. And when asked how the people could survive such hardships, the old men would tell their grandchildren that their forefathers had endured because their medicine was good, and because they were Mesquakies.[79]

But the old men also told their grandchildren that Wisaka was always a trickster and that he had saved his most cunning prank for the Foxes' greatest enemy. In 1750 Beauharnois, who had conducted the campaign of annihilation against Wisaka's people, had returned to France. His efforts had failed, but in 1734 he had treacherously sentenced the last of the great Fox patriots to slavery in the Indies; and when the planters on the islands had refused to accept the warrior and his wife, they had been carried by Onontio's servants to a yet-more-distant shore and abandoned near the mouth of a great river on a fetid, jungle-shrouded continent. But unknown to Beauharnois, when the warrior and his wife had given themselves up as hostages, they had left their son behind with their kinsmen. And in August 1750, when Foxes from the villages on the Rock River had met with a new Onontio, they informed him that another young war chief had arisen among Wisaka's people on the Rock River. And the young man had taken his father's name. And his people called him Kiala.[80]

CHAPTER SEVEN

REGENESIS

In the last half of the eighteenth century at least some Sacs and Foxes remained permanently in the lower Rock River Valley. Other Foxes periodically left the fertile bottomlands along the Rock River to form temporary settlements near modern Dubuque, Iowa, or along the lower Wisconsin. In 1755 a few Sac and Fox warriors from the Rock River fought beside other western tribesmen at Braddock's Defeat, and also during the French and Indian War another war party from the same location halfheartedly accompanied Montcalm down Lake Champlain in the successful campaign against Fort William Henry. In the 1760s some Foxes from a recently established village near the Fox-Wisconsin portage were carrying their fur to Green Bay, while others had erected a smaller village on the northern bank of the Wisconsin River, across from modern Muscoda.[1]

During the American Revolution, Fox warriors from the villages along the Wisconsin accompanied British agent Charles Gautier back to the Lake Champlain region, where they fought in Burgoyne's campaign, but their kinsmen near Dubuque, Prairie du Chien, and along the lower Rock River, had developed economic ties with the Spaniards in Louisiana and were less willing to support the Redcoats. Indeed, by the revolutionary period Fox women from villages near Dubuque were mining lead in such quantities that the commodity assumed an important place in the Indian trade of the region, and Spanish officials at St. Louis sent parties up the Mississippi to purchase the metal. Consequently, in 1779, when Lieutenant-Governor Henry Hamilton sought Sac and Fox assistance in his efforts to recapture Fort Vincennes, the tribesmen from the Mississippi and Rock river valleys refused, and one year later they only reluctantly joined British General Emmanuel Hesse as his armada of canoes descended the Mississippi to attack Louisiana. After reaching St. Louis, both the Sacs and the Foxes refused to fire on the Spaniards, and when Hesse's campaign floundered, the Foxes gladly retreated up the river to their villages. Although the Americans retaliated by burning a Sac village on the Rock River, the Foxes remained relatively unscathed and continued to trade with merchants from Louisiana.[2]

In the years following the American Revolution, the Foxes began a slow migration to the west. Abandoning their villages in central Wisconsin, some returned to the Rock River valley while others journeyed to Prairie du Chien and Dubuque, or established new villages on the Upper Iowa or the Turkey River in modern northeastern Iowa. Encouraged by the Spaniards, they joined with Sacs, Potawatomis, and Kickapoos to attack Osage villages in modern Missouri. They also acquired growing numbers of horses and hunted westward to the Missouri River, trading with the Otoes and the Omahas. In 1803, when the United States bought Louisiana from Napoleon, Sac and Fox leaders most certainly underestimated the significance of the purchase, but American officials in Missouri were eager to end the Osage wars, and one year later a delegation from the Sacs and Foxes journeyed to St. Louis, where they met with William Henry Harrison. In November 1804, either through ignorance or misunderstanding, they signed a treaty that ceded their claims to western Illinois.[3]

The treaty did not stop the Osage wars, but American attempts to intercede on the part of the Osages strengthened the position of those Foxes who championed closer ties with the British. In the postrevolutionary period both the Sacs and the Foxes had nurtured a "British party," and in the autumn of 1790 some Foxes had journeyed to Indiana to assist the Shawnees and the Miamis against an American military expedition led by Josiah Harmar. They arrived too late to participate in the battle, but they shared in the plunder from the encounter, and during the next decade, as other Foxes continued to visit the British Indian Department at Amherstburg, Ontario, their ties to the Crown increased. Although their lands in northern Illinois were not immediately threatened by American expansion, in the years preceding the War of 1812 many Foxes subscribed to the religious teachings of the Shawnee Prophet and joined with his brother Tecumseh in an intertribal attempt to retain the remaining Indian land base. In 1813 Fox warriors accompanied a party led by the Sac war chief Black Hawk to the Detroit frontier, where they fought at the battle of Frenchtown and participated in the ill-fated British invasion of northwestern Ohio. Others attacked Fort Madison, the American post on the Des Moines River, and assisted in the defeat of Zachary Taylor's expedition up the Mississippi in 1814.[4]

But not all the Foxes supported the Redcoats. As the war ended, many Foxes joined with Sacs led by the pro-American chief Keokuk and attempted to come to terms with the Long Knives. Moreover, in the postwar period the Foxes continued their westward migration, and as they established new villages on the lower Iowa, Wapsipinicon, Des Moines, and Cedar rivers they concentrated their hunting into northwestern Iowa. Unfortunately, this westward expansion brought them into conflict with the Sioux, who also hunted in the region, and with the Otoes and Omahas. By 1825 warfare between the Sacs and the Foxes, one one side, and the Sioux, on the other, reached such proportions that it threatened the peace of the entire upper Mississippi Valley until, in August of that year, several Fox leaders met with federal officials and delegates from other tribes to sign the treaty of Prairie du Chien. Although the agreement supposedly brought a permanent peace to the region, skirmishing resumed and the enmity between the Foxes and the Sioux continued.[5]

Conflicts between the Sacs and the Americans soon overshadowed the Sioux warfare. In the 1820s American settlement advanced north from the Illinois river valley, and at the end of the decade white miners threatened Fox control of the lead mines along the Fever River in extreme northwestern Illinois. Moreover, during the same period American farmers began to infiltrate the Rock river valley, and in September 1829 Keokuk led a large party of Sacs and a few remaining Foxes out of their old homeland on the Rock River to a new village in Iowa. But in 1830 Black Hawk brought his band of Sacs and a handful of Foxes back across the Mississippi, where they reoccupied the old Sac village at Saukenuk. The region was filling with American settlers, and Black Hawk and his followers spent a tense summer, tending their cornfields but brooding about the American homesteads that now encroached upon their village. In the fall they left the village to hunt in Iowa, and in the spring of 1831 when they again returned to Saukenuk, they were confronted by Keokuk and federal officials who warned that if they did not depart voluntarily, they would be forced across the Mississippi at bayonet point. Meanwhile, Governor John Reynolds of Illinois sent fifteen hundred militia to the Rock River to support the government's demands, and on June 26, 1831, Black Hawk's band retreated to Iowa.[6]

With the exception of a small village in the Fever River region, almost all of the Foxes already had relocated west of the Mississippi, and few could be found in Black Hawk's camp. Moreover, by 1830, although government officials still referred to "the Sac and Fox Indians" as one composite unit, most of the Foxes resented both Keokuk's and Black Hawk's assertions of intertribal leadership, preferring to follow leaders such as Wapello (He Who Is Painted White), Poweshiek (The Shaker), or the mixed-blood Manquopwan (Bear's Hip), also known as George Morgan.

Consequently, when Black Hawk's return to Illinois in April 1832 ignited the conflict known as the Black Hawk War, most Foxes remained neutral in action, if not in sentiment, and few accompanied the old Sac war chief. Yet when the conflict ended, the Foxes were forced to surrender their claims to the ore-rich Dubuque region as payment. Meanwhile, almost all Sac and Fox villages were consolidated into a series of separate settlements along the Upper Iowa and Des Moines rivers.[7]

In Iowa the split between the Sacs and the Foxes deepened. Although Fox leaders complained that most of the recently ceded Iowa lands had belonged to their people, most federal annuities were parcelled out through Keokuk's hegemony, and the majority went to the Sacs, not to the Foxes. Meanwhile, both tribes adamantly resisted the efforts of both Christian missionaries and federal Indian agents to introduce Euro-American concepts of education, religion, and agriculture. Warfare with the Sioux flared anew, and although the Foxes took many scalps, they suffered significant numbers of casualties. In addition, the problems that had plagued their residency in Illinois reemerged in Iowa. Although the 1832 treaty had opened eastern Iowa to American settlement, white farmers' demands for Indian lands remained unsatisfied. In 1836 the Sacs relinquished an additional 400 square miles of "Keokuk's Reserve" immediately abutting the 1832 cession, but federal officials clamored for more, even suggesting that both the Sacs and the Foxes give up all their remaining lands in Iowa.[8]

Most Foxes adamantly opposed any further land cessions, and when government agents met with tribal leaders during the late 1830s, the Foxes complained so bitterly that even Keokuk acquiesced to their wishes. Still, American settlement continually spilled over onto their lands, and they were in debt to white traders. Finally, in October 1842, delegations from both the Sacs and the Foxes signed a treaty relinquishing their remaining Iowa homelands in exchange for increased annuities and a new reservation on the Osage River, in eastern Kansas. Following Keokuk, most of the Sacs moved to their new home in Kansas, but the Foxes stubbornly refused to leave. Scattering into small camps along the upper Des Moines, Skunk, and Raccoon rivers, they eluded Indian agents assigned to supervise their removal. In response, in 1846 a contingent of U.S. Dragoons scoured north-central Iowa and forced the Foxes westward toward Kansas. Still, of the approximately 1,275 Foxes, only about 250 settled permanently with the Sacs on the Osage River. A small band, the 125 followers of Wetemah (Tobacco Smoker), settled among the Kickapoos in northeastern Kansas, while Poweshiek's band of 500 were given refuge on Potawatomi lands along the Nodaway River in southwestern Iowa and northwestern Missouri. Almost 400 other Foxes, still divided into small family groups, remained scattered across northern Iowa.[9]

During the next decade Foxes in growing numbers returned to their old homes. Camping along the Iowa River, they spent the summer hunting and growing corn. Then they dispersed into small camps for the winter. Many visited the Kickapoos in Kansas during the winter months, or even returned temporarily to the Osage River in an attempt to obtain their share of the "Sac and Fox" annuities. Then, when spring arrived and the maples along the Iowa

River could be tapped for sugar making, they returned to
their homeland. In the early 1850s federal troops repeatedly were dispatched to drive them back into Kansas, and
many fled before the mounted soldiers, but when the
troops returned to their barracks, the Foxes returned to
Iowa. Meanwhile, public sentiment in Iowa finally rallied
to the Foxes' defense. In 1856 the Iowa state legislature
authorized the Foxes to purchase lands in the state and requested that the federal government pay an appropriate
portion of the Sac and Fox annuity to the Foxes in Iowa.
One year later tribal leaders purchased the first eighty
acres of what eventually would become about thirty-five
hundred acres of tribally owned bottomlands along the
Iowa River, near modern Tama. Although the Bureau of
Indian Affairs at first refused to establish a separate agency
in Iowa, many of the Foxes had returned to the Tama settlement, and in 1866 Congress instructed the bureau to
establish an agency, appoint an agent, and pay an appropriate portion of the Sac and Fox annuities to the Foxes at
that location. The Bureau of Indian Affairs still refused to
recognize the Foxes as a separate tribe, but it did acknowl-
edge that they were a distinct band: the Sacs and Foxes of
Iowa.[10]

In Kansas the remainder of the Foxes lived with the
Sacs, but their tenure on the Osage River was an unhappy
one. Although they hunted buffalo in western Kansas and
defended themselves admirably from attacks by the Plains
Indians, the lands along the Osage lacked fertility and they
raised sparse crops of corn. Meanwhile, in the 1850s they
suffered repeatedly from plagues of measles, smallpox,
and cholera. Their numbers declined, and although Moses
Keokuk, who had succeeded his father as the government-
favored "agency chief," attempted "to walk the white
man's road," his half-hearted support of the government's
"civilization" programs attracted little adherence from his
followers. In contrast, many turned to Mokohoko, a leader

of the traditionalists, who was a shrewd politician and understood the intricacies of tribal politics.[11]

Succumbing to government pressure, in 1859 the Sacs and the Foxes in Kansas agreed to the allotment of their lands and the sale of the surplus acreage to non-Indians. The process proved disastrous. The Sacs and Foxes still refused to farm their allotments, and government-constructed houses on their plots proved to be so shoddy that the Indians either used the buildings for firewood or as shelter for their horses. Disillusioned, in 1867 most of the remaining Sacs and Foxes in Kansas relinquished their claims to their allotments and agreed to move to a new tract of land between the North Canadian and Cimarron rivers in Indian Territory. Predictably, Mokohoko refused to abide by the agreement, and in 1869 when most of the Sacs and Foxes left for the Indian Territory, the traditionalist chief and his two hundred followers remained in Kansas. In the aftermath of the exodus most of the Foxes who had followed Mokohoko returned to Iowa.[12]

In Indian Territory the majority of the Sacs and the Foxes still clung to their old ways. Although both federal agents and missionaries continued to champion acculturation, the Sacs and the Foxes disdained both agriculture and formal education, preferring to lease their land to white cattlemen rather than settle down as small yeomen farmers. Mokohoko died in 1878, and eight years later the remnants of his band were forced out of Kansas and relocated on the Oklahoma reservation, but they preferred to live separately and formed their own village near the reservation's northern borders. Like most other Sacs and Foxes, they opposed the allotment of the reservation in 1891, and when the allotments were assigned, Mokohoko's followers received contiguous tracts of land that they immediately enclosed with a single fence, still attempting to hold the land in common.[13]

During the twentieth century the pace of change has quickened, and now most Oklahoma Sacs and Foxes are integrated into both the pan-Indian and white cultures of Oklahoma. Organized under the Oklahoma Indian Welfare Act of 1936, the modern Sac and Fox tribal government consists of an elected chief and a business committee, and tribal offices are housed on Sac and Fox land near Stroud, in Lincoln County. Today many Oklahoma Sacs and Foxes have intermarried with whites or members of other tribes, and they pursue the broad spectrum of economic opportunities available to both Indians and non-Indians in eastern Oklahoma. Most participate in both tribal and pan-tribal dances and festivals, and in mid-July the annual Sac and Fox Powwow remains the center of much Sac and Fox activity. Although most of the Oklahoma Sacs and Foxes emphasize their Sac heritage, several families still boast of their Fox lineage. In 1990 the Sac and Fox Tribe of Oklahoma enrolled approximately 2,700 members.[14]

In Iowa the old ways still linger. Since the people who returned to Iowa were almost entirely of Fox descent, they proudly refer to themselves as Mesquakies. Moreover, because the tribal acreage near Tama was purchased by the Mesquakies with their own funds, the settlement is Indian land but not a "reservation." It was not subject to the 1887 Dawes Severalty Act, and it has never been allotted. And if the Sacs and Foxes in Oklahoma were at first reluctant to accept the federal government's programs, the Mesquakies have been even more recalcitrant. In 1896, when Indian agents opened a boarding school in the neighboring town of Toledo, the Mesquakies refused to enroll their children, and when Pushetonequa (Old Man's Eyes), a tribal leader, finally agreed that his children should attend, the decision engendered a quarrel in the tribal council that still plagues Mesquakie politics. Today Mesquakie children, like other children, are enrolled in school. Some attend classes in surrounding communities, but others are enrolled at the Mesquakie Day School at the settlement.[15]

When the Mesquakies first returned to Iowa they retained their communal villages, and throughout the second half of the nineteenth century most Mesquakies at the Tama settlement continued to live in a single village, many still residing in traditional wigwams. In 1902, however, in response to a smallpox epidemic, federal officials burned the village, and the population scattered to small individual homesteads within the settlement boundaries. Today over eight hundred Mesquakies live in mobile homes or small frame houses, and either farm part of the tribal lands or work at jobs in the white communities that surround the settlement. The Mesquakies retained their traditional form of government until 1937, when they adopted a formal constitution under the Indian Reorganization Act. Some of the old ways have been lost, but others continue. Many Mesquakies are Christians, but they also participate in the old medicine-bundle ceremonies. Others are members of the Medicine Drum Society or follow the peyote road. Some of the clans have been lost, but others remain. The Mesquakies are not a wealthy people, but they are self-sustaining. The old people die, but they are renewed in their grandchildren. The struggle has never been easy, but Pemoussa's defiant claim at the siege of the Fox village at Detroit in 1712 still rings true. His people still remain. "The Foxes are immortal."[16]

CHAPTER EIGHT

EPILOGUE

In July 1796, when Count Constantin F. S. Volney, a former official of the French government, visited the Wabash Valley, Indians from throughout Indiana and southern Illinois flocked to Vincennes to speak with the emissary. Eager to meet again with a spokesman from the Great Onontio, Miamis, Potawatomis, Shawnees, and the remnants of the Illinois Confederacy arrived in such numbers that Major Thomas Pasteur, the commanding officer at nearby Fort Knox, became alarmed for the safety of the post and forbade the Frenchman to address the throng. A decade later William Henry Harrison reported that "the happiness they [the Indians] enjoyed from their intercourse with the French is their perpetual theme—it is their golden age. Those who are old enough to remember it, speak of it with rapture." John Johnston, a contemporary of Harrison and an Indian agent at Fort Wayne, commented, "I have seen Indians burst into tears in speaking of the time when their French father had dominance over them." Indeed, many of the tribes upstream on the St. Lawrence from Montreal maintained close ties with Onontio throughout the French period, and after the French and Indian War their continued participation in Creole-French cultural patterns was an important facet of their acculturation. Tribes such as the Chippewas, the Potawatomis, and the Miamis periodically quarrelled with their French father, but their relationships with Onontio more often were characterized by cooperation or accommodation, rather than conflict.[1]

Not so the Foxes! More than any of the other midwestern tribes, the Foxes remained outside the realm of French hegemony, and their ability to maintain their independence in the face of growing French pressure was perceived by French officials as a direct threat to the stability and even the existence of New France. Afraid that Wisaka's people might provide a catalyst for rebellion among the other tribes, governors such as Callières, Vaudreuil, and Beauharnois cajoled, threatened, and finally attempted to coerce the Foxes to submit to French authority. The Foxes rejected such demands, and although they paid a heavy price for such independence, they remained free. Fox leaders such as Noro, Pemoussa, and Ouchala often walked a narrow and thorny path, yet they consistently championed the welfare of their people, adroitly maneuvering between Onontio's yoke and the antipathy of his allies. Only in 1730, after the defection of the Kickapoos, the Mascoutens, and the Winnebagos, were Fox leaders forced to make the ill-fated trek toward the Iroquois Country, and the resulting slaughter on the prairie, followed by the treacherous Huron and Christian Iroquois attack on their village in December 1731, finally brought them to their knees. But still the people persisted, and after 1732 their alliance with the Sacs provided both a refuge and an opportunity for regeneration.

In retrospect, several factors contributed to the Fox alienation from the French, and to their ability to function outside the French alliance. Unquestionably, the Fox-

Chippewa warfare, which forced the Foxes from Michigan and encouraged their emigration to Wisconsin, created a climate of Fox hostility toward the Chippewas and their Michigan allies (especially the Ottawas). Moreover, from the Fox perspective, "my enemy's friends shall also become my enemy," and as the Chippewas and their allies became associated with New France, Fox suspicion, if not hostility, also was projected toward Onontio.

This hostility was sharpened when the Potawatomis and several other French-allied tribes fled to the Green Bay region. The Foxes had migrated to Wisconsin well before the destruction of Huronia and the subsequent dispersal of the Michigan tribes. Early in the seventeenth century Wisaka's people already had become securely established at Ouestatimong and along the Wolf and Fox rivers in east-central Wisconsin. Consequently, after 1650, when many Petuns, refugee Hurons, Potawatomis, Miamis, and other Michigan tribes fled the onslaught of the Neutrals and the Iroquois, the Foxes considered the newcomers to be inter-lopers infringing on hunting lands that the Foxes regarded their own. In contrast, like the Chippewas, many of the more-recent emigrants still regarded the Foxes as Outa-gamis, or "people of the far shore": rude, unsophisticated folk who, though potentially hostile, offered opportunities for economic exploitation. Intertribal trade did develop between the newcomers and the Foxes, but the French-allied tribes were eager to ration the supply of trade goods available to the Foxes, forcing the latter to supply large numbers of pelts for a limited quantity of metal utensils, guns, ammunition, and other merchandise that reached Ouestatimong. In response, Fox resentment increased toward both the French and their allies.

The Foxes' hostility toward the Sioux also complicated their relationship with New France. Antoine Denis Raudot aptly reported that most of the French-allied tribes wished to trade with the Foxes, but they feared them and considered "the Outagamis [to be] so savage that they cannot stand them, but as they are so numerous, . . . they let them make war . . . on the Sioux . . . without interference." Indeed, in the late seventeenth century the Fox-Sioux warfare already seemed of considerable duration, and the Fox occupation of the Wolf and Fox rivers in east-central Wisconsin, which placed them on the Sioux frontier, made them vulnerable to Sioux retaliation.[2]

Yet, in that conflict, the Foxes were holding their own. In 1701, when Noro informed Callières that the Foxes were "much involved with the Sioux," he was reluctant to admit that the Foxes, although sometimes hard pressed, were capable of defending themselves. Their location in east-central Wisconsin gave them a better (if still somewhat limited) access to firearms than the Sioux, and their control of the portage between the Fox and Wisconsin rivers enabled them either to prevent or to limit the supply of guns and ammunition that reached their enemy. But they faced a marked demographic disadvantage. In the late seventeenth century the Foxes probably could muster between eight hundred and one thousand warriors, but the Sioux were much more populous, and although neither side could organize such a large war party, the Foxes were badly outnumbered. Their supply of firearms and metal weapons, although limited, helped to balance the scale, and the Foxes initially were reluctant to allow French traders or French-allied Indians to pass over the portage and trade with their enemies.

In contrast, French officials envisioned the Sioux as potentially a more lucrative market and as a medium through which French influence could penetrate the northern plains. The French were eager to establish trading posts along the upper Mississippi, and the Fox-Wisconsin portage offered the best access to these markets. In comparison to the Sioux, the Foxes offered only limited economic opportunities; moreover, the French-allied tribes initially described the Foxes in such negative terms that French officials considered their trade an economic backwater, a limited market that eventually would be absorbed into the general Indian trade in Wisconsin. Officials in Canada were incensed when Fox warriors either pillaged or exacted considerable tribute from the traders who ascended the Fox River, and they feared that Fox intransigence would prevent the growth of their economic and political influence on the upper Mississippi.

Obviously, for the Foxes the development of a strong French-Sioux relationship was disastrous. They already faced relatively well-armed, hostile tribes on their northern and eastern borders, and to the south the Illinois Confederacy, though declining in power, had direct access to traders from Louisiana. They maintained a perilous balance of power with the Sioux, but if the French-allied tribes and the traders—merchants who repeatedly charged exorbitant prices and refused to meet the Foxes' demands for arms and powder—carried such commodities to their Sioux enemies, then the Fox position would be untenable. They most certainly would be caught between the Sioux hammer and the French anvil, and if well-armed Sioux war parties descended on the Fox villages in Wisconsin, Noro and other Fox leaders knew they could expect little support from the French-allied tribes. Better, then, to soften the hammer and to stifle the flow of trade goods to their Sioux enemies. Obviously Onontio would be angered, but he lived in Montreal. The Sioux villages were in western Wisconsin.

If the stage for the Fox-French confrontation had been set by the Foxes' alienation from the Chippewas, by their early emigration to Wisconsin, and by their longstanding warfare with the Sioux, their quarrel with Onontio was exacerbated by ill-conceived French policies that only deepened the conflict. Surely, Cadillac's invitation to the Foxes to resettle in the Detroit region proved catastrophic for both sides. Although the French feared the spread of Iroquois influence, the migration of Pemoussa and his people back into eastern Michigan provided a medium for such infiltration and increased the contacts between the Foxes and the Senecas. Moreover, Vaudreuil's reversal of Cadillac's invitation was incomprehensible to the Foxes and violated their sense of both honor and hospitality.

The Foxes, however, contributed to the problem. Their assumption that Cadillac's invitation provided carte blanche to assume tribal hegemony over the Detroit region reflected both their own naïve egotism and their ignorance of the relationship between the French and the other tribes of Michigan. In Wisconsin, Fox-French relations had not always been amicable, but they had not been marred by full-scale, major confrontations. After 1711, however, conditions changed. Too much blood was spilled at Detroit. In the aftermath, political and kinship influences on both sides demanded a full retribution. From the French perspective, the remaining Foxes and their Kickapoo and Mascouten allies could not go unpunished, and from the Fox point of view, Cadillac, Dubuisson, and Onontio had betrayed them.

The boundary dispute between Canada and Louisiana also contributed to the Fox-French confrontation. After 1717, when Illinois was transferred from Canada to Louisiana, Vaudreuil became so apprehensive that Creole traders from the Illinois Country would siphon the fur trade off to Louisiana that he refused to use his influence to prevent the Foxes and their allies from attacking the Illinois Confederacy. Indeed, from Vaudreuil's perspective, the disruption resulting from Fox attacks in the Illinois Country forced merchants from Cahokia and Kaskaskia to trade with the Sioux via the Missouri River, at best a dangerous and circuitous route that discouraged such commerce. As a result, most of the pelts from the upper Mississippi Valley continued to flow eastward through the Great Lakes and

Canada. Meanwhile, many Foxes perceived Vaudreuil's inaction as tacit approval of their warfare. Commanders at several of the western posts continued clandestinely to trade military supplies to the tribe, and assurances by Canadian coureurs de bois that Creole traders in Illinois were not Onontio's children but "other white men," only added kindling to the conflagration. For the Kiyagamohag, the Fox warrior society, the Illinois were an available and vulnerable target. Elecevas and other young war chiefs needed little encouragement.[3]

French officials in Illinois intensified the conflict. Undoubtedly, they were enraged by the Fox attacks, but their retaliatory torture and execution of Fox captives, and their sanction of similar actions by the Illinois Confederacy, intensified the Fox campaign and undercut the influence of Ouchala and those Foxes who preferred a peaceful settlement. Like the siege at Detroit, the warfare in the Illinois Country engendered such bitterness that personal vendettas eventually became the cornerstones of intertribal relations. Once the warfare became general, it created a momentum of its own.[4]

Finally, the initial French campaigns against Fox villages in Wisconsin were marked by indecision and poor leadership. Louvigny's threatened campaign of 1715 failed to materialize, and one year later, when he invaded Wisconsin, the expedition degenerated into a trading mission so rapidly that it achieved little political or military success. Led by Pemoussa, the Foxes withstood the French siege and received such favorable terms that their respect for French military power only diminished. In 1728 Lignery traveled so slowly that the Foxes and their allies were able to abandon their villages and retreat over the Fox-Wisconsin portage. Of course, Lignery burned Fox wigwams and cut down their corn, but his claims that "one-half those people will die of hunger" during the following winter was only wishful thinking. His subsequent destruction of Fort

St. Francis and the French withdrawal from Green Bay provides a more accurate, if less sanguine, gauge of French influence in the region, for after his withdrawal many of the Foxes returned to their old homes in Wisconsin. Once again, from the Fox perspective, French military power in the west was less than pervasive.[5]

The Foxes also contributed to the difficulties. Political organization in all of the tribes of the western Great Lakes region was characterized by a lack of centralization, but by the early eighteenth century the authority of the Fox village chiefs had become particularly limited. Half a century of warfare had so disrupted the traditional clan system that the leadership of the Kiyagamohag was openly contested, and members of the Wahgohagi, or Fox clan, no longer dominated the warrior society. Warfare now permeated Fox politics, and attempts by Elecevas, Kansekoe, and other younger warriors to enhance their status as war chiefs completely disrupted the efforts of older leaders to reach an accommodation with Onontio. Ouchala and other village chiefs repeatedly complained that their "foolish young men" had "lost their senses" and refused all counsel. A century later Indian agent Thomas Forsyth reported that many Foxes still paid "no respect to their chiefs at any time, except necessity compels them." In 1729 this fragmentation proved disastrous, for the younger warriors' alienation of the Kickapoos and Mascoutens denied the Foxes their two most faithful allies and left the tribe surrounded by enemies. The subsequent flight toward the Senecas ended in catastrophe.[6]

Finally, why and how did the Foxes survive? What features account for their ability to persist against such overwhelming odds? Why did they reemerge as a viable tribal entity in the latter half of the nineteenth century? Obviously many elements contributed to their perseverance, but several emerge as primary factors in their regenesis. Ironically, Beauharnois's treachery and ultimately, his military successes proved to be a double-edged sword that destroyed yet sustained the Foxes. The French intransigence at the siege preceding the great battle on the prairie alarmed many of the western tribes, and as the siege continued, the Sacs, the Kickapoos, and some of the other erstwhile allies of New France developed second thoughts about their commitment to Beauharnois. How could Onontio, their "Great Father," destroy his children?. Within the framework of tribal society a "father" was a provider who cared for his family. He might become angered and even punish his children, but he would not destroy them. Beauharnois's admonition to exterminate the Foxes offended many of the western Indians and they were shocked by the subsequent slaughter on the prairie. Moreover, the destruction of the Fox emigrants emphasized the vulnerability of all the tribes. If Onontio could annihilate the Foxes, who would be next? Most of the western tribes grew apprehensive. The Sacs provided refuge; the Ottawas, the Potawatomis, and the Mascoutens were reluctant to participate in the Huron and Christian Iroquois attack on the Fox village; and in 1734 the Kickapoos attempted to lead Noyelles astray on the Grand Prairie of the Illinois, rather than guide him to the Sac and Fox villages.

The western tribes' alienation from Beauharnois also created a favorable climate for the return of Fox captives. Many of the survivors of the fight on the prairie, and of the subsequent winter campaign against the Fox village on the Wisconsin, passed into the hands of tribes now favorably inclined toward the Foxes, and those tribespeople eventually allowed the former prisoners to return to their village. In addition, as their friendship with the Foxes was rekindled, members of the neighboring tribes took Fox wives or husbands, and these newcomers and their children rapidly replenished the Fox population. Demographic figures at best are sketchy, but in the spring of 1732, after the Huron–Christian Iroquois attack on their village, the Fox population reached its nadir: about fifty men and adolescent boys, and approximately ninety women and children. Thirty years later, when Lieutenant James Gorrell arrived at Green Bay to formally extend British control over the post there, he estimated they could again raise three hundred and fifty warriors from a total population of just under twelve hundred.[7]

Finally, although encapsulations of national character currently are unfashionable, a particular quality of perseverance does seem to have permeated the Fox psyche, and it still can be found among the modern Mesquakie people. Like the oaks and hickories that grace the river valleys of their homeland, the Mesquakies possessed a tough resilience, a heartwood of inner strength that enabled them to cling to their sense of identity. In the face of insurmountable odds, they persisted. The French and their allies never described the Foxes as gregarious, effusive people eager to embrace new ideas or new ways. But they grudgingly admitted that Wisaka's people took care of their own, and their adherence to traditional values, those things that were Mesquakie, formed the core of their resistance.

And some things still remain. In February 1989 one of the authors had the opportunity to speak at two academic institutions in east-central Iowa and to visit the Mesquakie settlement at Tama. En route to the tribal offices, he passed through an adjoining non-Indian community where he stopped for coffee. Several local residents learned that he had been conducting research on the history of the Mesquakies. Most members of the coffee klatch at the local cafe freely volunteered advice or comments about the Mesquakies, and their various comments reflected the broad spectrum of attitudes toward the tribe held by the Mesquakies' non-Indian neighbors. Some thought the Mesquakies should become more "progressive," while others complained about the tribe's relationship with various branches of federal, state, and local governments. But on two things they all agreed. Many Mesquakies are still an inwardly focused people with a strong sense of tribal identity, and when the author described the Mesquakies' past struggles against the French, the coffee drinkers were not surprised. As one observer so aptly put it, "They don't have much, but they're tough as nails. I sure wouldn't want to have to move them off that settlement."[8]

NOTES

CHAPTER ONE
THE WEST IN CHAOS

1. Pierre-François-Xavier de Charlevoix, *History and General Description of New France* 5:99–111.

2. Ibid., 111–12, 135–40. Also see David Schyler and Lawrence Clease to Robert Livingston, June 2, 1701, in E. B. O'Callaghan, ed., *Documents Relative to the Colonial History of the State of New York* (15 vols.; Albany: Weed, Parsons and Co., 1857–93) (hereafter cited as *New York Colonial Documents*), 4:889–95; Conference of Lieutenant-Governor Nanfan with the Indians, July 1701, ibid., 896–908.

3. Charlevoix, *History* 5:141–43.

4. Speech by the Fox chief, July 29, 1701, Archives nationales, Colonies (Paris), series F³, vol. 8, folio 262 verso; speech by Callières, August 6, 1701, ibid., ff. 270v–71. Hereafter documents from the Archives nationales will be cited as AN, Col. Direct citations from French-language archival sources are translated by the present authors. Also see Charlevoix, *History,* 5:143–49.

5. Speech by Callières, August, 6, 1701, AN, Col., F³, vol. 8, ff. 270v–71; Introduction, Margry Manuscripts, Burton Historical Collections, Detroit, Public Library, Detroit, Michigan (microfilm). Hereafter materials from these translated manuscripts will be cited as "Margry Manuscripts." The term Onontio, meaning "great mountain," was given by the Indians to the first titular governor-general of New France (1636–48), whose French name, Montmagny, had that mean-

ing. All subsequent governors-general of New France were called Onontio by the Indians, whereas the king of France was referred to as "the Great Onontio." For further discussion of this term, see *Dictionary of Canadian Biography* (Toronto: University of Toronto Press, 1966–91), 1:373–74, and W. J. Eccles, *The Canadian Frontier, 1534–1760* (Albuquerque: University of New Mexico Press, 1983), 201n.15.

6. Charlevoix, *History* 5:149, 152.

7. Ibid., 150–51; Ratification of the Peace between the French and the Indians, August 4, 1701, *New York Colonial Documents* 9:722–25.

8. Charlevoix, *History* 5:151; Ratification of the Peace between the French and the Indians, August 4, 1701, *New York Colonial Documents,* 9:722–25.

9. Charlevoix, *History* 5:151.

10. Reuben G. Thwaites, ed., *Jesuit Relations and Allied Documents* 51:43–45, 44:245–51; Louise Phelps Kellogg, *The French Regime in Wisconsin and the Old Northwest,* 152–55.

11. William Jones, "Notes on the Fox Indians," *Journal of American Folklore* 24 (April-June, 1911): 211–12; Jedidiah Morse, "Memoirs Relating to the Sauks and Foxes, in Emma Hunt Blair, ed., *The Indian Tribes of the Upper Mississippi Valley and the Region of the Great Lakes* 2:146. Traditions from other tribes support the Fox argument. See Statement by Andrew Blackbird, in Fox File, Great Lakes–Ohio Valley Indian Archives, Glenn A. Black Laboratory of Archaeology, Indiana University, Bloomington. Hereafter materials from these archives will be cited as "Great Lakes Indian Archives." Also see Thwaites, *Jesuit Relations* 18:233–35.

12. Wittry, Warren L., "A Michigan Fox Hunt," *Newsletter of the Cranbrook Institute of Science* 32, no. 7: 74–77; Wittry, "The Bell Site, Wn9, an Early Historic Fox Village," *Wisconsin Archaeologist* 44 (March, 1963): 41. Also see statement by Andrew Blackbird, Fox File, Great Lakes Indian Archives; Jones, "Notes on the Fox Indians," 232; and William W. Warren, *History of the Ojibway Nation,* 95–96.

13. Charles Callender, "Fox," in Bruce Trigger, *Northeast,* vol. 15 of William C. Sturtevant, ed., *Handbook of North American Indians,* 636–37; Harold Hickerson, *The Southwestern Chippewa: An Ethnohistorical Study,* 92n.10; Thwaites, *Jesuit Relations* 54:223–25. George Quimby has shown that during the early seventeenth century southwestern Michigan was inhabited by the Sacs, the Kickapoos, and perhaps the Potawatomis, but archaeological evidence from the Dumaw Creek site does not indicate significant Fox occupancy of that location. See George I. Quimby, *The Dumaw Creek Site: A Seventeenth Century Prehis-*

toric Indian Village and Cemetery in Oceana County, Michigan, Fieldiana Anthropology 56, no. 1 (1966): 87–89. Although some archaeologists continue to argue that the Foxes did not emigrate to Michigan until the middle decades of the seventeenth century, there is considerable evidence that supports an earlier emigration. Both historians and anthropologists agree that Outagami, the common Algonquian term for the Foxes, means the "people of the opposite shore," but many have asserted that the term first was applied to the Foxes when they supposedly lived along the southern shores of Lake Erie, or that it was applied to the tribe when they still occupied the eastern shores of Lake Michigan (see Kellogg, *French Regime*, 87–88). But since most of the Algonquian-speaking tribes that used this term *were* residents of lower Michigan until driven westward by the Neutrals, their appellation for the Foxes makes little sense if the Foxes also shared the region. Moreover, basing her perspective upon La Potherie's narrative, Kellogg argued that the Foxes remained in Michigan until the middle 1640s, for she describes an abortive attempt by the Winnebagos to attack the Fox villages by crossing "Lake Michigan" during this period. But La Potherie only mentions that a large flotilla of Winnebago canoes was sunk by a storm as it attempted to reach the Foxes "who dwelt on the other shore of the lake." Neither La Potherie nor any of the other early sources specifically refer to "the lake" as "Lake Michigan." All available evidence indicates that Indian canoe routes followed the shores of Lake Michigan, and that neither the Winnebagos nor any of the other tribes indigenous to the region were foolish enough to risk a crossing of Lake Michigan in open, birchbark canoes. In contrast, it is more likely that the Winnebagos were attempting to cross Lake Winnebago, also a substantial body of water, where they were caught by the storm and their canoes swamped. Such a circumstance would, of course, indicate that by the late 1630s or early 1640s, the Foxes already had established permanent villages in Wisconsin.

Other evidence also supports the Foxes' early residence west of Lake Michigan. As Noro admitted in 1701, the Foxes did not share in their Algonquian neighbors' animosity for the Iroquois. Unlike the Sauks, Potawatomis, Miamis, and other tribes who had fled to Wisconsin because of Iroquois or Neutral expansion, the Foxes never had been substantially threatened by the Iroquois. In 1670, when Allouez first journeyed to Ouestatimong, he found the Foxes grieving for relatives recently killed by an Iroquois war party, but the Foxes were surprised at the attack and believed that Iroquois had mistaken their kinsmen for Potawatomis. Indeed, during the 1640s, when Neutral and Iroquois war parties had created havoc across Michigan, the Foxes had remained unscathed. They already were in Wisconsin.

In contrast, their enmity toward the Sioux reflected a conflict of some duration. Allouez reported that Ouestatimong had been fortified against Sioux attacks and that the two tribes had been at war for a considerable period. Fox warriors had contested Sioux control over central and western Wisconsin. Again, as Noro pointed out in 1701, the Sioux (a western tribe), not the Iroquois, were the Foxes' old enemies.

Finally, the other Algonquian tribes commonly referred to the Foxes as "barbarians," as a rude, unsophisticated people with little familiarity regarding the recent French-sponsored fur trade that earlier had been funneled through the Huron villages. If the Foxes had remained in Michigan with these other tribes until their dispersal by the Neutrals, there is no reason to assume that they would have been unfamiliar with the fur trade and its practices. But since they already were in Wisconsin, in a region more remote from the trade, they were less familiar with the new economic patterns that were penetrating the western Great Lakes in the seventeenth century. Unlike the Ottawas, Chippewas, or Potawatomis, they had little or no previous access to the fur trade in Michigan.

14. Thwaites, *Jesuit Relations* 54:205–207, 219–21; Wittry, "The Bell Site," 40–44. Also see Helen Hornbeck Tanner, ed., *Atlas of Great Lakes Indian History,* 32–33.

15. Thwaites, *Jesuit Relations* 54:215–27.

16. Ibid.

17. Ibid., 55:219–25. Also see Sebastian Messmer, "The Early Jesuit Missions in the Fox River Valley," *Proceedings of the State Historical Society of Wisconsin at its 47th Annual Meeting,* 147–52.

18. Thwaites, *Jesuit Relations* 56:143–45, 58:43–49.

19. Ibid., 56:145–47, 58:49–71; *Collections of the State Historical Society of Wisconsin* (hereafter cited as *Wisconsin Historical Collections*), 16:88. Jesuit accounts of the Fox-Sioux confrontation contain contradictory dates, although the skirmishes obviously took place in 1672–73.

20. Thwaites, *Jesuit Relations* 58:10, 51–53.

21. Ibid., 59:221–35.

22. Ibid., 60:149–51, 199–201.

23. Ibid., 60:199–201; Kellogg, *French Regime,* 166–68; Emily J. Blasingham, "The Depopulation of the Illinois Indians, Part 2, Concluded," *Ethnohistory* 3 (Fall 1956): 386. Also see Louis Hennepin, *A New Discovery of a Vast Country in America* 1:134–35.

24. *Wisconsin Historical Collections* 16:70; Claude Charles Le Roy Bacqueville de La Potherie, "History of the Savage People Who Are Allies of New France," in Blair, *Indian Tribes of the Upper Mississippi Valley* (hereafter cited as La Potherie, "History"), 1:316–19. Also see Antoine Denis Raudot, "Memoir Concerning the Different Indian Nations of North America," in W. Vernon Kinietz, *The Indians of the Western Great Lakes, 1615–1760*, 382–83.

25. La Potherie, "History," 1:357; Blair, *Indian Tribes of the Upper Mississippi Valley* 2:63–73; Jean Enjalran to Joseph-Antoine Lefebvre de La Barre, August 26, 1686, Margry Manuscripts.

26. Warren, *History of the Ojibway Nation*, 95–96, 190–191.

27. La Potherie, "History," 1:357–59; *Wisconsin Historical Collections*, 16: 101–102.

28. La Potherie, "History," 1:357–59; *Wisconsin Historical Collections*, 16: 101–102.

29. La Potherie, "History," 1:358–59.

30. La Potherie, "History," 1:359–63. Okimaouassen's name was transcribed in various ways in seventeenth- and eighteenth-century New France, including Okimaouasen, Okima8asen, 8ekima8esimme, and Ouikimaoucsime. English transliterations vary as well, including Onkimaouassan (*New York Colonial Documents* 9).

31. La Potherie, "History," 2:28–31.

32. Thwaites, *Jesuit Relations* 54:217–23. Allouez mistakenly believed that Ouestatimong was fortified against Iroquois attacks, but there is no record of Iroquois raids along the Wolf River.

33. Nicolas Perrot, "Memoir on the Manners, Customs, and Religion of the Savages of North America," in Blair, *Indian Tribes of the Upper Mississippi* 1:188–89. Hereafter the Perrot narrative will be cited as Perrot, "Memoir." Also see Thwaites, *Jesuit Relations* 56:145, 58:53–55, and 60:199.

34. Sieur Du Lhut to Frontenac, April 5, 1679, Margry Manuscripts; "Memoir of Duluth on the Sioux Country, 1678–1682," in Louise Phelps Kellogg, ed., *Early Narratives of the Northwest, 1634–1699*, 329–32. Also see Hennepin, *A New Discovery*, 307, and Gary Clayton Anderson, *Kinsmen of Another Kind: Dakota-White Relations in the Upper Mississippi Valley, 1650–1862*, 32–33.

35. Hennepin, *A New Discovery*, 278; Perrot, "Memoir," 245–49; Kellogg, *The French Regime*, 231–33.

36. La Potherie, "History," 2:23, 63–64. Also see Lahontan, *Some New Voyages to North America*, in Fox File, Great Lakes Indian Archives.

37. La Potherie, "History," 2:56–73; Memoir on Canada, 1694–1695, News from the Ottawas, National Archives of Canada, Manuscript

228

Group 1 (MG1), series C¹¹A, vol. 14, transcript pp. 169–70. Hereinafter materials from the National Archives of Canada will be cited as NAC.

38. La Potherie, "History," 2:97–109, 114–18; Memoir on Canada, 1696, AN, Col., series C¹¹A, vol. 14, f. 213; Anderson, *Kinsmen of Another Kind*, 34–35.

39. Thwaites, *Jesuit Relations* 54:225–27; *Wisconsin Historical Collections* 16:69–70. This attack has been discussed earlier; see the text supported by n. 15, above.

40. Thwaites, *Jesuit Relations* 56:143, 58:51–53; *Wisconsin Historical Collections* 16:88; La Potherie, "History," 1:349–350.

41. Narrative of Governor de Courcelle, Margry Manuscripts; Thwaites, *Jesuit Relations* 58:51.

42. Expense Account of La Durantaye, 1683, 1684, in *Collections of the Illinois State Historical Library* 23:60–67; Perrot, "Memoir," 1:232–43.

43. Cadwallader Colden, *The History of the Five Indian Nations*, 58; La Potherie, "History," 2:20–21; Francis Parkman, *Count Frontenac and New France under Louis XIV*, 107–19, 132–37; *Wisconsin Historical Collections* 16:134, 141.

44. Lefebvre de La Barre to unknown, November 4, 1683, Margry Manuscripts; extract of a "Mémoire" of what took place in Canada, 1690, ibid. French documents from the 1680s contain limited reports that some of the Iroquois (especially the Oneidas) "planned" to attack the Foxes during this period, but there are no records that these attacks ever occurred. See Father de Lamberville to Frontenac, September 20, 1682, *New York Colonial Documents* 9:192; Claude Chauchetière to Unknown, October 14, 1682, Fox File, Great Lakes Indian Archives; Account of a Journey in the Country of the Islinois by M. M. Beauvais, Prevost, and Des Posiers, 1683–1684 Margry Manuscripts.

45. La Potherie, "History," 2:54–56; Memoir on Canada, 1694–95, News from the Ottawas, NAC, MG1, series C¹¹A, vol. 14, transcript pp. 169–70; Champigny to the Minister, August 17, 1695, NAC, MG1, C¹¹A, vol. 13, transcript pp. 403–404.

46. Thwaites, *Jesuit Relations* 55:187–89, 219; *Wisconsin Historical Collections* 16:80; Memoir by M. Du Chesneau, September 13, 1681, in *New York Colonial Documents* 9:161–62.

47. Narrative of the Most Remarkable Occurrences in Canada, 1694, 1695, in *New York Colonial Documents* 9:619.

48. La Potherie, "History," 2:62–63; in Blair, *Indian Tribes of the Upper Mississippi*, 2:62–63; Narrative of the Most Remarkable Occurrences in Canada, 1694, 1695, in *New York Colonial Documents* 9:621.

49. Narrative of the Most Remarkable Occurrences in Canada, 1694, 1695, in *New York Colonial Documents* 9:621.

50. Ibid., 621–26.; La Potherie, "History," 2:105–107.

51. Narrative of the Most Remarkable Occurrences in Canada, 1696, 1697, in *New York Colonial Documents* 9:674–75; La Potherie, "History," 2:109–11.

52. Kellogg, *The French Regime*, 257–60; Narrative of the Most Remarkable Occurrences in Canada, 1696, 1697, in *New York Colonial Documents* 9:673.

53. La Potherie, "History," in 2:122–32; Introduction, in Margry Manuscripts; M. Jean-François Buisson de St. Cosme to Unknown, January 2, 1699, in Kellogg, *Early Narratives*, 344; speeches by the Ottawas to Callières, July 12, 1699, AN, Col., series F³, vol. 8, f. 136; speech by the Fox chief, July 29, 1701, ibid., f. 262v. Also see Jacob Van der Zee, "French Discovery and Exploration of the Eastern Iowa Country Before 1763," *Iowa Journal of History and Politics* 12 (July 1914): 338.

54. Charlevoix, *History* 5:151.

CHAPTER TWO
PEOPLE OF THE RED EARTH

1. William Jones, "Episodes in the Culture-Hero Myth of the Sauks and Foxes," *Journal of American Folklore* 14 (October-December 1901): 237–39; William Jones, "Notes on the Fox Indians," *Iowa Journal of History and Politics* 10 (January 1912): 74–75.

2. Jones, "Notes on the Fox Indians," 74–75.

3. Thwaites, *Jesuit Relations* 54:197–227; *Wisconsin Historical Collections* 16:50–59; Jones, "Episodes," 239.

4. Carl F. Voegelin and E. W. Voegelin, "Linguistic Considerations of Northeastern North America," in Frederick Johnson, ed., *Man in Northeastern North America: Papers of the Robert S. Peabody Foundation for Archaeology* 3:191–92; Ives Goddard, "Central Algonquian Languages," in Trigger, ed., *Northeast*, 584–86. Also see Thomas Forsyth, "An Account of the Manners and Customs of the Sauk and Fox Nations of Indians Tradition," in Blair, *Indian Tribes of the Upper Mississippi Valley* 2:239–45.

5. Natalie E. Joffe, "The Fox of Iowa," in Ralph Linton, ed., *Acculturation in Seven American Indian Tribes*, 264; William Jones, *Ethnography of the Fox Indians*, 50–51. Also see Forsyth, "An Account of the Manners and Customs," in Blair, *Indian Tribes of the Upper Mississippi Valley* 2:227.

6. Thwaites, *Jesuit Relations* 51:43–45; Forsyth, "An Account of the Manners and Customs," in Blair, *Indian Tribes of the Upper Mississippi Valley* 2:228–29.

7. Unquestionably the best description of the Foxes' broad spectrum of indigenous vegetable foods can be found in Huron H. Smith, *Ethnobotany of the Meskwaki Indians. Bulletin of the Public Museum of the City of Milwaukee* 4, (no. 2): 252–65. Also see "Antoine Le Claire's Statement," in *Wisconsin Historical Collections* 11:241; Hickerson, *The Southwestern Chippewas*, 92 n.10; and Jones, *Ethnography of the Fox Indians*, 51.

8. Thwaites, *Jesuit Relations* 51:43–45; Joffe, "The Fox of Iowa," 263–64; Forsyth, "An Account of the Manners and Customs," in Blair, *Indian Tribes of the Upper Mississippi Valley* 2:229.

9. Jones, *Ethnography of the Fox Indians*, 88–106; Truman Michelson, "The Mythical Origin of the White Buffalo Dance of the Fox Indians," in *Fortieth Annual Report of the Bureau of American Ethnology*, 23–289; Truman Michelson, "Notes on the Fox Society Known as Those Who Worship the Little Spotted Buffalo," ibid., 497–539; Mark R. Harrington, *Sacred Bundles of the Sac and Fox Indians, University of Pennsylvania Museum Anthropological Publications* 4 (1914): 130–262.

10. Forsyth, "An Account of the Manners and Customs," in Blair, *Indians of the Upper Mississippi Valley*, 227–28; Joffe, "The Fox of Iowa," 264.

11. Joffe, "The Fox of Iowa." For a more contemporary discussion of Mesquakie elders' use of traditional stories as a medium for imparting tribal values, see Fred McTaggart, *Wolf That I Am: In Search of the Red Earth People.*

12. Gary Nash, *Red, White, and Black: The Peoples of Early America*, 22; Forsyth, "An Account of the Manners and Customs," in Blair, *Indian Tribes of the Upper Mississippi Valley* 2:212–13; Joffe, "The Fox of Iowa," 272.

13. Sol Tax, "The Social Organization of the Fox Indians," in Fred Eggan, ed., *Social Anthropology of North American Tribes*, 255–62.

14. Ibid.; Joffe, "The Fox of Iowa," 268.

15. Jones, *Ethnography of the Fox Indians*, 62–64; Truman Michelson, ed., "The Autobiography of a Fox Indian Woman," in *Fortieth Annual Report of the Bureau of American Ethnology*, 305–309, 339–30.

16. Tax, "Social Organization," 275–76; Forsyth, "An Account of the Manners and Customs," in Blair, *Indian Tribes of the Upper Mississippi Valley* 2:195–97, 210; Joffe, "The Fox of Iowa," 273.

17. Callender, "Fox," 638–39; Jones, *Ethnography of the Fox Indians*, 55–61; Forsyth, "An Account of the Manners and Customs," in Blair, *Indian Tribes of the Upper Mississippi* 2:165–67, 212, 216; Thwaites, *Jesuit Relations* 54:219.

18. Callender, "Fox," 638–39.

19. Truman Michelson, "Notes on Fox Mortuary Customs and Beliefs," *Fortieth Annual Report of the Bureau of American Ethnology*, 435–51, 55–61,

485–91; Michelson, "Autobiography of a Fox Woman," 329–33; Jones, *Ethnography of the Fox Indians,* 64–70.

20. Joffe, "The Fox of Iowa," 273–74; Michelson, "Notes on Fox Mortuary Customs," 405–406; Jones, *Ethnography of the Fox Indians,* 16–17.

21. Thwaites, *Jesuit Relations* 51:45; Jones, *Ethnography of the Fox Indians,* 13–14.

22. Jones, "Notes on the Fox Indians," 75–79; Jones, *Ethnography of the Fox Indians,* 18–20.

23. There is extensive information upon the place of manitous within Fox religious beliefs. See Michelson, "The Mythical Origin," 23–290 passim; Jones, *Ethnography of the Fox Indians,* 20–23; Michelson, *Notes on the Fox Wâpanôwiweni,* 3–195 passim; Michelson, *Fox Miscellany,* 18–118 passim; Jones, "Notes on the Fox Indians," 79–80; Thwaites, *Jesuit Relations* 50:285–89.

24. Eugene Fugler, "Mesquakie Witchcraft Lore," *Plains Anthropologist* 6 (February 1961): 31–39. Also see Jones, *Ethnography of the Fox Indians,* 26–30, and Thwaites, *Jesuit Relations* 50:291–93, and 61: 149–51.

25. Forsyth, "An Account of the Manners and Customs," in Blair, *Indian Tribes of the Upper Mississippi,* 2:235–37; Wittry, "A Michigan Fox Hunt," 77; Thwaites, *Jesuit Relations* 54:207; *Wisconsin Historical Collections,* 16:39; Jones, *Ethnography of the Fox Indians,* 54–55; Kinietz, *Indians of the Western Great Lakes,* 169.

26. Marston, "Memoirs of the Sauk and Foxes," in Blair, *Indian Tribes of the Upper Mississippi* 2:151–53; Gary A. Wright, "Some Aspects of Early and Mid-seventeenth Century Exchange Networks in the Western Great Lakes," *Michigan Archaeologist* 13 (December 1967): 181–94.

27. Wittry, "The Bell Site," 17–50; Joe Bauxar, "The Historic Period," *Illinois Archaeology,* 46–47. Also see George Irving Quimby, *Indian Culture and European Trade Goods: The Archaeology of the Historic Period in the Western Great Lakes Region,* 117–25. Richard White recently has argued that the Great Lakes tribes did not become dependent on European goods until late in the eighteenth century, and that in an emergency the "Algonquians remained able to feed, clothe, and shelter themselves without European assistance." But there is strong evidence to suggest that the tribespeople desperately wanted such merchandise, particularly firearms, and when their access to such goods was denied, they complained bitterly. In 1697, after the French limited the supply of trade goods reaching the West, Potawatomi and Ottawa leaders from Lake Michigan journeyed to Montreal, where

they charged that "formerly you furnished us powder and iron to conquer our enemies, but now we are in want of everything. Since we want powder, iron, and every other necessary which you were formerly in the habit of sending us, what do you expect us to do?" Obviously, the western tribes believed that they needed European goods and were willing to exert considerable effort both to acquire them and to keep them from their enemies. See White, *The Middle Ground: Indians, Empires, and Republics in the Great Lakes Region, 1650–1815* (Cambridge: Cambridge University Press, 1991), 140; and Report of a Conference at Montreal, 1697, *Wisconsin Historical Collections* 16:166–73.

28. Thwaites, *Jesuit Relations* 51:45, 55:187–89, 219; Memoir by M. Du Chesneau, September 13, 1681, in *New York Colonial Documents*, 9:161–62.

29. Memoir by Antoine Denis Raudot, 1710, in Kinietz, *Indians of the Western Great Lakes*, 382–83; *Wisconsin Historical Collections* 16:39; La Potherie, "History," in Blair, *Indian Tribes of the Upper Mississippi* 1:316–22; Warren, *History of the Ojibway*, 147–48.

30. Raudot Memoir, 1710, in Kinietz, *Indians of the Western Great Lakes*, 382–83; La Potherie, "History," in Blair, *Indian Tribes of the Upper Mississippi* 1:316–22.

31. Extracts from the Instructions of the King to Sieur de Meules, May 10, 1682, in Margry Manuscripts; Extract from the Account of the Events that took place in Canada from 1694 to 1695, ibid.; M. Jean Frs. Buisson de St. Cosme to Unknown, January 2, 1699, in Kellogg, *Early Narratives of the Northwest*, 344; La Potherie, "History," in Blair, *Indian Tribes of the Upper Mississippi* 2:27.

32. Forsyth, "An Account of the Manners and Customs," in Blair, *Indian Tribes of the Upper Mississippi* 2:103; Jones, *Ethnography of the Fox Indians*, 72–78. Other clans also may have been present at that time. Some evidence suggests that the Eagle clan, an important group in the nineteenth century, may have originated from the Thunder clan. Other prominent nineteenth century clans such as the Bear, Potato, or Sturgeon groups may have originated among the Sacs.

33. Marston, "Memoirs of the Sauk and Foxes," in Blair, *Indian Tribes of the Upper Mississippi* 2:162, 213, 196–97; Michelson, "Fox Mortuary Customs," 359–64, 385, 425–27; Joffe, "The Fox of Iowa," 267; Anthony F. C. Wallace, *The Death and Rebirth of the Seneca*, 44–48, 102–103.

34. Callender, "Fox," 640; Tax, "Social Organization of the Fox Indians," 268–69; Joffe, "The Fox of Iowa," 270; Jones, "Notes on the Fox Indians," 87–90.

35. Forsyth, "An Account of the Manners and Customs," in Blair, *Indian Tribes of the Upper Mississippi* 2:186–87; Callender, "Fox," 640–41.

36. Jones, *Ethnography of the Fox Indians*, 84–87; Tax, "Social Organization of the Fox Indians," 259.

37. Callender, "Fox," 640–41; Joffe, "The Fox of Iowa," 271; Forsyth, "An Account of the Manners and Customs," in Blair, *Indian Tribes of the Upper Mississippi* 2:227. Also see Walter B. Miller, "Two Concepts of Authority," *American Anthropologist* 57 (1955) 271–89.

38. Jones, *Ethnography of the Fox Indians*, 73; Forsyth, "An Account of the Sauk and Foxes," in Blair, *Indian Tribes of the Upper Mississippi* 2: 194–95. The Foxes were not the only tribe whose political structure was changed by warfare during these decades. Wallace describes the increased role of war chiefs among the Iroquois in *Death and Rebirth of the Seneca*, 39–48.

39. Jones, "Notes on the Fox Indians," 90–91; Forsyth, "An Account of the Sauks and Foxes," in Blair, *Indian Tribes of the Upper Mississippi* 2:197–98. Also see Truman Michelson, *The Owl Sacred Pack of the Fox Indians*, 19–21, 33, 35.

40. Forsyth, "An Account of the Sauks and Foxes," in Blair, *Indian Tribes of the Upper Mississippi* 2:161–62; Callender, "Fox," 640–42; Joffe, "The Fox of Iowa," 276–78.

41. The Iroquois called their league the Hodenosaunee, or People of the Longhouse. See William Fenton, "Northern Iroquoian Culture Patterns," in Trigger, *Northeast*, 320.

42. The Foxes and many of their Algonquian-speaking neighbors referred to the Iroquois as the Machi Nodaway, or "Bad Snakes." See ibid.

CHAPTER THREE
REAPING THE WHIRLWIND

1. C. M. Burton, "Fort Pontchartrain du Detroit—1701 to 1710—under Cadillac," *Collections of the Michigan Pioneer and Historical Society* (hereafter cited as *Michigan Historical Collections*), 24:240–42, 250–54; C. M. Burton, "Detroit Rulers: French Commandants in this Region from 1701 to 1760," ibid., 34:303–305; Kellogg, *French Regime in Wisconsin,* 254.

2. Memorandum of Lamothe Cadillac on the foundation of a post at Detroit, forwarded to Canada, May 27, 1699, in Margry Manuscripts; Memorandum of Cadillac concerning the Establishment of Detroit, from Quebec, November 19, 1704, in *Michigan Historical Collections,* 33:198–99.

3. Cadillac to Phillip de Rigault, Marquis de Vaudreuil, August 31, 1703, *Michigan Historical Collections* 33:161–62; First Council held at Fort Pont-

chartrain, October 3, 1701, in Margry Manuscripts; Council of the Hurons at Detroit, December 4, 1701, ibid.

4. Speeches by the Hurons, February 17, 1702, in Margry Manuscripts; Speech by Michipichy to the Miamis, February 27, 1702, ibid.; Council with the Miamis, June 1702, ibid.; Cadillac to Vaudreuil, August 31, 1703, *Michigan Historical Collections* 33:161–63. Also see Burton, "Fort Pontchartrain du Detroit," 260–62, and R. David Edmunds, "Miami Tribal Movements, 1670–1750," 6–7 (unpublished manuscript in author's possession).

5. Council with the Iroquois, December 7, 1701, in Margry Manuscripts; Council between the Ottawas and Iroquois, May 4, 1702, ibid.; Council between the Iroquois, Ottawas, Hurons, Nipissings, and Mississaugas, July 1702, ibid.

6. Cadillac to Vaudreuil, August 31, 1703, *Michigan Historical Collections* 33:166–68; C. M. Burton, "Early Detroit," ibid., 24:225–29; Burton, "Fort Pontchartrain du Détroit," 263–73.

7. Observations by Cadillac, 1705, *Michigan Historical Collections* 33: 233–36; Speeches of the Ottawas at Michilimackinac, September 27, 1703, *Wisconsin Historical Collections* 16:221–27; Summary of an Inspection of the Posts of Detroit and Michilimackinac, by D'Aigremont, November 14, 1708, ibid., 251–60.

8. Joseph Marest to Vaudreuil, August 27, 1706, *Michigan Historical Collections* 33:269–70; Cadillac to Vaudreuil, August 27, 1706, ibid., 272–85; Speech of Miscoukay, September 27, 1706, ibid., 288–96; Speech by Jean Leblanc, June 23, 1707, ibid., 326–27. Also see Marest to Vaudreuil, August 14, 1706, *Wisconsin Historical Collections* 16:232–38.

9. Speech by Leblanc, June 23, 1707, *Michigan Historical Collections* 33:326–27; Speech by Miscoukay, September 27, 1706, ibid., 288–96; Cadillac to Vaudreuil, August 27, 1706, ibid., 272–85. For a detailed discussion on the negotiations surrounding this affair, see White, *The Middle Ground,* 82–90.

10. Memorandum by Vaudreuil, November 13, 1708, *Michigan Historical Collections* 33:399–400; Summary of an Inspection of the Posts of Detroit and Michilimackinac, November 14, 1708, *Wisconsin Historical Collections* 16:251–60; Vaudreuil to Pontchartrain, July 24, 1707, *New York Colonial Documents* 9:810–11. Also see Charlevoix, *History* 5:187–90. Written by a Jesuit, Charlevoix's account of these events exonerates the priests and is very critical of Cadillac.

11. Report of a Conference at Montreal, September 27, 1703, *Wisconsin Historical Collections* 16:221–27; Marest to Vaudreuil, August 14, 1706, ibid., 232–39.

12. Extract from the memoir of the Chevalier de Baurain on Louisiana, 1702, Margry Documents; Diron d'Artaguette to Pontchartrain, February 12, 1710, ibid.; Raudot Memoir, 1710, in Kinietz, *Indians of the Western Great Lakes,* 382–83; Cadillac to Vaudreuil, August 31, 1703, *Michigan Historical Collections* 33:161–81.

13. Minutes of a Council with the Hurons, May 14, 1703, Margry Documents; Speeches of the Ottawas, September 27, 1703, *Wisconsin Historical Collections* 16:221–27; Report by Dubuisson, June 15, 1712, ibid., 267–87; Perrot, "Memoir," in Blair, *Indians of the Upper Mississippi* 1:260–61; Report by Vaudreuil, November 8, 1711, *Michigan Historical Collections* 33:528–36. "Sauganash" was the Fox term for the English.

14. Memorandum on the settlement of Mobile and the Mississippi, Margry Documents; Gaspard Chaussegros de Léry to Unknown, 1712, *Wisconsin Historical Collections* 16:293–95.

15. Speech by Vaudreuil to the Indians, March 1711, *Michigan Historical Collections* 33:503–506; Memorandum by Vaudreuil, March 10, 1711, ibid., 497–502; Dubuisson to Vaudreuil, June 15, 1712, *Wisconsin Historical Collections* 16:267–87.

16. Speech by Vaudreuil to the Indians, March 1711, *Michigan Historical Collections* 33:503–506; Dubuisson to Vaudreuil, June 15, 1712, *Wisconsin Historical Collections* 16:267–87; Speech by Makisabi, August 17, 1712, NAC, MG1, C¹¹A, vol. 33, transcript pp. 130–42.

17. Speech by Vaudreuil to the Indians, March 1711, *Michigan Historical Collections* 33:503–506. Also see William A. Hunter, "Refugee Fox Settlements among the Senecas," *Ethnohistory* 3 (Winter 1956): 11–12.

18. Dubuisson to Vaudreuil, June 15, 1712, *Wisconsin Historical Collections* 16:267–87; Vaudreuil to Pontchartrain, November 6, 1712, *New York Colonial Documents* 9:862–65; Speech by Makisabi, August 17, 1712, NAC, MG1, C¹¹A, vol. 33, transcript pp. 130–42.

19. De Léry to Unknown, 1712, *Wisconsin Historical Collections* 16:293–95; Dubuisson to Vaudreuil, June 15, 1712, ibid., 267–87; Speech by Makisabi, August 17, 1712, NAC, MG1, C¹¹A, vol. 33, transcript pp. 130–42.

20. Marest to Vaudreuil, June 21, 1712, *Wisconsin Historical Collections* 16:288–90; Speech by Makisabi, August 17, 1712, NAC, MG1, C¹¹A, vol. 33, transcript pp. 130–42.

21. Dubuisson to Vaudreuil, June 15, 1712, *Wisconsin Historical Collections* 16:267–87; De Léry to Unknown, 1712, ibid., 293–95.

22. Dubuisson to Vaudreuil, June 15, 1712, *Wisconsin Historical Collections* 16:267–87.

23. Ibid.

24. Ibid.

25. Ibid.; Speech by Makisabi, August 17, 1712, NAC, MG1, C¹¹A, vol. 33, transcript, pp. 130–42.

26. Ibid.; Dubuisson to Vaudreuil, June 15, 1712, *Wisconsin Historical Collections* 16:267–87.

27. Dubuisson to Vaudreuil, June 15, 1712, *Wisconsin Historical Collections* 16:267–87; Statement of what Mons. Dubuisson expended for the services of the King . . . at Detroit, October 14, 1712, *Michigan Historical Collections*, 33:568.

28. Dubuisson to Vaudreuil, June 15, 1712, *Wisconsin Historical Collections* 16:267–87.

29. De Léry to Unknown, 1712, ibid., 293–95.

30. Dubuisson to Vaudreuil, June 15, 1712, ibid., 267–87.

31. Ibid.

32. De Léry to Unknown, 1712, ibid., 293–95.

33. Dubuisson to Vaudreuil, June 15, 1712, ibid., 267–87.

34. Ibid. Italics added for ironic emphasis.

35. Ibid.

36. Ibid.

37. Ibid.

38. Ibid.

39. De Léry to Unknown, 1712, ibid., 293–95.

40. Ibid.; Dubuisson to Vaudreuil, June 15. 1712, ibid., 267–87.

41. De Léry to Unknown, 1712, ibid., 293–98; Dubuisson to Vaudreuil, June 15, 1712, ibid., 288–92.

42. Marest to Vaudreuil, June 21, 1712, ibid., 288–92; Dubuisson to Vaudreuil, June 15, 1712, ibid., 267–87; De Léry to Unknown, 1712, ibid., 293–98.

43. Dubuisson to Vaudreuil, June 15, 1712, ibid., 267–87; Marest to Vaudreuil, June 21, 1712, ibid., 288–92; Vaudreuil to Pontchartrain, September 6, 1712, *Michigan Historical Collections* 33:559–67; Speech by Chachagouesse, August 20, 1712, NAC, MG1, C¹¹A, vol. 33, transcript pp. 145–46, 149–50; Hunter, "Refugee Fox Settlements among the Senecas," 11–12.

44. Vaudreuil to Pontchartrain, September 6, 1712, *Michigan Historical Collections* 33:559–67; Vaudreuil to Pontchartrain, October 15, 1712, ibid., 569–71; Vaudreuil to Pontchartrain, November 6, 1712, *New York Colonial Documents* 9:862–65; Speeches of the Senecas to the Governor General and his reply, September 10, 1712, NAC, MG1, C¹¹A, vol. 33, transcript pp. 151, 157–63.

45. Vaudreuil to the Minister, November 15, 1713, *Wisconsin Historical Col-*

lections 16:298–99; Claude de Ramezay to the Minister, September 18, 1714, ibid., 300–303; Letter to the Minister, November 12, 1714, Fox File, Great Lakes Indian Archives; Extracts from letters of Ramezay and Begon to the Minister, September 13 and September 16, 1715, *Wisconsin Historical Collections* 16:311–22.

46. Ramezay to the Minister, September 18, 1714, *Wisconsin Historical Collections* 16:300–303.

47. Ibid.; Vaudreuil to the Minister, November 15, 1713, ibid., 298–99; Vaudreuil to the Minister, September 6, 1712, *Michigan Historical Collections* 33:559–67.

48. Vaudreuil and Bégon to the French Minister, September 20, 1714, *Wisconsin Historical Collections* 16:303–307; Ramezay and Bégon to the French Minister, September 1714, ibid., 311–22; Kellogg, *French Regime in Wisconsin*, 252, 299; Anderson, *Kinsmen of Another Kind*, 38–48. Anderson illustrates that considerable Sioux-Chippewa conflict emerged in the 1720s and 1730s.

49. In 1713–1714 the Tuscaroras moved from the Carolinas to New York, where they became associated with the Iroquois confederacy. After that date the Iroquois League, or Five Nations, became known as the Six Nations.

50. Speech of the Seneca delegates, September 25, 1714, AN, Col., C¹¹A, vol. 34, ff. 297–98v; Letter to the French Minister, October 23, 1714, Fox File, Great Lakes Indian Archives; Letters and Papers of Cadwallader Colden, vol. 9, 418, Great Lakes Indian Archives; Message of the Far Indians to Governor Hunter, August 29, 1715, *New York Colonial Documents* 5:445–46.

51. Vaudreuil and Bégon to the French Minister, September 20, 1714, *Wisconsin Historical Collections* 16:303–307; Ramezay and Bégon to the French Minister, September, 1715, ibid., 311–22.

52. Entry for June 14, 1715, in "An Abridgment of Indian Affairs," Fox File, Great Lakes Indian Archives; "Statement by Colden," Letters and Papers of Cadwallader Colden, Great Lakes Indian Archives; Vaudreuil to the Council of the Marine, October 14, 1716, AN Col. C¹¹A, vol. 36, ff. 71–76; Ramezay to the French Minister, November 3, 1715, *Wisconsin Historical Collections* 16:322–26; Ramezay and Bégon to the French Minister, November 7, 1715, ibid., 327–28.

53. Ramezay to the French Minister, September 13, 1715, Fox File, Great Lakes Indian Archives.

54. Wittry, "The Bell Site," 3–6, 43–46; Louvigny to the Council, October 14, 1716, *Wisconsin Historical Collections* 5:78–80; Charlevoix, *History* 5:306. Some local historians and antiquarians have argued that the

village was located on the Little Butte des Morts Lake. See Publius Lawson, "The Outagamie Village at West Menasha," *Proceedings of the State Historical Society of Wisconsin at Its 47th Annual Meeting* (Madison: Democrat Printing Co., 1900), 204–11.

55. Vaudreuil to the Council of Marine, October 14, 1716, AN, Col., C¹¹A, vol. 36, ff. 71–76.

56. Ibid.

57. List of Expenses incurred on the occasion of the Renard War, and in 1715, 1716, and 1717, *Wisconsin Historical Collections* 16:400–407; Kellogg, *The French Regime,* 285–87.

58. Louvigny to the Council, October 14, 1716, *Wisconsin Historical Collections* 5:78–80; Vaudreuil to the Council, October 30, 1716, ibid., 80–81; Vaudreuil to the Council, October 14, 1716, *Michigan Historical Collections* 33:576–79.

59. Proceedings in the French Council of Marine, March 28, 1716, *Wisconsin Historical Collections* 16:338–40; Louvigny to the Council, October 14, 1716, ibid., 5:78–80; Vaudreuil to the Council, October 14, 1716, *Michigan Historical Collections* 33:576–79.

60. Louvigny to the Council, October 14, 1716, *Wisconsin Historical Collections* 5:78–80; Vaudreuil to the Council, October 14, 1716, *Michigan Historical Collections* 33:576–79; Council of Marine to François de Beauharnois, May 2, 1716, NAC, MG1, AN Col. B, vol. 38, f. 111 (microfilm F224).

61. Louvigny to the Council, October 14, 1716, *Wisconsin Historical Collections* 5:78–80.

62. Kellogg, *The French Regime,* 287–88.

63. Ibid.; Charlevoix, *History* 5:306–307; Louvigny to the Council, October 14, 1716, *Wisconsin Historical Collections* 5:78–80.

64. Vaudreuil to the Council, October 14, 1716, *Michigan Historical Collections* 33:576–79.

65. Louvigny to the Council, October, 14, 1716, *Wisconsin Historical Collections* 5:78–80; Vaudreuil to the Council, October 30, 1716, ibid., 80–81; Statement by Pierre Lestage, 1716, *Bulletin des recherches historiques* 35 (1929): 287; Charlevoix, *History* 5:309; Perrot, "Memoir," in Blair, *Indian Tribes of the Upper Mississippi* 1:268–72.

CHAPTER FOUR
BITTER INTERLUDE

1. Vaudreuil to the Council of the Marine, October 12, 1717, *Michigan Historical Collections* 33:588–90.

2. Louvigny to Louis Alexandre de Bourbon, October 1, 1717, *Wisconsin Historical Collections* 16:346–49.

3. Ibid.

4. Ibid.; Vaudreuil to the Council of the Marine, October 12, 1717, *Michigan Historical Collections* 33:588–90.

5. Vaudreuil to the Council of the Marine, October 12, 1717, ibid., 33:588–90.

6. Ibid.; Louvigny to Louis Alexandre de Bourbon, October 1, 1717, *Wisconsin Historical Collections* 16:346–49.

7. Vaudreuil to the Council of the Marine, October 12, 1717, *Michigan Historical Collections* 33:588–90; Louvigny to Louis Alexandre de Bourbon, October 1, 1717, *Wisconsin Historical Collections* 16:346–49.

8. Memoir of the Savages of Canada, 1718, *New York Colonial Documents* 9:885–92; Vaudreuil to the Council, October 30, 1718, *Wisconsin Historical Collections* 16:377–79.

9. Vaudreuil to the Council, October 30, 1718, *Wisconsin Historical Collections* 16:377–79.

10. Ibid. The identity of White Robe remains open to question. Although the modern Mesquakie people consider him to be of Fox or Mesquakie descent, contemporary French documents repeatedly refer to him as a Kickapoo. See Fred McTaggart, *Wolf That I Am: In Search of the Red Earth People,* 167–73; and Jones, "Fox Notes," 103–104. Both of the above references describe White Robe as a member of the Fox or Mesquakie tribe. Documents describing him as a Kickapoo include Proceedings of a Council, October 6, 1721, *Wisconsin Historical Collections* 16:395–400; Narrative of De Boucherville's "Captivity among the Kickapoos, 1728–1729," ibid, 17:36–56; Lespervenche to Beauharnois, June 11, 1728, AN Col., C¹¹A, vol. 50, f. 398v; and Vaudreuil to the Council, October 6, 1721, AN, Col., C¹¹A, vol 44, ff. 72–84. Vaudreuil's letter of October 6, 1728, is published in Joseph L. Peyser, *Letters from New France,* 105–108. Since the Foxes, the Kickapoos, and the Mascoutens were closely allied, and since these tribes frequently intermarried during this period, White Robe may have been of Fox lineage but living among the Kickapoos.

11. Vaudreuil to the Council, October 28, 1719, *Wisconsin Historical Collections* 16:380–83.

12. Ibid.; Vaudreuil to the Council, October 22, 1720, ibid., 392–95; Vaudreuil and Bégon to the Council of the Marine, October 26, 1719, NAC, MG1, C¹¹A, vol. 40, transcript p. 16.

13. Vaudreuil to the Council, October 28, 1719, *Wisconsin Historical Collections* 16:380–83.

14. Ibid.; Vaudreuil to the Council, October 22, 1720, ibid., 392–95.

15. Excerpt from Charlevoix's *Journal Historique,* in *Wisconsin Historical Collections* 16:417; Vaudreuil to the Minister, October 11, 1723, ibid.,

16:433–41; Report from Canada, 1726, ibid., 16:463–68; Vaudreuil and Bégon to the Minister, October 14, 1725, Margry Manuscripts; Charles Le Moyne, Baron de Longueuil, to Bégon, October 31, 1725, ibid.

16. Vaudreuil to the French Minister, October 2, 1723, *Wisconsin Historical Collections* 16:428–31; Vaudreuil to the French Minister, October 11, 1723, ibid., 433–41; C. C. Du Tisné to Vaudreuil, January 14, 1725, ibid., 450–53; ibid., 443 n.2. Also see Vaudreuil to the Council, November 4, 1720, Margry Translation, Fox File, Great Lakes Indian Archives.

17. Entry for May 27, 1722, in Stanley Faye, ed., "A Search for Copper on the Illinois River: The Journal of Le Gardeur Delisle, 1722," *Journal of the Illinois State Historical Society* 38 (March 1945), 52–53; Nicolas Michael Chassin to Father Bobe, July 1, 1722, in Dunbar Rowland, A. G. Sanders, and Patricia Galloway, eds., *Mississippi Provincial Archives: French Dominion* 2:274–79.

18. Entries for June 9–14, 1722, in Faye, "Delisle Journal," 54–56; entry for October 23, 1722, in the Journal of Diron d'Artaguiette, in Fox File, Great Lakes Indian Archives; Speech by Ouchala, September 6, 1722, in *Wisconsin Historical Collections* 16:418–20. Although local traditions suggest that the Illinois Confederacy was besieged on Starved Rock by the Ottawas and the Potawatomis after Pontiac was killed by an Illinois warrior, contemporary documents make no mention of such an incident following Pontiac's death. The legend of Starved Rock may very well have originated from Ouchala's raid.

19. Speech by Ouchala, September 6, 1722, *Wisconsin Historical Collections* 16:418–20.

20. Speech by Elecevas, September 6, 1722, ibid., 420.

21. Speech by Montigny, September 6, 1722, ibid., 421–22.

22. Proceedings of a Council, December 2, 1721, ibid., 395–400; Speeches of the Foxes in Council, September 6, 1722, ibid., 418–22; Vaudreuil to the French Minister, October 2, 1722, ibid., 428–31; entry for April 30, 1723, in Journal of Diron d'Artaguiette, Fox File, Great Lakes Indian Archives; Vaudreuil to the Council, October 6, 1721, in Peyser, *Letters from New France*, 105–108.

23. Joseph Aubry to Vaudreuil, October 3, 1723, in Thwaites, *Jesuit Relations* 67:128–31; ibid., 56:267, n.22; Vaudreuil to the Minister, October 11, 1723, *Wisconsin Historical Collections* 16:433–41.

24. Vaudreuil to the Minister, October 11, 1723, *Wisconsin Historical Collections* 16:433–41.

25. Vaudreuil to Boisbriant, May 20, 1724, ibid., 441–42; Lignery to Boisbriant, August 23, 1724, ibid., 444–46.

26. Lignery to Boisbriant, August 23, 1724, ibid., 444–46.

27. Vaudreuil to the Minister, October 11, 1723, ibid., 433–41; Vaudreuil to Boisbriant, May 20, 1724, ibid., 441–42; Vaudreuil to Boisbriant, August 17, 1724, ibid., 442–44; Jean Le Boullenger and Joseph François Kereben to Claude Charles Du Tisné, January 10, 1725, ibid., 453–56. Boullenger and Kereben were priests at Kaskaskia. Du Tisné was the French commander at Fort de Chartres, in the Illinois Country.

28. Du Tisné to the Minister, January 14, 1725, *Wisconsin Historical Collections* 16:450–53; Speech by the Illinois Indians, January 14, 1725, ibid., 456–63.

29. Lignery to De Siette *(sic)*, June 19, 1726, ibid., 3:153–56; Memoir from Boisbriant, February 1725, NAC, MG1, C^{13}A, vol. 8, ff. 447–50 (microfilm F-1048).

30. Étienne de Bourgmont to the Commissioners, January 11, 1724, Margry Manuscripts; Speeches of the Missouria, Osage, and Otoe tribes, November 19, 1724, ibid.; entry for April 19, 1723, Journal of Diron d'Artaguiette, Fox File, Great Lakes Indian Archives; Boullenger and Kereben to Du Tisné, January 10, 1725, *Wisconsin Historical Collections* 16:453–56; Speeches of the Illinois, January 14, 1725, ibid., 456–63. Also see Henri Folmer, "Étienne Veniard de Bourgmond in the Missouri Country," *Missouri Historical Review* 36 (April 1942): 280; and Blasingham, "Depopulation of the Illinois Indians," 403–405.

31. Entry for June 2, 1723, Journal of Diron d'Artaguiette, Fox File, Great Lakes Indian Archives; entry for September 9, 1723, ibid.; Lignery to Boisbriant, August 23, 1724, *Wisconsin Historical Collections* 16: 444–46; Boullenger and Kereben to Du Tisné, January 10, 1725, ibid., 453–56; Du Tisné to the Minister, January 14, 1725, ibid., 450–53.

32. Charles Michel Messager to the Commandant at Kaskaskia, October 2, 1724, *Wisconsin Historical Collections* 16:446–48; Memoir Concerning the Peace Made by Monsieur de Lignery with the Chiefs of the Foxes, Sauks, and Winnebagos, June 7, 1726, ibid., 148–150.

33. Superior Council of Louisiana to the General Directors of the Company of the Indies, February 27, 1725, in Rowland, Sanders, and Galloway, *Mississippi Provincial Archives* 2:399–418; "An Account of the Arrival in France of Four Mississippi Savages," December 1725, in Richard Ellis and Charlie E. Steen, eds., "An Indian Delegation in France, 1725," *Journal of the Illinois State Historical Society* 67 (September 1964): 389–405; Folmer, "Étienne Veniard de Bourgmond," 295–97; Kellogg, *French Regime*, 307.

34. Report from Canada, 1726, *Wisconsin Historical Collections* 16:463–68; Longueuil to the Minister, July 25, 1726, ibid., 3:156–59.

35. Report of a Council held at Green Bay, June 7, 1726, Ibid., 150–53.

36. Ibid.; Lignery to De Siette (*sic*), June 19, 1726, ibid., 153–156.

37. Ibid.; Memoir Concerning the Peace made by Monsieur Lignery with the Chiefs of the Foxes, Sauks, and Winnebagos, June 7, 1726, ibid., 148–50; Report from Canada, 1726, ibid., 16:463–68.

38. Longueuil to Chippewas, 1726, ibid., 3:165–66; Longueuil to the Minister, July 25, 1726, ibid., 156–59.

39. Longueuil to the Minister, July 25, 1726, ibid., 156–59; Articles of the Trading Company for the Post among the Sioux, June 6, 1727, Margry Manuscripts; Beauharnois to the Minister of the Navy, September 25, 1727, ibid.; Guignas to Beauharnois, May 29, 1728, ibid.

40. Longueuil to the Minister, July 25, 1726, *Wisconsin Historical Collections* 3:156–59; Beauharnois to the Minister, October 1, 1726, ibid., 159–60; Résumé of French Relations with the Foxes, April 27, 1727, ibid., 17:1–7.

41. Guignas to Beauharnois, May 29, 1728, Margry Manuscripts.

42. Affidavit of Mssrs. Groesbeck and Schyler, February 15, 1724, *New York Colonial Documents* 5:743–44; Cadwallader Colden's Memoir on the Fur Trade, November 11, 1724, ibid., 726–33; Speeches by the Hurons, August 9, 1727, *Michigan Historical Collections* 34:49–51; Beauharnois to the Minister, September 25, 1727, ibid., 51–53; Beauharnois and De Argemait (*sic*) to the Minister, September 1, 1728, *Wisconsin Historical Collections* 5:92–95.

43. Beauharnois to the Minister, May 18, 1727, *Wisconsin Historical Collections* 16:468–70; Beauharnois to De Siette (*sic*), August 20, 1727, ibid., 3:163; Beauharnois and Depuy to the Minister, October 25, 1727, ibid., 16:476–77; Beauharnois and D'Aigremont to the Minister, October 1, 1728, *Michigan Historical Collections* 34:63–64; Speech of 8ekima8esimme, 1727, AN, Col. C^{11}A, vol. 49, f. 521; excerpts from letters by La Perrière and La Fresnière, September 10 and 13, 1728, NAC, MG1, C^{11}A, vol. 50, transcript pp. 66–68.

44. Beauharnois to De Siette (*sic*), August 20, 1727, *Wisconsin Historical Collections* 3:163–64; Beauharnois to Unknown, September 25, 1727, ibid., 162; Beauharnois and Depuy to the Minister, October 25, 1727, ibid., 16:476–77; Beauharnois and De Argemait (*sic*) to the Minister, September 1, 1728, ibid., 5:92–95.

45. Conference between Governor Montgomery and the Indians, October, 1728, *New York Colonial Documents* 5:859–70; excerpts from letters by La Perrière and La Fresnière, September 10, 1728, NAC, MG1, C^{11}A, vol. 50, transcript pp. 66–68; Beauharnois to the French Minister, August 4, 1728, *Wisconsin Historical Collections* 17:28–29.

46. Perier and La Chaise to the Minister, January 30, 1729, AN, Col. C^{13}A,

vol. 11, f. 309; Perier to Le Pelletier, April 1, 1729, AN Col. C¹¹A, vol. 12. ff. 7, 13; excerpts from letters by La Perrière and Lafresnière, September 10 and 13, 1728, NAC, MG1, C¹¹A, 50:66–68.

47. Lignery to Beauharnois, August 30, 1728, *Wisconsin Historical Collections* 17:31–35; Emanuel Crespel's Narrative, 1728, ibid., 10:47–53.

48. Emanuel Crespel's Narrative, ibid., 10:47–53; Lignery to Beauharnois, August 30, 1728, ibid., 17:31–35.

49. Crespel's Narrative, ibid., 10:47–53; Lignery to Beauharnois, August 30, 1728, ibid., 17:31–35.

50. Beauharnois and De Argemait (*sic*) to the Minister, September 1, 1728, ibid., 5:92–95; Crespel's Narrative, ibid., 10:47–53; Lignery to Beauharnois, August 30, 1728, ibid., 17:31–35.

51. Lignery to Beauharnois, August 30, 1728, ibid., 17:31–35.

52. Extract of a Memoir from the King to the Governor General and Intendant of New France, May 14, 1728, *New York Colonial Documents* 9:1004–1005; S. Dale Standen, "Charles, Marquis de Beauharnois de La Boische, Governor General of New France, 1726–1747," Ph.D. diss. University of Toronto, 1975, 175–82. Although Standen defends Beauharnois from charges that he often acted rashly and out of self-interest, he does discuss the many allegations that seem to have plagued Beauharnois through much of his career.

53. Beauharnois and De Argemait (*sic*) to the French Minister, September 8, 1728, *Wisconsin Historical Collections* 5:93–95; Beauharnois and Gilles Hocquart to the French Minister, October 25, 1729, ibid., 17:73–76; Beauharnois and De Aigremont (*sic*) to the Minister, October 1, 1728, *Michigan Historical Collections* 34:63–64.

54. Beauharnois and De Argemait (*sic*) to the French Minister, September 1, 1728, *Wisconsin Historical Collections* 5:92–93; Narrative of De Boucherville, 1728–1729, ibid., 17:36–56; Beauharnois to the French Minister, September 1, 1729, ibid., 67–69; Perrier, De Salvert, and De La Chaise to the Directors of the Company of the Indies, March 25, 1729, in Fox File, Great Lakes Indian Archives.

55. Beauharnois to the French Minister, July 21, 1729, *Wisconsin Historical Collections* 17:62–65; Beauharnois to the French Minister, August 17, 1729, ibid., 65–66; Beauharnois to the French Minister, September 1, 1729, ibid., 67–69; De Léry to Unknown, 1712, ibid., 16:293–95.

CHAPTER FIVE
ARMAGEDDON

1. Boucherville Narrative, 1728–1729, *Wisconsin Historical Collections* 17:36–37.

2. Ibid.

3. Ibid.

4. Ibid., 37–39.

5. Ibid. Also see A. M. Gibson, *The Kickapoos: Lords of the Middle Border,* 18.

6. Boucherville Narrative, 1728–1729, *Wisconsin Historical Collections* 17:39–40.

7. Ibid., 40–43.

8. Ibid., 43–45; Beauharnois to the Minister, March 24, 1729, ibid., 58–59.

9. Beauharnois to the Minister, March 24, 1729, *Wisconsin Historical Collections* 17:58–59; Guignas to Villiers, December 5, 1728, AN, Col., C¹¹A, vol. 51, f. 436.

10. Boucherville Narrative, 1728–1729, *Wisconsin Historical Collections* 17:45; Beauharnois to the Minister, March 24, 1729, ibid., 58–59.

11. Boucherville Narrative, 1728–1729, ibid., 45–47.

12. Ibid., 47; Guignas to Villiers, December 5, 1728, AN, Col., C¹¹A, vol. 51, f. 436.

13. Boucherville Narrative, 1728–1729, *Wisconsin Historical Collections* 17:47.

14. Ibid.

15. Ibid., 47–48; Guignas to Villiers, December 5, 1728, AN, Col., C¹¹A, vol. 51, f. 436.

16. Boucherville Narrative, *Wisconsin Historical Collections* 17:48–51.

17. Ibid., 52–55; Perrier, De Salvert, and De La Chaise to the Directors of the Company of the Indies, April 22, 1729, in Rowland and Sanders, *Mississippi Provincial Archives* 2:642–44; Perrier, De Salvert, and De La Chaise to the Directors of the Company of the Indies, August 16, 1729, ibid., 669.

18. Beauharnois to the French Minister, August 17, 1729, *Wisconsin Historical Collections* 17:65–66; Beauharnois to the French Minister, September 1, 1729, ibid., 67–70.

19. Beauharnois to the French Minister, July 21, 1729, *Wisconsin Historical Collections* 17:62–64; Beauharnois to the French Minister, September 1, 1729, ibid., 67–70; Report by Beauharnois, May 6, 1730, ibid., 3:104, 208–11; Beauharnois to the Minister, August 17–October 25, 1729, AN, Col., C¹¹A, vol. 52, ff. 254–257v.

20. Beauharnois to the French Minister, September 1, 1729, *Wisconsin Historical Collections* 17:67–69; Marin to Beauharnois, May 11, 1730, ibid., 88–100; Beauharnois to the Minister, October 25, 1729, AN, Col. C¹¹A, vol 52, ff. 254–57v. The French-allied Indians boasted that in the ambush of the Fox buffalo hunters, the Foxes lost 77 men and 300 women and children. Although the Foxes undoubtedly suffered significant losses in this attack, the claims of their enemies probably

were exaggerated.

21. Report by Beauharnois, May 6, 1730, *Wisconsin Historical Collections* 5:104–106.

22. Beauharnois to the French Minister, July 21, 1729, *Wisconsin Historical Collections* 17:62–64; Marin to Beauharnois, May 11, 1730, ibid., 88–100.

23. Marin to Beauharnois, May 11, 1730, ibid., 88–100.

24. Ibid.

25. Ibid.

26. Ibid.

27. Ibid.

28. Ibid. A Winnebago account of these incidents can be found in Paul Radin, "A Semi-historical Account of the War of the Winnebago and the Foxes," *Proceedings of the State Historical Society of Wisconsin at Its Sixty-second Annual Meeting,* 192–207.

29. Marin to Beauharnois, May 11, 1730, *Wisconsin Historical Collections* 17:88–100.

30. Report by Beauharnois, May 6, 1730, ibid., 5:104–106.

31. Beauharnois to the French Minister, May 19, 1729, ibid., 17:59–62; Beauharnois to the Minister, June 25, 1730, ibid., 5:106–107; Abstract of Beauharnois's and Hocquart's Dispatches, October 25, 1729, *New York Colonial Documents* 9: 1014–19.

32. Beauharnois and Hocquart to the French Minister, November 2, 1730, *Wisconsin Historical Collections* 17:109–18; Beauharnois to the French Minister, November 9, 1730, ibid., 118–19; Minutes of the Commissioner of Indian Affairs, November 23, 1730, *New York Colonial Documents* 5:910–12. Also see excerpt from Peter Wraxall, *An Abridgement of Indian Affairs,* in Fox File, Great Lakes Indian Archives; and speech of the Foxes and reply of the Governor-General, September 1731, AN, Col., C¹¹A, vol. 50. f. 381. The speech of the Foxes and subsequent reply by Beauharnois originally were misfiled by an archivist with correspondence received in 1730, but internal evidence indicates the speeches took place in 1731.

33. Minutes of the Commissioners for Indian Affairs, November 23, 1730, *New York Colonial Documents* 5:910–12; speech of the Foxes and reply of the Governor-General, September 1731, AN, Col., C¹¹A, vol. 50, f. 381; Beauharnois and Hocquart to the French Minister, November 2, 1730, *Wisconsin Historical Collections* 17:109–18; Beauharnois to the French Minister, November 9, 1730, ibid., 118–19.

34. Beauharnois and Hocquart to the French Minister, November 2, 1730, *Wisconsin Historical Collections* 17:109–19.

35. Ibid.

36. Letter by D'Auteuil de Monceaux, November 7, 1730, AN, Col., series F³ (Moreau de Saint-Méry collection), vol. 24, ff. 196–98v. This letter also can be found NAC, MG1, F³24 (part 3), transcript pp. 525–35; and in Paris, Bibliothèque nationale, Manuscrits français, nouvelles acquisitions, vol. 2551, ff. 100–103. The letter has been translated and analyzed in Joseph L. Peyser, "The Fate of the Fox Survivors: A Dark Chapter in the History of the French in the Upper Country, 1726–1737," *Wisconsin Magazine of History* 73 (Winter 1989–90): 82–110.

37. Ibid.

38. Ibid.; Beauharnois and Hocquart to the French Minister, November 2, 1730, *Wisconsin Historical Collections* 17:109–18.

39. European and American travelers described the Illinois prairies and often mentioned the clouds of flies and mosquitoes that inhabited the region. See journal of George Winter, March 1836–August 1837, George Winter Papers, Tippecanoe County Historical Association, Lafayette, Indiana; Ferdinand Ernst, "Travels in Illinois in 1819," *Transactions of the Illinois State Historical Society for the Year 1903*, 150–65; entry for September 12, 1835, in the journal of Frederick Julius Gustorf, in Fred Gustorf, ed., "Frontier Perils Told by an Early Illinois Visitor," *Journal of the Illinois State Historical Society* 55 (Summer 1962): 146–47. Also see Charles Dickens, *American Notes,* 166–68; William Oliver, *Eight Months in Illinois,* 56–60; and John Woods, *Two Years' Residence on the English Prairie of Illinois,* 199–200.

40. Commandant at Detroit to Beauharnois, August 22, 1730, *Michigan Historical Collections* 34:67–69; De Villiers to Beauharnois, September 23, 1730, *Wisconsin Historical Collections,* 17:113–17. The location of this grove of trees and the subsequent battle has been the subject of considerable inquiry and debate among historians and archaeologists. Although amateur historians and archaeologists in the first half of the twentieth century argued for a variety of sites, including some north of the Illinois River, more recent and professional investigation has ascertained that the site probably was on the Grand Prairie of the Illinois, in either modern McLean, or possibly Champaign, county. Local traditions and some historical evidence suggest that the site was on the headwaters of the Sangamon River near modern Arrowsmith, Illinois. For documents supporting this location see William H. Keating, *Narrative of an Expedition to the Source of the St. Peter's River* 1:171; Lenville J. Stelle, "History and Archaeology: New Evidence of the 1730 Mesquakie Fort"; and Paul Sweich, "Dig Seeking Proof of Old Indian Fort," *Bloomington Pantagraph,* July 20, 1988, A2. Archaeologist Lenville Stelle has recently conducted a series of excavations

at the Arrowsmith site, and although there is considerable archaeological evidence to suggest that an eighteenth-century military action took place there, the evidence is still too limited to prove conclusively that the Arrowsmith site is the location of the great Fox battle on the prairie. Perhaps additional archaeological excavation will provide such evidence. Meanwhile, after extensive historical research in the Archives nationales in Paris, Joseph L. Peyser has argued that the site more likely was farther southeast. Peyser has meticulously examined and compared contemporary eighteenth-century reports of the engagement (including several eyewitness accounts) with recently discovered maps of the site, one of which (pp. 142–43, above) states that the stream that traversed the location flowed into the Great Wabash. See Peyser, "The 1730 Fox Fort: A Recently Discovered Map Throws New Light on Its Siege and Location," *Journal of the Illinois State Historical Society* 73 (Autumn 1980): 201–13; and "The 1730 Siege of the Foxes: Two Maps by Canadian Participants Provide Additional Information on the Fort and Its Location," ibid., 80 (Autumn 1987): 147–54. Peyser's articles contain a thorough discussion and analysis of the literature focusing on this problem.

41. Commandant at Detroit to Beauharnois, August 22, 1730, *Michigan Historical Collections* 34:67–69; De Villiers to Beauharnois, September 23, 1730, *Wisconsin Historical Collections* 17:113–18.

42. D'Auteuil de Monceaux to the Minister, November 7, 1730, AN, Col., F³, vol. 24, ff. 196–98v.

43. Ibid.

44. Letter by an Unknown French Officer, September 9, 1730, *Wisconsin Historical Collections* 17:109–13.

45. Villiers to Beauharnois, September 23, 1730, ibid., 113–18; letter by Monceaux, November 7, 1730, AN, Col., F³, vol. 24, ff. 196–98v; Commandant of Detroit to Beauharnois, August 22, 1730, *Michigan Historical Collections* 34:67–69. Also see Joseph Peyser, "The 1730 Fox Fort," 206–207.

46. Villiers to Beauharnois, September 23, 1730, *Wisconsin Historical Collections*, 7:115; Letter by Monceaux, November 7, 1730, AN, Col., F³, vol. 24, ff. 196–98v.

47. Letter by Unknown, September 9, 1730, *Wisconsin Historical Collections*, 17:109–13; Sieur de Villiers to Beauharnois, September 23, 1730, ibid., 113–18; Letter by Monceaux, November 7, 1730, AN, Col., F³, vol. 24, ff. 196–98v.

48. Villiers to Beauharnois, September 23, 1730, *Wisconsin Historical Collections* 17:113–18.

49. Letter by Unknown, September 9, 1730, *Wisconsin Historical Collec-*

tions 17:109–13; Villiers to Beauharnois, September 23, 1730, ibid., 113–18; Letter by Monceaux, November 7, 1730, AN, Col., F³, vol. 24, ff. 196–98v.

50. Report by Unknown, 1731 (misdated on the manuscript in the archives as 1730), AN, Col., C¹¹A, vol. 50, ff. 378–380v; Villiers to Beauharnois, September 23, 1730, *Wisconsin Historical Collections* 17: 113–18. Also see Peyser, "The 1730 Siege of the Foxes," 148–50. For an interesting discussion of French siege machines utilized against Indians in the Mississippi Valley, see Joseph Peyser, "The Chickasaw Wars of 1736 and 1740: French Military Drawings and Plans Document the Struggle for the Lower Mississippi," *Journal of Mississippi History* 44 (February 1982): 1–25.

51. Villiers to Beauharnois, September 23, 1730, *Wisconsin Historical Collections* 17:113–18. Also see Peyser, "The 1730 Siege of the Foxes," 147–54.

52. Villiers to Beauharnois, September 23, 1730, *Wisconsin Historical Collections* 17:113–18.

53. Letter by Unknown, 1730, ibid., 109–13; Commandant at Detroit to Beauharnois, August 22, 1730, *Michigan Historical Collections* 34:67–69.

54. Villiers to Beauharnois, September 23, 1730, *Wisconsin Historical Collections* 17:113–18; McTaggart, *Wolf That I Am,* 170–71.

55. Villiers to Beauharnois, September 23, 1730, *Wisconsin Historical Collections,* 17:113–18; Letter by Monceaux, November 7, 1730, AN, Col., F³, vol. 24, ff. 196–98v; Letter by Unknown, 1731 (misdated on the manuscript as 1730), AN, Col., C¹¹A, vol. 50, ff. 378–380v.

56. Letter by Monceaux, November 7, 1730, AN, Col., F³, vol. 24, ff. 196–98v; De Villiers to Beauharnois, September 23, 1730, *Wisconsin Historical Collections* 17:113–18; McTaggart, *Wolf That I Am,* 170–71; Peyser, "The 1730 Siege of the Foxes," 149. Also see Jones, "Notes on the Fox Indians," 231–32.

57. Villiers to Beauharnois, September 23, 1730, *Wisconsin Historical Collections* 17:113–18.

58. Letter by Monceaux, November 7, 1730, AN, Col., F³, vol. 24, ff. 196–98v. Monceaux reported that during the night the Sacs and a few small parties of other Indians captured almost three hundred Fox prisoners, but that number may have been exaggerated.

59. Letter by Unknown, September 9, 1730, *Wisconsin Historical Collections* 17:109–13.

60. Ibid.

61. Ibid.; Villiers to Beauharnois, September 23, 1730, ibid., 113–18, letter by Monceaux, November 7, 1730, AN, Col., F³, vol. 24, ff. 196–98v. The estimates of Fox losses in this battle and of the number of

Fox prisoners burned in the aftermath vary considerably. An unnamed member of St. Ange's force listed the Fox losses as "300 warriors, besides the women and children." Villiers reported 200 Fox warriors killed in the battle. Monceaux mentions 200 dead warriors and 300 dead women and children. Beauharnois mentions 200 warriors either slain in the battle or killed in the aftermath, and also claims that the French and their allies killed an additional 600 women and children. See Beauharnois and Hocquart to the Minister, November 2, 1730, *Michigan Historical Collections* 5:107–108. For a comprehensive analysis of the fate of those Foxes who survived this holocaust, see Peyser, "The Fate of the Fox Survivors," 83–110.

62. Letter by Monceaux, November 7, 1730, AN, Col., F³, vol. 24, ff. 196–98v; letter by unknown, fall, 1731, AN, Col., C¹¹A, vol. 50, ff. 378–380v; Report by Beauharnois and Hocquart, October 12, 1731, *Wisconsin Historical Collections* 17:142–47; Beauharnois and Hocquart to the Minister, 1732, ibid., 163–64.

CHAPTER SIX
GENOCIDE

1. Beauharnois and Hocquart to the Minister, November 2, 1730, *Wisconsin Historical Collections* 5:107–08; Beauharnois and Hocquart to the Minister, October 12, 1731, ibid., 17:142–47; Letter by Monceaux, November 7, 1730, AN, Col., F³, vol. 24, ff. 196–98v; Report by Unknown, 1731, AN, Col., C¹¹A, vol. 50, ff. 378–380v.

2. Hocquart to the French Minister, January 15, 1731, *Wisconsin Historical Collections* 17:129–30; Report by Unknown, 1731, AN, Col., C¹¹A, vol. 50, ff. 378–380v.

3. Speech of the Foxes to Sieur de Villiers and Reply to the Foxes by Villiers, January 19, 20, 1731, AN, Col., C¹¹A, vol. 54, ff. 395, 397–98; Report by Unknown, 1731, AN, Col., C¹¹A, vol. 50, ff. 378–80v; Boishébert to Beauharnois, February 28, 1732, *Wisconsin Historical Collections* 17:148–54. Also see Peyser, "Fate of the Fox Survivors," 91–97, and Tanner, *Atlas of Great Lakes Indian History*, 40–42.

4. Report by Unknown, 1731, AN, Col., C¹¹A, vol. 50, ff. 378–380v; Speech of the Foxes to Sieur de Villiers, January 19, 20, 1731, AN, Col., C¹¹A, vol. 54, ff. 395, 397–398.

5. Speech of the Foxes, January 19, 20, 1731, AN, Col., C¹¹A, vol. 54, ff. 395, 397–398.

6. Speech of the Foxes and the Reply of the Governor General, September 1731 (misdated on the manuscript in the archives as 1730), AN, Col., C¹¹A, vol. 50, f. 381; Report on the arrival of the Fox chiefs, September 1731, Bibliothèque nationale, Fonds français, nouvelles

acquisitions, vol. 2551, f. 136.

7. Speech of the Foxes and the Reply of the Governor-General, September 1731, AN, Col., C¹¹A, vol. 50, f. 381; Beauharnois to the French Minister, October 1, 1731, *Wisconsin Historical Collections* 17:139–41.

8. Boishébert to Beauharnois, February 28, 1732, *Wisconsin Historical Collections* 17:148–52; Beauharnois to the French Minister, 1732, ibid., 152–53.

9. Beauharnois to the French Minister, May 23, 1732, *Wisconsin Historical Collections* 17:153–54; Beauharnois to the French Minister, October 15, 1732, ibid., 167–69.

10. Sieur de Douville to Boishébert, July 1731, Fox File, Great Lakes Indian Archives; Beauharnois to the Minister, October 10, 1731, *Wisconsin Historical Collections* 17:148; Beauharnois and Hocquart to the French Minister, October 12, 1731, ibid., 142–47.

11. Boishébert to Beauharnois, February 28, 1732, *Wisconsin Historical Collections* 17:148–52.

12. Ibid.

13. Boishébert to Beauharnois, February 28, 1832, *Wisconsin Historical Collections* 17:148–52.

14. Ibid.

15. Ibid.

16. Ibid.

17. Ibid.; Beauharnois to the French Minister, May 23, 1732, ibid., 153–54.

18. Beauharnois to the French Minister, May 23, 1732, ibid., 152–54.

19. Ibid.; Beauharnois to Maurepas, October 15, 1732, *New York Colonial Documents* 9:1035–37; Beauharnois to the French Minister, October 15, 1732, AN Col., C¹¹A, vol. 57, f. 340. Also see Peyser, "Fate of the Fox Survivors," 96–97.

20. Boishébert to Beauharnois, February 28, 1732, *Wisconsin Historical Collections* 17:148–52; Beauharnois to the Minister of the Navy, Margry translation, 6:574–75, in Fox File, Great Lakes Indian Archives.

21. Beauharnois to the French Minister, October 15, 1732, *Wisconsin Historical Collections* 17:167–69; Beauharnois to the Minister of the Navy, October 15, 1732, Margry translation, 6:574–75, Fox File, Great Lakes Indian Archives. The site of this village remains uncertain. Contemporary reports mention that the village was located near "Lake Maramek," and a French map from the late seventeenth century places such a lake on the Fox River, west of Lake Michigan, but considerable confusion exists over the precise location. See *Wisconsin Historical Collections* 17:173, n.1; John F. Steward, *Lost Maramech and Earliest Chicago*, 302; and Steward, "The Fox River of Illinois,"

Transactions of the Illinois State Historical Society for the Year 1916 22:107.

22. Boishébert to Beauharnois, November 7, 1732, *Wisconsin Historical Collections* 17:173–74.

23. Beauharnois to the French Minister, October 15, 1732, *Wisconsin Historical Collections,* 17:167–69.

24. Boishébert to Beauharnois, November 7, 1732, ibid., 173–74; Beauharnois to the French Minister, May 1, 1733, ibid., 172–73.

25. Boishébert to Beauharnois, November 7, 1732, ibid., 173–74.

26. Ibid. Also see Hauser, "The Illinois Indian Tribe," *Journal of the Illinois State Historical Society* 69 (May 1976): 134, and Wayne C. Temple, *Indian Villages of the Illinois Country,* 43, 91.

27. Boishébert to Beauharnois, November 7, 1732, *Wisconsin Historical Collections* 17:173–74.

28. Ibid.; Beauharnois to the French Minister, May 1, 1733, ibid., 172–73. Also see Beauharnois to the French Minister, May 30, 1733, AN, Col., C¹¹A, vol. 59, ff. 8–9.

29. Beauharnois to the French Minister, July 1, 1733, *Wisconsin Historical Collections* 17:182–83.

30. Beauharnois to the French Minister, October 15, 1732, ibid., 167–69; Beauharnois to the French Minister, October 1, 1733, ibid., 182–83.

31. Enumeration of the Indian tribes connected with the government of Canada, 1736, *New York Colonial Documents* 9:1055; Tanner, *Atlas of Great Lakes Indian History,* 41–42.

32. Beauharnois to the French Minister, July 1, 1733, *Wisconsin Historical Collections* 17:182–83.

33. Ibid.; Beauharnois and Hocquart to the French Minister, October 14, 1733, ibid., 184–87.

34. Beauharnois and Hocquart to the French Minister, November 11, 1733, ibid., 188–91. Also see Lyle M. Stone, *Fort Michilimackinac, 1715–1781: An Archaeological Perspective on the Revolutionary Frontier,* 8.

35. Beauharnois and Hocquart to the French Minister, November 11, 1732, *Wisconsin Historical Collections* 17:188–89.

36. Ibid.

37. Ibid.

38. Ibid.; Beauharnois to the French Minister, October 5, 1734, AN, Col., C¹¹A, vol. 61, ff. 287–91v. Also see Augustin Grignon's Memoirs, *Wisconsin Historical Collections* 3:205–206. Although Grignon presents a confused account of these events, his narration does include much detailed information.

39. Beauharnois and Hocquart to the French Minister, November 11, 1733, *Wisconsin Historical Collections* 17:188–91.

40. Ibid.

41. Ibid. Augustin Grignon's memoirs contain a sketchy account of these events, but it is flawed by considerable confusion regarding dates and personnel. See Grignon's Memoirs, ibid., 3:197–211.

42. King's Communication to Beauharnois and Hocquart, April 27, 1734, AN, Col., Series B, vol. 61, ff. 543v-44v; Beauharnois to the French Minister, October 5, 1734, AN, Col., C¹¹A, vol. 61, ff. 287–91v.

43. King's communication to Beauharnois and Hocquart, April 27, 1734, AN, Col., B, vol. 61, ff. 543v-44v; French Minister to Champigny and Dorgeville, May 6, 1734, AN, Col., B, vol. 60, f. 311; Beauharnois and Hocquart to Officials in Martinique, September 16, 1734, *Rapport concernant les Archives canadiennes pour l'année 1905* (Ottawa: Public Archives of Canada, 1906), 1:lxxi; Beauharnois and Hocquart to the Minister, October 7, 1734, AN, Col., C¹¹A, vol. 61, ff. 84–85v, 89v-90.

44. Beauharnois and Hocquart to the French Minister, October 7, 1734, AN, Col., C¹¹A, vol. 61, ff. 84v–85v, 89v–-90v; Minister to Champigny and Dorgeville, December 28, 1734, AN, Col., B, vol. 60., f. 311; Champigny and Dorgeville to the Minister, March 12, 1735, AN, Col., C⁸A, vol. 46, n.p.; Minister to Champigny and Dorgeville, May 31, 1735, AN Col., B, vol. 62, f. 278v.

45. Minister to Beauharnois, July 20, 1734, NAC, MG1, B, vol. 61–1, transcript p. 235; Beauharnois and Hocquart to the French Minister, October 7, 1734, AN, Col., C¹¹A, vol. 61, ff. 84v–85v.

46. Yearly Report of Beauharnois and Hocquart, October 7, 1734, *Wisconsin Historical Collections* 17:206–213.

47. Copy of the Relation of the Journey of the Sieur de Noyelle, Commanding of the War-Party against the Renards and Sakis, sent to Monsieur the Marquis de Beauharnois, April 24, 1734, *Michigan Historical Collections* 34:122–28. French officers on the St. Joseph River intervened and dissuaded the Hurons from attacking this small village of Sacs. See Hocquart to the Controller General, October 26, 1735, ibid., 130–33.

48. Hocquart to the Controller General, October 26, 1735, *Michigan Historical Collections* 34:130–33; Beauharnois to the French Minister, October 9, 1735, *Wisconsin Historical Collections* 17:216–221.

49. Account of Noyelles' Journey, April 23, 1735, *Michigan Historical Collections* 34:122–28; Beauharnois to the French Minister, October 9, 1735, *Wisconsin Historical Collections* 17:216–21.

50. Account of Noyelles' Journey. April 23, 1735, *Michigan Historical Collections* 34:122–28. Local historians have speculated that the location of this village probably was near the site of modern Des Moines. See Jacob Van der Zee, "French Expedition against the Sac and Fox Indians in the Iowa Country, 1734–1735," *Iowa Journal of History and*

Politics 12 (April 1914): 250–51nn.13–16.

51. Account of Noyelles' Journey, April 23, 1735, *Michigan Historical Collections* 34:122–28.

52. Ibid.

53. Ibid.; L. F. Nau to Bonin, October 3, 1735, in Thwaites, *Jesuit Relations* 68:261–85.

54. Account of Noyelles' Journey, April 23, 1735, *Michigan Historical Collections* 34:122–28.

55. Ibid.

56. Ibid.

57. Ibid.

58. Ibid.; Hocquart to the Minister, October 26, 1735, ibid., 230–33; Beauharnois to the French Minister, October 17, 1736, ibid., 255–60; L. F. Nau to Bonin, October 2, 1735, in Thwaites, *Jesuit Relations* 68: 275–77.

59. Hocquart to the Minister, October 26, 1735, *Wisconsin Historical Collections* 17:230–33; Beauharnois to the French Minister, October 17, 1736, ibid., 255–60; Beauharnois and Hocquart to the King, October 13, 1735, Margry Documents; Bienville to Maurepas, August 20, 1735, Rowland, Sanders, and Galloway, *Mississippi Provincial Archives* 1:264–69; Bienville to Maurepas, February 10, 1736, ibid., 276–94; Census of the Indian Nations which are connected to the Government of Canada, October 12, 1736, AN, Col., C¹¹A, vol. 66, ff. 236, 242, 252.

60. Minister to Beauharnois, April 30, 1737, AN, Col., B, vol. 65, ff. 415–415v.; Beauharnois's Reply to the King's Memoir, 1737, AN, Col., C¹¹A, vol. 67, f. 139; Beauharnois to the French Minister, October 16, 1737, *Wisconsin Historical Collections* 17:274–76. Also see George Paré, "The St. Joseph Mission," *Mississippi Valley Historical Review* 17 (June 1930): 24–54.

61. Tanner, *Atlas of Great Lakes Indian History,* 44; Peyser, "The Chickasaw Wars of 1736 and 1740," 5–6; St. Pierre to Beauharnois, October 14, 1737, *Wisconsin Historical Collections* 17:269–74.

62. Speech by the Six Nations, June 28, 1737, Fox File, Great Lakes–Ohio Valley Archives, Bloomington; Conference between Lieutenant Governor Clarke and the Indians, June 24–July 2, 1737, *New York Colonial Documents* 25:98–109; Beauharnois to the French Minister, October 16, 1737, *Wisconsin Historical Collections* 17:274–76; List of Gifts to the Sacs and Foxes, October 15, 1737, AN, Col., C¹¹A, vol. 78, f. 286r and v; Memorial on Indians in Canada, 1738, AN, Col., C¹¹A, vol. 70, f. 257.

63. Statement of La Martinière's expenditures, July 22, 1738, AN, Col.,

C¹¹A, vol. 69, ff. 84–85.

64. Beauharnois to the Minister, October 4, 1738, AN, Col., C¹¹A, vol. 69, ff. 115–19; Speech by the Fox chiefs, November 17, 1738, *Wisconsin Historical Collections* 17:318–20.

65. Speeches of Winnebagos, Foxes, and Sacs to Marin at the Rock River, November 17, 1738, to May 10, 1739, AN, Col., C¹¹A, vol. 71, ff. 54–56v.; Beauharnois to the French Minister, October 12, 1739, AN, Col., C¹¹A, vol. 71, ff. 52–53v; Beauharnois to the French Minister, June 30, 1739, *Wisconsin Historical Collections* 17:315–16.

66. Speech by the Sacs, January 22, 1739, *Wisconsin Historical Collections* 17: 319; Memoir on the Indians and their Relations, 1740, ibid., 335–38; Beauharnois to the French Minister, October 12, 1739, AN, Col., C¹¹A, vol. 71, ff. 52–53v. Also see Donald Jackson, ed., *Black Hawk: An Autobiography* (Urbana: University of Illinois Press, 1964), 88–89.

67. Memoir on the Indians, 1740–1741, *Wisconsin Historical Collections* 17: 335–38; Beauharnois to the French Minister, September 26, 1741, ibid., 360–66; French Minister to Beauharnois, May 31, 1743, ibid., 18:1–3.

68. Beauharnois to the French Minister, September 26, 1741, ibid., 17:360–66; Speeches of the Sioux, Sacs, Foxes, Winnebagos, Chippewas, and Menominees to Beauharnois, and his replies, July 1742, AN, Col., C¹¹A, vol. 77, ff. 213–18, 233–40v.

69. Abstract of Dispatches from Canada, respecting Oswego and the Western Tribes, 1741, *New York Colonial Documents* 9:1085–1086; Speeches of the Sioux, Sacs, Foxes, Winnebegos, Chippewas, and Menominees to Beauharnois, and his replies, July 1742, AN Col., C¹¹A, vol. 77, ff. 213–18, 233–240v.

70. Speeches of the Sioux, Sacs, Foxes, Winnebagos, Chippewas, and Menominees to Beauharnois, and his replies, July 1742, AN, Col., C¹¹A, vol. 77, ff. 213–18, 233–40v.

71. Ibid.; Beauharnois to the French Minister, September 24, 1742, *Wisconsin Historical Collections* 17:111–12.

72. Speeches of the Sioux, Sacs, Foxes, Winnebagos, Chippewas, and Menominees to Beauharnois, and his reply, July 1742, ibid., ff. 213–18, 233–40v; Beauharnois to the French Minister, September 24, 1742, ibid., 111–12. Also see Speeches of Sac and Fox Chiefs and Marin's reply, April 25, 1743, AN, Col., C¹¹A, vol. 79, ff. 126–27; and Beauharnois to the French Minister, October 12, 1742, *Wisconsin Historical Collections* 17:424–29.

73. Speeches of the Sacs, Foxes, Menominees, and Winnebagos to Marquis de Beauharnois, Governor-General of New France, and his replies, July 1743, AN, Col., C¹¹A, vol 79, ff. 128–32.

74. Ibid.; Beauharnois to the French Minister, September 18, 1743,

Wisconsin Historical Collections 17:435–38; Beauharnois to the French Minister, October 13, 1743, ibid., 439–40.

75. French Minister to Beauharnois, March 24, 1744, *Wisconsin Historical Collections* 18:3–5; French Minister to Beauharnois, April 28, 1745, ibid., 5–7; trading contract for La Baye, April 4, 1747, ibid., 7–10. Also see Kellogg, *French Regime in Wisconsin,* 373–77; and R. David Edmunds, "Old Briton," in Edmunds, ed., *American Indian Leaders: Studies in Diversity,* 1–5.

76. Vaudreuil to the Minister, March 22, 1747, AN, Col., C¹³A, vol. 31, f. 46; Beauharnois to the Minister, October 9, 1744, *Wisconsin Historical Collections* 17:440–43; Vaudreuil to Maurepas, March 25, 1747, *Illinois Historical Collections* 29:19–22.

77. Vaudreuil to the Minister, March 22, 1747, AN Col., C¹³A, vol. 31, f. 46; Kellogg, *French Regime in Wisconsin,* 379–80.

78. Jonquière to the French Minister, September 16, 1751, *Wisconsin Historical Collections* 18:76–80.

79. As Fred McTaggart has illustrated in *Wolf That I Am,* many members of the modern Mesquakie community near Tama, Iowa, still retain an oral tradition focusing on their struggle against the French. When one of the authors visited this community in February 1989, he heard a tribal administrator quote, verbatim, part of the speech that Pemoussa delivered at Detroit in May 1712. See De Léry to Unknown, 1712, *Wisconsin Historical Collections* 16:293–95.

80. Excerpt from the Council held by Marquis de La Jonquière with the Menominees, Sioux, Foxes, Sacs, and Winnebagos, and the Replies of the Governor-General, July-August, 1750, AN, Col., C¹¹A, vol. 95, ff. 190–95v.

CHAPTER SEVEN
REGENESIS

1. Entries for July 27 and August 29, 1757, in Edward P. Hamilton, ed., *Adventure in the Wilderness: The American Journals of Louis Antoine de Bougainville, 1756–1760,* 149, 179; Memoir by Louis Billouart de Kerlérec, December 12, 1758, in Rowland, Sanders, and Galloway, *Mississippi Provincial Archives,* 5:203–27; Ian K. Steele, *Betrayals: Fort William Henry and the Massacre,* 80–82. Also see Zachary Gussow, "An Ethnological Report on the Historic Habitat of the Sauk, Fox, and Iowa Indians," in Gussow and Raleigh Barlowe, eds., *Sac, Fox, and Iowa Indians* 1:142–44.

2. Jonathan Carver, *Travels through the Interior Parts of North America in the Years 1766, 1767, and 1768,* 50; "Summary of Documents," *Wisconsin Historical Collections* 18:357–58; Louise Phelps Kellogg, *The British*

Regime in Wisconsin and the Northwest, 142–68 passim, 202.

3. Gussow, "Ethnological Report," 25–27; Gilbert Din and A. P. Nasatir, *Imperial Osage: Spanish-Indian Diplomacy in the Mississippi Valley,* 14, 227n.17; A Treaty between the United States of America and the United Tribes of the Sac and Fox Indians, November 3, 1804, in Charles J. Kappler, ed., *Indian Affairs: Laws and Treaties,* 2:74–77.

4. Wiley Sword, *President Washington's Indian War: The Struggle for the Old Northwest, 1790–1795,* 111; William T. Hagan, *The Sac and Fox Indians,* 18:37–72 passim; Jackson, *Black Hawk,* 53–71 passim. Also see R. David Edmunds, "Black Hawk," *Timeline* 5 (May 1988): 25.

5. Zachary Gussow, "Before the Indian Claims Commission: An Anthropological Report on Indian Use and Occupancy of Royce Areas 69 and 120 which were ceded to the United States by the Sac, Fox, and Iowa Indians under the Treaty of August 4, 1824," in Gussow and Barlowe, *Sac, Fox, and Iowa Indians* 1:69–77; Hagan, *Sac and Fox Indians,* 86–91, 97–100. Also see "Treaty with the Sioux and Chippewa, Sacs and Fox . . . , " August 19, 1825, in Kappler, *Indian Affairs* 1:250–55.

6. Hagan, *Sac and Fox Indians,* 115–37 passim; Edmund Gaines to Hugh L. White, July 6, 1831, *Illinois Historical Collections* 36:102–103.

7. *Illinois Historical Collections* 36:19n.8, 50–51n.5, 37:1169–70n.3; Michael D. Green, "'We Dance in Opposite Directions': Mesquakie (Fox) Separatism for the Sac and Fox Tribe," *Ethnohistory* 30 (Summer 1983): 132. Excellent accounts of the Black Hawk War are in Hagan, *Sac and Fox Indians,* 141–91 passim, and in Anthony F. C. Wallace, "Prelude to Disaster: The Course of Indian-White Relations Which Led to the Black Hawk War of 1832," *Illinois Historical Collections* 35:1–51, and in Roger Nichols, *Black Hawk and the Warrior's Path.*

8. Hagan, *Sac and Fox Indians,* 205–18; Green, "'We Dance in Opposite Directions,'" 133–34. The treaties that ceded these lands in Iowa can be found in Kappler, *Indian Affairs* 1:473–78.

9. Hagan, *Sac and Fox Indians,* 219–24; Green, "'We Dance in Opposite Directions,'" 134–35. "Articles of a treaty made and concluded . . . between the United States of America . . . and the confederated tribes of Sac and Fox Indians," October 11, 1842, Kappler, *Indian Affairs* 1:546–49.

10. Green, "'We Dance in Different Directions,'" 137–38; Callender, "Fox," 644–45; Hagan, *Sac and Fox Indians,* 232–33; Josiah Bushnell Grinnell, *Men and Events of Forty Years: Autobiographical Reminiscences of an Active Career from 1850 to 1890* (1891), 274–79. The Fox account of these events can be found in William Jones, *Fox Texts* 1:35–37. Also

see Fred Gearing, Robert McC. Netting, and Lisa R. Peattie, eds., *Documentary History of the Fox Project, 1948–1959*, 66–67.

11. Hagan, *Sac and Fox Indians*, 225–38; H. Craig Miner and William E. Unrau, *The End of Indian Kansas: A Study of Cultural Revolution, 1854–1871*, 103–105; Joseph Herring, *The Enduring Indians of Kansas*, 98–100.

12. Hagan, *Sac and Fox Indians*, 238–44; Miner and Unrau, *The End of Indian Kansas*, 77–78, 135–37; "Articles of agreement and convention made and concluded at the Sac and Fox agency . . . ," October 1, 1859, in Kappler, *Indian Affairs* 1:796–99. A traditional Fox account of these events can be found in Jones, *Fox Texts*, 31–35. For an excellent discussion of Mokohoko's fight to remain in Kansas, see Herring, *Enduring Indians of Kansas*, 98–118.

13. Hagan, *Sac and Fox Indians*, 245–60.

14. Hagan, *Sac and Fox Indians*, 260–65; Muriel H. Wright, *A Guide to the Indian Tribes of Oklahoma*, 227–28; telephone interview with Juanita Goodreau, Sac and Fox Tribal Offices, June 6, 1991.

15. McTaggart, *Wolf That I Am*, 10, 131–32; Gearing, Netting, and Peattie, *Documentary History*, 72–74.

16. Joffe, "The Fox of Iowa," 290–325; Callender, "Fox," 644–45; McTaggart, *Wolf That I Am*, 8–192 passim; Gearing, Netting, and Peattie, *Documentary History*, 39–59, 75–79; De Léry to Unknown, 1712, *Wisconsin Historical Collections* 16:293–95.

CHAPTER EIGHT
EPILOGUE

1. Constantin François Chasseboeuf Volney, "A View of the Soil and Climate of the United States of America," in Harlow Lindley, *Indiana as Seen by Early Travelers*, 21–24; Harrison to the Secretary of War, July 5, 1809, in Logan Esarey, ed., *Messages and Letters of William Henry Harrison* 1:349–55; John Johnston's Recollections, Frank J. Jones Collection, Cincinnati Historical Society. Also see R. David Edmunds, "'Unacquainted with the Laws of the Civilized World': American Attitudes toward the Métis' Communities in the Old Northwest," in Jacqueline Peterson and Jennifer S. H. Brown, eds., *The New Peoples: Being and Becoming Métis in North America*, 185–93.

2. Raudot, "Memoir," in Kinietz, *Indians of the Western Great Lakes*, 382; Charlevoix, *History* 5:151.

3. Du Tisné to the Minister, January 4, 1725, *Wisconsin Historical Collections* 16:450–53; Speech by the Illinois Indians, January 14, 1725, ibid., 456–63.

4. Lignery to De Siette *(sic)*, June 19, 1726, *Wisconsin Historical Collections*

3:153–56; Résumé for the Council of the Marine, 1726, ibid., 16:463–68; Memoir by Broisbriant, February, 1725, NAC, MG1, C¹³A, vol. 8, ff. 447–450v (microfilm F-1048).

5. Lignery to Beauharnois, August 30, 1728, *Wisconsin Historical Collections* 17:31–35.

6. Vaudreuil to the Council, October 22, 1720, AN, Col., C¹¹A, vol. 42, ff. 164–74v; Forsyth, "An Account of the Manners and Customs," in Blair, *Indian Tribes of the Upper Mississippi* 2:227; Miller, "Two Concepts of Authority," 271–89.

7. Beauharnois to the French Minister, July 1, 1733, *Wisconsin Historical Collections* 17:182–83; David B. Stout, Erminie Wheeler-Voegelin, and Emily J. Blasingham, "Indians of Eastern Missouri, Western Illinois, and Southern Wisconsin from the Proto-Historic Period to 1804," in *Sac and Fox Indians* 2:142–44.

8. Interview with anonymous informants, Tama County, Iowa, February 1989.

BIBLIOGRAPHY

PRIMARY SOURCES
MANUSCRIPT MATERIALS

Basse-Terre. Archives régionales de la Guadeloupe.

Bloomington. Indiana University. Glenn A. Black Laboratory of Archaeology. Great Lakes–Ohio Valley Indian Archives Project. Fox File. Kickapoo File. Potawatomi File. Sac File.

Chicago. Chicago Historical Society. Archives and Manuscripts Department. Beauharnois Collection.

Chicago. The Newberry Library. Edward E. Ayer Manuscripts.

Cincinnati. Cincinnati Historical Society. Frank J. Jones Collections.

Detroit. Detroit Public Library. Burton Historical Collections. Margry Manuscripts.

Fort-de-France. Archives départementales de la Martinique.

Lafayette, Indiana. Tippecanoe County Historical Association. George Winter Papers.

Ottawa. National Archives of Canada.

  Archives françaises, Division des manuscrits. Manuscript Group 1 (MG1), Archives des Colonies (Paris).

  Serie C^{11}A, Correspondance générale, Canada. Vols. 14, 33, 40, 50.

  Série C^{13}A, Correspondance générale, Louisiane, vol. 8.

  Série F^3, Collection Moreau de Saint-Méry, vol. 24–3.

  Série B, Lettres envoyées, vol. 61–1.

  Cartographic and Architectural Archives Division. Early Canadian Cartography Section. Ph/1250/Renards/1731 (DFC 46C, 46bisC, and 47C).

Bibliography

Paris. Archives nationales

Les fonds des Colonies antérieurs à 1815

Correspondance au départ, Série B, vols. 60–62, 65.

Correspondance à l'arrivée. Sous-série C⁸ᴬ, Martinique, vol. 46.

Sous-série C¹¹A, Canada et colonies d'Amérique du Nord, vols. 12, 14, 33–36, 42, 44, 49–52, 54, 57, 59, 61, 66–67, 69–71, 77–79, 95.

Sous-série C¹³A, Louisiane, vols. 8, 11, 13.

Document divers. Sous-série F³, Collection Moreau de Saint-Méry, vols. 8, 24.

Section Outre-mer (now in Aix-en-Provence). Dépôt des fortifications des Colonies (Louisiane).

Paris. Bibliothèque nationale.

Département des manuscrits. Manuscrits français, nouvelles acquisitions. Liasse 2551.

Département des estampes. Vd.20.b, Amérique septentrionale: Canada, tome II.

Québec. Archives du Séminaire de Québec. Fonds Verreau.

Québec. Archives nationales du Québec.

Saint-Jérôme, P.Q. Archives de La Compagnie de Jésus. Fonds Rochemonteix, boîte 4005.

INTERVIEWS

Anonymous. Interviews, Tama, Iowa, February 1989.

Campeau, Lucien. Interview, Maison des Pères Jesuites, Saint-Jérôme, P.Q., July 5, 1991.

Goodreau, Juanita. Telephone interview, June 1991.

Whistler, Jeri. Telephone interview, June 1991.

Wannatee, Donald. Interview, Mesquakie Administrative Office, Tama, Iowa, February 1989.

ARTICLES

Ellis, Richard N., and Charles R. Steen, eds. "An Indian Delegation in France, 1725." *Journal of the Illinois State Historical Society* 67 (September 1974): 385–405.

Ernst, Ferdinand. "Travels in Illinois in 1819." *Transactions of the Illinois State Historical Society for the Year 1903*, 150–65. Springfield: Phillips Bros., 1904.

Faye, Stanley, ed. "A Search for Copper on the Illinois River: The Journal of Le Gardeur de Lisle, 1722." *Journal of the Illinois State Historical Society* 38 (March 1945): 38–57.

Gustorf, Fred, ed. "Frontier Perils Told by an Early Illinois Visitor." *Journal of the Illinois State Historical Society* 55 (Summer 1962): 136–56.

Volney, Constantin François Chasseboeuf. "A View of the Soil and Climate of the United States of America." In Harlow Lindley, ed., *Indiana as Seen by Early Travelers*, 17–24. Indianapolis: Indiana Historical Commission, 1916.

BOOKS

Blair, Emma Hunt, ed. *The Indian Tribes of the Upper Mississippi Valley and the Region of the Great Lakes.* 2 vols. Cleveland: Arthur H. Clark Co., 1911.

Carver, Jonathan. *Travels through the Interior Parts of North America in the Years 1766, 1767, and 1768.* London: Jonathan Carver, 1779.

Colden, Cadwallader. *The History of the Five Indian Nations Depending on the Province of New York in America.* 1747. Reprint. Ithaca: Great Seal Books, 1958.

Collections of the Illinois State Historical Library. 38 vols. Springfield: Illinois State Historical Library, 1903–.

Collections of the Michigan Pioneer and Historical Society. 40 vols. Lansing: Thorp and Godfrey and others, 1874–1929.

Collections of the State Historical Society of Wisconsin. 25 vols. Madison: State Historical Society, 1854–.

Dickens, Charles. *American Notes.* Reprint. New York: St. Martins Press, 1985.

Esarey, Logan, ed. *Messages and Letters of William Henry Harrison.* 2 vols. Indianapolis: Indiana Historical Commission, 1922.

Grinnell, Josiah Bushnell. *Men and Events of Forty Years: Autobiographical Reminiscences of an Active Career from 1850–1890.* Boston: D. Lathrop and Company, 1891.

Hamilton, Edward P., ed. and trans. *Adventure in the Wilderness: The American Journals of Louis Antoine de Bougainville, 1756–1760.* Norman: University of Oklahoma Press, 1964, 1990.

Hennepin, Louis. *A New Discovery of a Vast Country in America.* Edited by Reuben Gold Thwaites. 2 vols. Chicago: A. C. McClurg and Company, 1903.

Jackson, Donald, ed. *Black Hawk: An Autobiography.* Urbana: University of Illinois Press, 1964.

Kappler, Charles J., ed. *Indian Affairs: Laws and Treaties.* 2 vols. Washington: U.S. Government Printing Office, 1904.

Keating, William H. *Narrative of an Expedition to the Source of the St. Peters River.* 2 vols. London: George P. Whittaker, 1825.

Kellogg, Louise Phelps, ed. *Early Narratives of the Northwest, 1634–1699.* New York: Charles Scribner's Sons, 1917.

Kinietz, W. Vernon. *The Indians of the Western Great Lakes, 1615–1760.* Ann Arbor: University of Michigan Press, 1965.

Bibliography

262

O'Callaghan, Edward B. *Documents Relative to the Colonial History of the State of New York*. 15 vols. Albany: Weed, Parsons, and Company, 1853–87.

Oliver, William. *Eight Months in Illinois*. Reprint. Chicago: Walter M. Hill, 1924.

Peyser, Joseph L., ed. and trans. *Fort St. Joseph Manuscripts: Chronological Inventory and Translations*. Niles, Mich.: City of Niles and Joseph L. Peyser, 1978.

————. ed. and trans. *Letters from New France: The Upper Country, 1686–1783*. Urbana: University of Illinois Press, 1992.

Rowland, Dunbar, A. G. Sanders, and Patricia Galloway, eds. *Mississippi Provincial Archives: French Dominion*. 5 vols. Jackson: Press of the Mississippi Archives and History, 1927–1984.

Thwaites, Reuben G., ed. *Jesuit Relations and Allied Documents*. 73 vols. Cleveland: Burrows Brothers, 1896–1901.

Woods, John. *Two Years' Residence on the English Prairie of Illinois*. Chicago: R. R. Donnelly, 1968.

SECONDARY SOURCES
UNPUBLISHED MATERIALS

Edmunds, R. David. "Miami Tribal Movements, 1670–1750." Unpublished manuscript in author's possession.

THESES AND DISSERTATIONS

Hauser, Raymond E. "An Ethnohistorical Approach to the Study of the Fox Wars, 1712–1735." M.A. thesis, Northern Illinois University, 1966.

Lortie, Richard. "La Guerre des Renards, 1700–1740, ou Quatre décennies de résistance à l'expansionnisme français." M.A. thesis, Université Laval, 1988.

Standen, S. Dale. "Charles, Marquis de Beauharnois de La Boische, Governor General of New France, 1726–1747." Ph.D. diss., University of Toronto, 1975.

ARTICLES AND ESSAYS

Bauxar, Joe. "The Historic Period." In *Illinois Archaeology*, 40–58. Illinois Archaeological Survey Bulletin no. 1. Urbana: Illinois Archaeological Survey, 1959.

Blasingham, Emily J. "The Depopulation of the Illinois Indians," parts 1 and 2. *Ethnohistory* 3 (Summer 1956): 193–223; 3 (Fall 1956): 361–412.

Borkowski, Kathryn. "The 1712 Siege of Detroit: The French and the Fox Indians.' *St. Joseph Valley Record,* Spring 1990, 1–5.

Brose, David S. "The Direct Historic Approach to Michigan Archaeology." *Ethnohistory* 18 (Winter 1971): 51–61.

Burnham, John H. "Mysterious Indian Battle Grounds in McLean County, Illinois." *Transactions of the Illinois Historical Society for the Year 1908,* 184–91. Springfield: Illinois Historical Society, 1909.

Burton, C. M. "Detroit Rulers: French Commandants in the Region from 1701–1760." *Collections of the Michigan Pioneer and Historical Collections* 34:303–40. Lansing: Thorp and Godfrey, 1905.

———. "Early Detroit." *Collections of the Michigan Pioneer and Historical Society* 24:225–39. Lansing: Thorp and Godfrey, 1900.

———. "Fort Pontchartrain du Detroit—1701–1710—under Cadillac." *Collections of the Michigan Pioneer and Historical Collections* 24:240–320. Lansing: Thorp and Godfrey, 1900.

Busch, Francis X. "The French in Illinois." *Transactions of the Illinois State Historical Society for the Year 1922,* 90–101. Springfield: Illinois Historical Society, 1922.

Callender, Charles. "Fox." In Bruce Trigger, ed., *Northeast. Handbook of the North American Indians,* edited by William C. Sturtevant, 15:636–47. Washington, D.C.: Smithsonian Institution, 1978.

Edmunds, R. David. "Black Hawk." *Timeline* 5 (May 1988): 24–27.

———. "Old Briton." In Edmunds, ed., *American Indian Leaders: Studies in Tribal Diversity,*1–20. Lincoln: University of Nebraska Press, 1980.

———. "'Unacquainted with the Laws of the Civilized World': American Attitudes toward the Métis Communities in the Old Northwest." In Jacqueline Peterson and Jennifer S. H. Brown, eds., *The New Peoples: Being and Becoming Métis in North America,* 185–94. Winnipeg: University of Manitoba Press, 1985.

Faye, Stanley. "The Foxes' Fort—1730." *Journal of the Illinois State Historical Society* 28 (October 1935): 123–63.

Fenton, William N. "Northern Iroquoian Culture Patterns." In Bruce Trigger, ed., *Northeast. Handbook of North American Indians,* edited by William C. Sturtevant, 15:296–321. Washington: Smithsonian Institution, 1978.

Folmer, Henri. "Étienne Veniard de Bourgmond in the Missouri Country." *Missouri Historical Review* 36 (April 1942): 279–98.

Fugler, Eugene. "Mesquakie Witchcraft Lore." *Plains Anthropologist* 6 (February 1961): 31–39.

Goddard, Ives. "Central Algonquian Languages." In Bruce Trigger, ed., *Northeast. Handbook of North American Indians,* edited by William C. Sturtevant, 15:583–87. Washington: Smithsonian Institution, 1978.

Bibliography
264

Green, Michael. "'We Dance in Opposite Directions'": Mesquakie (Fox) Separatism from the Sac and Fox Tribe." *Ethnohistory* 30 (Summer 1983): 129–40.

Gussow, Zachary. "Before the Indian Claims Commission: An Anthropological Report on Indian Life and Occupancy of Royce Areas 69 and 120, Which Were Ceded to the United States by the Sac, Fox, And Iowa Indians under the Treaty of August 4, 1824." In Gussow and Barlowe, eds., *Sac, Fox, and Iowa Indians* 1:29–120. New York: Garland Publishing, 1974.

———. "An Ethnological Report on the Historic Habitat of the Sauk, Fox, and Iowa Indians." In Gussow and Raleigh Barlowe, eds., *Sac, Fox, and Iowa Indians* 1:121–85. New York: Garland Publishing, 1974.

Habig, Marion. "The Site of the Great Illinois Village." *Mid-America*, n.s., 16 (July 1933): 3–13.

Hauser, Raymond. "The Illinois Indian Tribe: From Autonomy and Self-sufficiency to Dependency and Depopulation." *Journal of the Illinois State Historical Society* 69 (May 1976): 127–38.

Hunter, William A. "Refugee Fox Settlements among the Senecas." *Ethnohistory* 3 (Winter 1956): 11–20.

Joffe, Natalie F. "The Fox of Iowa." In Ralph Linton, ed., *Acculturation in Seven American Indian Tribes*, 259–329. New York: D. Appleton-Century Co. 1963.

Jones, William. "The Algonkin Manitou." *Journal of American Folklore* 18 (1905): 183–90.

———. "Episodes in the Culture-Hero Myth of the Sauks and Foxes." *Journal of American Folklore* 14 (October–December 1901): 225–39.

———. "Notes on the Fox Indians." *Iowa Journal of History and Politics* 10 (January 1912): 70–112.

———. "Notes on the Fox Indians." *Journal of American Folklore* 24 (April–June 1911): 209–37.

Kellogg, Louise Phelps. "The Fox Indians during the French Regime." *Proceedings of the State Historical Society of Wisconsin at Its 55th Annual Meeting*, 142–78. Madison: State Historical Society, 1908.

Lawson, Publius V. "The Outagamie Village at West Menasha." *Proceedings of the State Historical Society of Wisconsin at Its 47th Annual Meeting*, 204–11. Madison: Democrat Printing Co., 1900.

Messmer, Sebastian G. "The Early Jesuit Missions in the Fox River Valley." *Proceedings of the State Historical Society at Its 47th Annual Meeting*, 147–52. Madison: Democrat Printing Co., 1900.

Michelson, Truman. "The Autobiography of a Fox Indian Woman." *Fortieth Annual Report of the Bureau of American Ethnology*, 295–349. Washington: U.S. Government Printing Office, 1925.

———. "The Mythical Origin of the White Buffalo Dance of the Fox Indians." *Fortieth Annual Report of the Bureau of American Ethnology,* 23–289. Washington: U.S. Government Printing Office, 1925.

———. "Notes on Fox Mortuary Customs and Beliefs." *Fortieth Annual Report of the Bureau of American Ethnology,* 351–496. Washington: U.S. Government Printing Office, 1925.

———. "Notes on the Fox Society Known as Those Who Worship the Little Spotted Buffalo." *Fortieth Annual Report of the Bureau of American Ethnology,* 497–539. Washington: U.S. Government Printing Office, 1925.

———. "The Traditional Origin of the Fox Society Known as 'The Singing Around Rite.'" *Fortieth Annual Report of the Bureau of American Ethnology,* 541–615. Washington: U.S. Government Printing Office, 1925.

Miller, Walter B. "Two Concepts of Authority." *American Anthropologist* 57 (1953): 271–89.

Palm, Mary Borgias. "Kaskaskia Indian Mission Village, 1703–1718." *Mid-America* 16 (July 1933): 14–25.

Paré, George. "The St. Joseph Mission." *Mississippi Valley Historical Review* 17 (June 1930): 24–54.

Peyser, Joseph L. "The Chickasaw Wars of 1736 and 1740: French Military Drawings and Plans Document the Struggle for the Lower Mississippi." *Journal of Mississippi History* 44 (February 1982): 1–25.

———. "The Fate of the Fox Survivors: A Dark Chapter in the History of the French in the Upper Country, 1726–1737." *Wisconsin Magazine of History* 73 (Winter 1989–90): 83–110.

———. "The 1730 Fox Fort: A Recently Discovered Map Throws New Light on Its Siege and Location." *Journal of the Illinois State Historical Society* 73 (Autumn 1980): 201–13.

———. "The 1730 Siege of the Foxes: Two Maps by Canadian Participants Provide Additional Information on the Fort and its Location." *Illinois Historical Journal* 80 (Autumn 1987): 147–54.

Radin, Paul. "A Semi-historical Account of the War of the Winnebago and the Foxes." *Proceedings of the State Historical Society of Wisconsin at Its Sixty-second Annual Meeting,* 192–207. Madison: State Historical Society, 1915.

Steward, John F. "Destruction of the Fox Indians in 1730." *Transactions of the Illinois State Historical Society for the Year 1902,* 148–54. Springfield: State Historical Society, 1903.

———. "The Fox River of Illinois." *Transactions of the Illinois State Historical Society for the Year 1916* 22:107–16. Springfield: State Historical Society, 1917.

Bibliography

———. "Further Regarding the Destruction of a Branch of the Fox Tribe of Indians." *Transactions of the Illinois State Historical Society for the Year 1914,* 175–85. Springfield: State Historical Society, 1915.

Stout, David B., Erminie Wheeler-Voegelin, and Emily Blasingham. "Indians of Eastern Missouri, Western Illinois, and Southern Wisconsin, from the Proto-historic Period to 1804." In Gussow. *Sac, Fox, and Iowa Indians* 2:3–319.

Sweich, Paul. "Dig Seeking Proof of Old Indian Fort." *Bloomington (Ill.) Pantagraph,* July 20, 1988, sec. A2.

Tax, Sol. "The Social Organization of the Fox Indians." In Fred Eggan, ed., *Social Anthropology of North American Tribes,* 243–82. Chicago: University of Chicago Press, 1955.

Van der Zee, Jacob. "French Discovery and Exploration of the Eastern Iowa Country Before 1763." *Iowa Journal of History and Politics* 12 (July 1914), 323–44.

———. "French Expedition against the Sac and Fox Indians in the Iowa Country." *Iowa Journal of History and Politics* 12 (April 1914): 245–61.

Voegelin, Carl F., and Erminie Wheeler-Voegelin. "Linguistic Considerations of Northeastern North America." In Frederick Johnson, ed., *Man in Northeastern North America: Papers of the Robert S. Peabody Foundation for Archaeology* 3:178–94. Andover, Mass.: Peabody Foundation, 1946.

Wallace, Anthony F. C. "Prelude to Disaster: The Course of Indian-White Relations Which Led to the Black Hawk War of 1832." *Collections of the Illinois State Historical Society* 35 (1970): 1–51.

Wittry, Warren L. "The Bell Site Wn9, an Early Historic Fox Village." *Wisconsin Archaeologist,* n.s., 44 (March 1963): 1–58.

———. "A Michigan Fox Hunt." *Newsletter of the Cranbrook Institute of Science* 32, no. 7: 74–77.

Wright, Gary. "Some Aspects of Early and Mid-seventeenth Century Exchange Networks in the Western Great Lakes." *Michigan Archaeologist* 13 (December 1967): 181–94.

BOOKS

Anderson, Gary Clayton. *Kinsmen of Another Kind: Dakota-White Relations in the Upper Mississippi Valley, 1650–1862.* Lincoln: University of Nebraska Press, 1984.

Callender, Charles. *Social Organization of the Central Algonkian Indians.* Milwaukee Public Museum Publications in Anthropology, no. 7. Milwaukee: Public Museum Board of Trustees, 1962.

Charlevoix, Pierre-François-Xavier. *History and General Description of New France.* Translated and edited by John Gilmary Shea. 1870. 6 vols. Chicago: Loyola University Press, 1962.

Cleland, Charles E. *The Prehistoric Animal Ecology and Ethnozoology of the Upper Great Lakes Region.* Museum of Anthropology, University of Michigan Anthropological Papers, no. 29. Ann Arbor: University of Michigan, 1966.

Din, Gilbert, and A. P. Nasatir. *Imperial Osage: Spanish-Indian Diplomacy in the Mississippi Valley.* Norman: University of Oklahoma Press, 1983.

Edmunds, R. David. *American Indian Leaders: Studies in Diversity.* Lincoln: University of Nebraska Press, 1980.

———. *The Potawatomis: Keepers of the Fire.* Norman: University of Oklahoma Press, 1978.

Gearing, Fred, Robert McC. Netting, and Lisa R. Peattie, eds. *Documentary History of the Fox Project, 1948–1959.* Chicago: University of Chicago, 1960.

Gibson, A. M. *The Kickapoos: Lords of the Middle Border.* Norman: University of Oklahoma Press, 1963.

Gussow, Zachary. *Sac, Fox, and Iowa Indians.* 3 vols. New York: Garland Publishing, 1974.

Hagan, William T. *The Sac and Fox Indians.* Norman: University of Oklahoma Press, 1958, 1980.

Harrington, Mark R. *Sacred Bundles of the Sac and Fox Indians, University of Pennsylvania Museum Anthropological Publications* 4, no. 2. Philadelphia: University Museum, 1914.

Herring, Joseph B. *The Enduring Indians of Kansas: A Century and a Half of Acculturation.* Lawrence: University Press of Kansas, 1990.

Hickerson, Harold. *The Southwestern Chippewas: An Ethnohistorical Study.* Memoirs of the American Anthropological Association, no. 92. Menasha, Wis.: George Banta Company, 1962.

Hunt, George T. *The Wars of the Iroquois: A Study in Intertribal Trade Relations.* Reprint. Madison: University of Wisconsin Press, 1967.

Jones, William. *Ethnography of the Fox Indians.* Bureau of American Ethnology Bulletin 125. Washington: U.S. Government Printing Office, 1939.

———. *Fox Texts.* Publications of the American Ethnological Society, vol. 1. Leyden: E. J. Brill, 1907. Reprint. New York: AMS Press, 1974.

Kellogg, Louise Phelps. *The British Regime in Wisconsin and the Northwest.* 1935. New York: Da Capo Press, 1971.

———. *The French Regime in Wisconsin and the Northwest.* 1925. New York: Cooper Square, 1986.

Bibliography

268

McTaggart, Fred. *Wolf that I Am: In Search of the Red Earth People.* Reprint. Norman: University of Oklahoma Press, 1976.

Mason, Ronald J. *Great Lakes Archaeology.* New York: Academic Press, 1981.

Mathews, Joseph. *The Osages: Children of the Middle Waters.* Norman: University of Oklahoma Press, 1961.

Michelson, Truman. *Fox Miscellany.* Bureau of American Ethnology Bulletin 114. Washington: U.S. Government Printing Office, 1927.

———. *Notes on the Fox Wâpanôwiweni.* Bureau of American Ethnology Bulletin 105. Washington: U.S. Government Printing Office, 1932.

———. *The Owl Sacred Pack of the Fox Indians.* Bureau of American Ethnology Bulletin no. 72. Washington: U.S. Government, 1921.

Miner, H. Craig, and William E. Unrau. *The End of Indian Kansas: A Study of Cultural Revolution, 1854–1871.* Lawrence: Regents Press of Kansas, 1978.

Nash, Gary B. *Red, White, and Black: The Peoples of Early America.* 2d ed. Englewood Cliffs, N.J.: Prentice-Hall, 1982.

Nichols, Roger. *Black Hawk and the Warrior's Path.* Arlington Heights, Ill.: Harlan Davidson, 1992.

Parkman, Francis. *Count Frontenac and New France under Louis XIV.* New York: Library of America, 1983.

Quimby, George I. *The Dumaw Creek Site: A Seventeenth Century Prehistoric Indian Village and Cemetery in Oceana County, Michigan. Fieldiana Anthropology* 56, no 1. Chicago: Field Museum of Natural History, 1966.

———. *Indian Culture and European Trade Goods: The Archaeology of the Historic Period in the Western Great Lakes Region.* Madison: University of Wisconsin Press, 1966.

Smith, Huron H. *Ethnobotany of the Mesquakie Indians. Bulletin of the Public Museum of the City of Milwaukee* 4, no. 2. Milwaukee: Public Museum Board of Trustees, 1928.

Steele, Ian K. *Betrayals: Fort William Henry and the "Massacre."* New York: Oxford University Press, 1990.

Stelle, Lenville J. *History and Archaeology: New Evidence on the 1730 Mesquakie Fort.* Champaign: Lenville J. Stelle, 1989.

Steward, John F. *Lost Maramech and Earliest Chicago.* Chicago: Fleming H. Revell Co., 1903.

Stone, Lyle M. *Fort Michilimackinac, 1715–1781: An Archaeological Perspective on the Revolutionary Frontier.* Michigan State Anthropological Series, no. 2. East Lansing: Michigan State Museum of Anthropology, 1974.

Sword, Wiley. *President Washington's Indian War: The Struggle for the Old Northwest, 1790–1795.* Norman: University of Oklahoma Press, 1985.

Tanner, Helen Hornbeck, ed. *Atlas of Great Lakes Indian History.* Norman: University of Oklahoma Press, 1987.

Temple, Wayne C. *Indian Villages of the Illinois Country,* Illinois State Museum Scientific Papers, no. 2, pt. 2. Springfield: Illinois State Museum, 1966.

Trigger, Bruce G. *Northeast.* Vol. 15, *Handbook of North American Indians,* edited by William C. Sturtevant. Washington: Smithsonian Institution, 1978.

Wallace, Anthony F. C. *The Death and Rebirth of the Seneca.* New York: Alfred A. Knopf, 1970.

Warren, William W. *History of the Ojibway Nation.* Minneapolis: Ross and Haines, 1957.

Wheeler-Voegelin, Erminie, and J. A. Jones. *Indians of Western Illinois and Southern Wisconsin.* New York: Garland Publishing, 1974.

White, Richard. *The Middle Ground: Indians, Empires, and Republics in the Great Lakes Region, 1650–1815.* Cambridge, England: Cambridge University Press, 1991.

Wright, Muriel H. *A Guide to the Indian Tribes of Oklahoma.* Norman: University of Oklahoma Press, 1951.

INDEX

Index